Praise for

The World's Wealthiest Women

"I love women's stories, non-fiction and memoirs, and tales that inspire so I am a dedicated fan of Marlene Wagman-Geller's amazing work. Just when I think I have read my favorite book of hers, she writes another one that becomes a favorite and captures my interest and most importantly my heart. Her latest The World's Wealthiest Women is filled with professionally researched facts along with the most fascinating tidbits all told in the author's unique fashion and entertaining voice. This book explores the lives of twenty-five women from businesswomen to heiresses and there is something here for everyone. The readers learn behind the scenes secrets and stories of unbelievable, yet true wealth that these women obtained, created, and lived with. Many still do today. I have to say, The World's Wealthiest Women is now my favorite Marlene Wagman-Geller's book."

—Laura L. Engel, *Author of You'll Forget This Ever Happened-secrets, shame, and adoption in the 1960's*

"In this, her twelfth book, Marlene Wagman shows that she is still the reigning advocate for forgotten, misunderstood, or misrepresented women. With its rags-to-riches stories of scrappy entrepreneurs, women who married into wealth, and women who were born rich and got richer, this book is almost impossible to put down."

—Laurel Corona Weeks, author of *The Mapmaker's*

Daughter

"Engaging writing, intriguing characters, and well-placed humor bring to life this collection of stories about The World's Wealthiest Women, the latest in Marlene Wagman-Geller's acclaimed series on notable women. Through meticulous research, Wagman-Geller offers intimate glimpses into the extravagant lives of international heiresses and wildly successful businesswomen, delivering stories that delight, entertain, and illuminate the fascinating world of women of extraordinary wealth."

—Judy Reeves, author of *When Your Heart Says Go*

"Wagman-Geller has done it again—delivering another dazzling collection of mini-biographies brimming with fabulous and fascinating women. Some built their fortunes from nothing, while others inherited wealth or gained it through marriage, but all lived lives that astound the imagination. With vivid detail and powerful prose, she sweeps readers into opulent worlds where extravagance reigns. A page-turner from start to finish, this book is as irresistible as it is unforgettable."

—Jill G. Hall, author of *On a Sundown Sea: A Novel of Madame Tingley and the Origins of Lomaland*

"How did I not know about these women? This was the question that kept going through my mind as I finished each chapter and began a new one in a much more rapid succession than I had initially planned. A chapter a night was my thought as I began "The World's Wealthiest Women," because each chapter is a self-contained biography. Instead, I quickly amended my plan to half the book and I had it finished in two nights.

In all honesty, the lives of these wealthy women were what I had anticipated. Many of them struggled initially with poverty and family tragedy, either self-made or awarded to them by fate. What all these women had in common was chutzpah, or as other cultures would say, gumption, but I don't want to give their amazing stories away.

As stated, I had never heard of the existence of many of these women. For example, who knew about Hetty Green or Madame C.J. Walker? Although I'm sure many of us have heard the names Imelda Marcos, Athina Onassis, or Soraya Khashoggi, it was fascinating to know more about them and how they handled their inherited wealth.

Many of us have daughters, and granddaughters who are growing up, and will assume positions of responsibility, power, and perhaps wealth. I think books like these are important for them to have access to. As I stated, I didn't know about these women, but I'm glad I do now. Marlene Wagman-Geller has authored a collection of books about the lives of women that provide important information and are also thoroughly enjoyable to read. cannot wait to pass them on to my granddaughter, who turned five this year, when she gets a little bit older. Then there's my grandson, who will read them, too. You can trust me on that one."

—Lynne Marino, author of *Third Time's a Charm: Romance Over 50.*

"Reading Marlene Wagman-Geller's new collection of biographies provides delightful glimpses into the lives of fabulously, eye-poppingly, staggeringly wealthy women. From a tale of a self-made girl-boss to a gossipy piece on a silver-spoon heiress, each bon-bon of a story can be read in a sitting. However, Wagman-Geller's quirky, tongue-in-cheek writing style–reminiscent of a Dorothy Parker quip or a Hedda Hopper gossip column–will tempt you to indulge in just one more. If you can't live like the diverse, rich, and famous women profiled, you can, at least, peek into their histories. Hours of vicarious indulgence here. Fascinating and fabulous!"

—Shelley Burbank, author of *Final Draft: An Olivia Lively Mystery*

"Marlene Wagman-Geller has written another gem! The World's Wealthiest Women: Fascinating Biographies of Heiresses, Royals, Entrepreneurs, and Entertainers is extraordinarily fascinating. Wagman-Geller's way of writing these mini-biographies packs so much in such a small space. I felt like I got to see these women in a more vulnerable way. I stayed completely invested from start to finish!"

—Rachael Wolff, Podcaster and Author of *Tending Your Inner Garden* and *Letters from a Better Me*

The World's Wealthiest Women

Books by Marlene Wagman-Geller

A Room of Their Own: Home Museums of Extraordinary Women Around the World (2024)

The Secret Lives of Royal Women: Fascinating Biographies of Queens, Princesses, Duchesses, and Other Regal Women (2022)

Unabashed Women: The Fascinating Biographies of Bad Girls, Seductresses, Rebels, and One-of-a-Kind Women (2021)

Fabulous Female Firsts: Because of Them We Can (2020)

Women of Means: Fascinating Biographies of Royals, Heiresses, Eccentrics, and Other Poor Little Rich Girls (2019)

Great Second Acts: In Praise of Older Women (2018)

Women Who Launch: Women Who Shattered Glass Ceilings (2018)

Still I Rise: The Persistence of Phenomenal Women (2017)

Behind Every Great Man: The Forgotten Women Behind the World's Famous and Infamous (2015)

And the Rest Is History: The Famous (and Infamous) First Meetings of the World's Most Passionate Couples (2011)

Eureka!: The Surprising Stories Behind the Ideas That Shaped the World (2010)

Once Again to Zelda: The Stories Behind Literature's Most Intriguing Dedications (2008)

The World's Wealthiest Women

Fascinating Biographies of Heiresses, Royals, Entrepreneurs, and Entertainers

by Marlene Wagman-Geller

Published by Books That Save Lives, an Imprint of Jim Dandy Publishineg LLC.

Cover Design: Maclin Lisle

For permission requests, please contact the publisher at:
Jim Dandy Publishing LLC
6252 Peach Ave.
Van Nuys, CA 91411
info@jimdandypublishing.com

For special orders, quantity sales, course adoptions and corporate sales, please email the publisher at info@jimdandypublishing.com. For trade and wholesale sales, please contact Ingram Publisher Services at customer.service@ingramcontent.com or +1.800.509.4887.

The World's Wealthiest Women: Fascinating Biographies of Heiresses, Royals, Entrepreneurs, and Entertainers

ISBN: (print) 9781684818211

BISAC category code BIO022000

Printed in the United States of America

To the women who have added wealth to my life: my mother, Gilda Wagman, my daughter, Jordanna Geller, and my dearest friend, Jamie Lovett

"Money makes the world go around
It makes the world go round
The clinking, clanking sound"

—FROM THE FILM CABARET**; PERFORMED BY JOEL GREY/LIZA MINNELLI (MUSIC JOHN KANDER/ LYRICS FRED EBB)**

◇◇◇◇◇◇◇◇◇◇◇◇◇◇◇◇◇◇

"Money is the best deodorant."

—ELIZABETH TAYLOR

◇◇◇◇◇◇◇◇◇◇◇◇◇◇◇◇◇◇◇◇

TABLE OF CONTENTS

PREFACE

What God Thinks of Money

Since time immemorial, the wealthy have played a starring societal role. The Queen of Sheba dazzled Solomon as she entered the gates of Jerusalem at the head of a procession "with camels bearing spices, and very much gold and precious stones." The queen's fabled treasure added panache to a love story that has endured for three thousand years. Had the affair been between servants, the fame of their relationship would have evaporated in the desert sands.

The rich have received a bad rap since ancient times. Greek slave Aesop wrote his famous fable of the lust for gold as a metaphor warning of the danger associated with greed. King Midas, the ruler of ancient Phrygia in Asia Minor, had one fatal flaw: avarice. When Dionysus, the god of wine, offered to grant him one wish, Midas asked that everything he touch be transformed to gold. He was thrilled with his power until he no longer had the ability to eat, to drink, or even to love. When his daughter Marigold embraced him, she turned into a golden statue.

The New Testament also cautioned against avarice. Jesus warned of the evils of Mammon with the words, "It is easier for a camel to pass through the eye of a needle than for a rich man to enter the Kingdom of God." And then there was the episode when Christ expelled the money changers from the temple, referring to them as a "den of thieves." St. Timothy reinforced the concept by preaching that "the love of money is the root of all evil."

Throughout the millennium, the public has been mesmerized with royalty—partially due to their magnificent castles and crowns. Queen Letizia takes the cake for the most expensive royal wedding gown, whose price tag was a whopping $8 million. But even this Spanish royal did not swallow a pearl to prove her wealth. Cleopatra bet Mark Antony, her Roman lover and partner in world domination, that she could spend the equivalent of 60,000 pounds of gold on one meal. During the dinner, it seemed no more lavish than others and Antony assumed he had won the wager. His smugness disappeared when the wily Cleopatra took off her pearl earring—the world's most valuable—and dropped it in a cup of vinegar. After the jewel had dissolved, the Queen of the Nile drank the mixture. Mark Antony was left to eat a banquet of crow.

Elizabeth I of England used pearls to cement her image as both the Virgin Queen and absolute monarch. A portrait by Marcus Gheeraerts the Younger showcases the ruler, whose queenly gown was decorated with hundreds of the precious adornment. One storied gem is La Peregrina, a fifty-one-carat pearl discovered in the sixteenth century which was once the possession of French and Spanish royals. In 1969, Richard Burton presented the storied jewel to Elizabeth Taylor. Moments after, one of her Lhasa Apsos decided the treasure was edible; fortunately, she was able to pry the glorious gift from its mouth. In 2011, Christie's auction house sold La Peregrina for $11.8 million. As First Lady Jacqueline Kennedy pronounced, "Pearls are always appropriate."

The French empress Josephine was likewise no slouch when it came to conspicuous consumption; in one year, she purchased nine hundred dresses. After her husband, Emperor Napoleon, gave her diamond necklace to his sister Caroline as a wedding present, Josephine retaliated by buying pearls once owned by Marie Antoinette. However, Josephine's skills in spending were perhaps exemplified by her expenditures for Malmaison, her estate outside Paris; she filled her home with paintings by da Vinci, Titian, and Raphael.

Historically, women of fabulous fortunes owed their luxuriant lifestyles to inherited wealth or marriage, but neither was the case with one self-made billionaire of the nineteenth century. Although she was the financial peer of robber barons Andrew Carnegie, John D. Rockefeller, and Cornelius Vanderbilt, the eccentric Hetty Green, who was the richest woman in America, spent her seventy-seventh birthday clipping coupons. Taking to heart the Benjamin Franklin admonition that "A penny saved is a penny earned," she pulled the screws from an old sled so that they could be saved to reuse. Despite her memorably Scrooge-like tendencies that earned her the moniker "The Witch of Wall Street," Hetty Green was a financial genius who truly would have qualified for the title of "The Wizard of Wall Street."

We continue to be fascinated by money; one intriguing heiress with an abundance of green was cereal czarina Marjorie Merriweather Post, whose inheritance was founded on breakfast foods like Grape-Nuts. Marjorie's manses were an ode to twentieth-century Downtown Abbeys: Hillwood in Washington, DC; Mar-a-Lago in Palm Beach; Topridge in the Adirondacks; and a triplex in Manhattan—New York City's first penthouse. Her yacht, the *Sea Cloud*, eclipsed those of J. P. Morgan, the Vanderbilts, and the British royals.

For Barbara Amiel, Lady Black of Crossharbour, her variation of the words of Saint Timothy could have been, "The lack of money is the root of all evil." At age fourteen, home was a boarding house favored by prostitutes. Armed with beauty and brains, Barbara used men as stepping stones to enter the land of milk and honey-slash-money. After her marriage to media mogul Conrad Black, she moved in circles populated by Rothschilds and royalty, flitting between multimillion-dollar properties in Toronto, Manhattan, Palm Beach, and London. Her Marie Antoinette moment occurred when she showed a *Vogue* reporter her Kensington, England closets, and disclosed, "My extravagance knows no bounds." Lady Black ended up flying too near the sun: one by one her treasures vanished, like priceless pearls dropping from a necklace.

While well-heeled ladies receive realms of ink, fabulously wealthy sisters have often taken center stage. There are heiresses, and then there are billionaire heiresses. But when it comes to serious spending, it is hard to beat British siblings Tamara and Petra, the daughters of Formula One head honcho Bernie Ecclestone and his starter wife, Slavica, a former Armani model from Croatia. The doting dad set up Bambino Holdings, a trust fund for his girls, and christened his $20 million yacht the *Petara*, so called after an amalgam of his daughters' names. While most twentysomethings live in starter homes they cannot wait to vacate, twenty-two-year-old Petra purchased the 123-room Spelling Manor in Los Angeles' Holmby Hills for $85 million. Not one to embrace something as pedestrian as a mortgage, she paid cash. In case of company, the home driveway has space for a hundred cars. Petra, who thought of the mega-mansion as a fixer-upper, spent an additional $20 million renovating the 57,000-square-foot home. Some additions: a gym, a beauty salon replete with massage area and tanning room, a wine cellar with tasting room, a two-lane bowling alley, and a night club. One of the mega-mansion's selling points: It provided ample room for her five miniature dogs. She described her acquisition as "homey and livable." When spending time across the pond, Petra owns Sloane Lodge in the heart of London's Chelsea district, which she purchased for $90 million.

Not to be overshadowed by her younger sister, Tamara renovated her $70 million, fifty-seven-room Kensington Palace Gardens—located on the most expensive street in London—for $27 million. One darling decorative touch was the installation of a crystal bathtub that set her back $1,245,700; its ambience aligns with her Lucite piano. The backyard holds a three-story play area, constructed for $62,000 for her daughter, Sofia. Home improvements consisted of the addition of a bowling alley, a hair salon, and a dog spa. When her five canine companions needed relaxation, Tamara took them to Harrods for manicures and coatings of a shimmering spray. An episode of the British show *Billion $$ Girl* captured a page in the diary of the pampered pooches.

Given her lavish digs, it was not surprising that Petra ponied up quite the chunk of change for her wedding to James Stunt. Despite her protest that she was no Bridezilla, her big day came with a multimillion-dollar price tag, one that even papa Bernie declared "excessive." The ceremony took place in Odescalchi Castle, the same Italian medieval castle where Tom Cruise and Katie Holmes tied the knot. Among the nuptial touches: a $130,000 Vera Wang gown, performances by Eric Clapton and Alicia Keyes, white roses from France, acrobats, and fireworks. The divorce that followed also had the force of a full-fledged fireworks display. Petra hired Baroness Fiona Shackleton (known as 'the Steel Magnolia'), the attorney for the most expensive divorces in British history. James Stunt's stunts that led to the break-up included spousal violence and multiple overdoses. In a message of support, Tamara wrote her sister, "You're a diamond, dear, they can't break you." In an interview in *Tatler*, James referred to his ex as a "C-list celebrity's daughter," his former father-in-law as "a dwarf," and former mother-in-law Slavica as "a Lady Macbeth."

In spite of all their untrammeled wealth, the piper demands to be paid. Tamara has revealed that due to the constant threat of being targeted for home invasion, she lives mainly behind high walls, protected by alarms and four ever-present security guards. As Petra stated, "Money can't buy happiness. It buys things." She also remarked of her lifestyle, "It's an extraordinary world, and a lonely one." There are other sets of conspicuous consumption sisters: Eva, Zsa Zsa, and Magda Gabor; Jaqueline and Lee Bouvier; Paris and Nicky Hilton; Pia, Marie-Chantal, and Alexandra Miller; and Khloé, Kim, Kendall, Kylie, and Kourtney Kardashian.

In keeping with the rivalry that has existed since 1776 between England and her former colony across the pond, Jackie Siegel, the poster woman for conspicuous consumption, built the country's largest home on ten lakeside acres in Orlando, Florida. Jackie and her husband, timeshare mogul David Siegel, decided to pattern their dream home on the Palace of Versailles after a trip to France. The result was their 90,000-square-foot McMansion equipped with a thirty-car garage, a bowling alley, ten kitchens, thirty bathrooms, a health spa, a movie theater modeled on the Paris Opera House, a 20,000-bottle wine cellar, two tennis courts, several swimming pools, an ice skating rink, and a baseball field. The pièce de résistance is an observation deck that affords a panoramic view of the nightly fireworks over Disney World. Versailles II provided ample room for their eight children, staff of nineteen, and fourteen white fluffy dogs—none of whom are housebroken. A former canine companion named Channel resides in a taxidermized state in a glass cabinet. For times when it isn't convenient for Jackie to be on her private jet, she had a model of an airplane installed in her living room that provides mile-high ambience in which to sip champagne and nibble on caviar. For verisimilitude, the jet interior has an authentic airplane seat, and a "window" offers a cloud-filled backdrop.

Insofar as weddings go, even more elaborate than big, fat Greek weddings are those held in India. In 2018, Mukesh and Nita Ambani threw a gala for their daughter Isha. The proud papa was well able to pick up the $100 million bill since his personal fortune is $122 billion (give or take a few billions). How many celebrations can boast of entertainment provided by Queen Bee Beyoncé? How many wedding planners have provided jewel-bedecked elephants and 5,500 drones? Guests included Mark Zuckerberg, Bill Gates, Ivanka Trump, and the king and queen of Bhutan. The celebrations took place in venues such as Mumbai and Lake Como. The event was on par with the Ambanis' twenty-seven-story residence that towers over Mumbai. Their palatial $1-billion abode boasts a six-level parking garage and three helipads.

The rich know how to overshadow even the Grim Reaper. Contemporary royal Queen Margrethe of Denmark spent $5 million on a modernist silver and glass coffin designed by sculptor Bjørn Nórgarrd; currently, the coffin waits for the queen in St. Birgitta Chapel in Roskilde Cathedral. But no one knew how to send off a loved one as Shah Jahan did for his wife, Mumtaz Mahal, affectionately known as Taj, "ornament of the palace." For her, this besotted husband waived his polygamous rights with his other two wives. When his beloved died giving birth to their fourteenth child, her dying wish was that he erect a monument to their love. The Shah constructed the Taj Mahal, a mausoleum for the ages. From the four corners of his far-flung empire, transported on the backs of a thousand elephants, came priceless treasures of marble, gold, and jewels. A labor force of 20,000 men labored on the tomb for twenty years. The crowning touch on the edifice is its dome, reminiscent of a giant pearl floating above the building's four minarets, echoing the prophet Muhammad's vision of the throne of God as a pearl surrounded by four pillars. A tale surrounding the love story immortalized in marble is that during the rainy season, only one droplet falls on the queen's tomb, which is why the poet Rabindranath Tagore described it as "one teardrop...upon the cheek of time."

In her novel *Shirley*, Charlotte Brontë wrote, "I'll borrow of imagination what reality will not give me." For those not to the manor born can engage in daydreams of what it would be like to spend with abandon—without repercussion. In her 1927 short story, "The Standard of Living," Dorothy Parker describes two office workers strolling along Fifth Avenue in a manner befitting young heiresses. On their afternoon promenade, Annabelle and Midge engaged in "the ancient sport of what-would-you-do-if-you-had-a-million-dollars?" They stopped in front of a store window that displayed a double row of pearls with an emerald clasp. Annabelle bet the strand cost $1,000 and then upped her guesstimate to $10,000. When the salesman informed them that the cost was $250,000, their regal manner gave way to slumped shoulders. The precious pearls were even further removed from their orbit than they had imagined.

In the 1971 musical *Fiddler on the Roof*, Tevye is a milkman who cannot afford dowries for his five daughters. Taking some time from his chores, he breaks into a song, "If I Were a Rich Man." He fantasizes how if he were wealthy, he would have a big house with rooms by the dozen; his wife, Goldie, would scream orders at the servants day and night; and he would have time to sit in the synagogue and pray. His last lyric poses the question, "Would it spoil some vast eternal plan/If I were a wealthy man?"

Those who did not have to rely on imagination to understand the realm of the rich have been found in various and sundry countries. The profiled women have tended to reside in the world's ritziest zip codes.

The World's Wealthiest Women is a sequel to my book *Women of Means*, insofar as both revolve around fabulously rich women and their singular destinies. However, there is a major difference. My earlier book dealt only with the "poor little rich girls:" those who had lives that delivered all the unhappiness that money can buy. My current book does not hold that distinction as some of the heiresses herein made it to the finish line without misfortune trailing in hot pursuit.

Both volumes raise the overreaching question: What is society's knee-jerk reaction to the chosen few who dwell in the economic stratosphere? Some rubberneckers harbor the utmost disdain for those who possess the lion's share of the pie, leaving everyone else to claw for the remaining slices. They view the oligarchs, tycoons, and heirs as scavengers, zealously guarding their kill. Others peer through the peepholes of the mansions with open-mouthed respect; they are avid fans of those who command the best of everything and lap up media coverage of their storied lifestyles. Celebrity blogger Hung Huang stated that those who cast aspersion on those in better circumstances are best described by the Chinese phrase "xianmu-jidu-hen," which translates to "envy-jealousy-hatred."

Two twentieth-century wits held different philosophies regarding money. Sophie Tucker declared, "From birth to age eighteen, a girl needs good parents; from eighteen to thirty-five, she needs good looks; from thirty-five to fifty-five, she needs a good personality; and from fifty-five on, she needs good cash." Rather than idolizing money, Dorothy Parker's acerbic take was, "If you want to know what God thinks of money, just look at the people he gave it to."

PART ONE

Businesswomen

CHAPTER 1

Hetty Green: The Wizard of Wall Street (1834)

"A good businesswoman is often sharper than a good businessman."

—HETTY GREEN

Martin Scorsese's 2013 film portrayed Jordan Belfort, a real-life Jay Gatsby and a rapacious predator who earned the sobriquet "The Wolf of Wall Street." Preceding the tale of Jordan

Belfort was the nineteenth-century true story of Hetty Green, whose detractors dubbed her "The Witch of Wall Street."

This Victorian magician of money, Hetty Howland Robinson, was born in New Bedford, Massachusetts, in 1834. Herman Melville, the author of *Moby Dick*, spent time in the town as well and could perhaps have bumped into her father. Before people learned how to bring oil up from the ground, they extracted it from whales, and men like Edward Robinson made a fabulous fortune. Melville set sail on the *Acushnet*, an experience that led to his seafaring novel of Captain Ahab's obsession with Moby Dick, the great white whale. Henrietta (Hetty) Howland Robinson's obsession, however, was with money. She was the daughter of Quaker parents whose affluence stemmed from maternal ancestor Isaac Howland, Jr., the owner of a fleet of whaling ships and the scion of a family that had come to America aboard the Mayflower. The Robinsons were deeply disappointed at the birth of a daughter. Their second-born was the long-awaited son, Isaac, but he died before his first birthday. Since her mother Abby was consumed with grief and her father was occupied with work, Hetty lived mainly with her grandfather, Gideon Howland, and her aunt.

Because Gideon and Edward suffered from poor eyesight, Hetty read them stock quotes and the rest of the newspaper's financial section, from which she learned "what stocks and bonds were, how the market fluctuated, and the meaning of 'bulls' and 'bears.' " Another lesson she learned was from her father's admonition, "Never owe anyone anything. Not even a kindness." At age eight, Hetty told the Howland family driver to hitch the horses and take her to the bank where, using the coins saved from her weekly allowance, she opened her own account. Her father Edward, whose motto could have been, "Miserliness is next to godliness," was pleased. Due to his position at the Bedford Commercial Bank,

Edward welcomed Congressman Abraham Lincoln when he came to New Bedford to speak at Liberty Hall.

Hetty's happiest childhood times were spent at Round Tree Farm, the Robinson clan's 100-acre summer retreat at the seaside. Her unhappiest were during her time attending Eliza Wing's boarding school in Sandwich, Massachusetts. Quaker discipline ruled, and classes centered on scripture and rote memorialization. On a vacation, she was delighted when her grandfather Gideon purchased a piano, something not sanctioned by the Society of Friends. This conflict with Quaker morés was seen one day when Hetty had a visitor and the piano caused a contretemps: Mary Swift was playing a tune on it when Abby berated Mary, yelling, "Take thy music, thy person, and thy furbelows and begone!" The girl rushed from the house.

Hetty's Aunt Sylvia, a semi-invalid who never married or had children, insisted her niece spend time with their wealthy Manhattan relatives Henry and Sarah Grinnell, who could introduce her to eligible bachelors. Henry was friends with Whig party senators Henry Clay and Daniel Webster and had served as the first president of the American Geographical Society. Before his daughter's departure, Edward gave her $1,200 for a new wardrobe; Hetty spent only $200 on clothes, the rest on purchasing bonds.

In 1860, Abby passed away, little mourned by her only daughter or her distant husband. She died without leaving a will, and when Edward claimed her money, Hetty was infuriated since the wealth had come from the Howlands. The twenty-six-year-old Hetty took the case to attorney B. F. Thomas for arbitration: Edward proved the victor; Hetty received an $8,000 home.

After the loss of his wife, Edward, endowed with clarity as to the demise of the whaling industry, sold his business and moved to Saratoga Springs, a popular place for Wall Street tycoons and industrialists and their kin to take the waters. With the relationship between father and daughter now mended, Hetty arrived for a vacation whose highlight was when former US President Martin van Buren invited her to a dinner party at his home on Lake Saratoga. Other guests were Baroness Stoeckel, the wife of the Russian ambassador, Lord Althorpe, the future Duke of Northumberland, and van Buren's son John.

Upon her return to Manhattan, the city was in a frenzy over the imminent arrival of the Prince of Wales, the future King Edward VII of England. On the day of his arrival, businesses closed and a crowd of hundreds of thousands thronged the streets. The crowd cheered, and cannons boomed as Queen Victoria's son waved from the balcony of his Fifth Avenue hotel. On the evening of the ball, Hetty cut a striking figure in her low-cut white gown. When an official introduced her to the Prince of Wales, Hetty responded, "And I am the Princess of Whales." The future king replied, "Ah, I have heard that all of Neptune's daughters are beautiful. You are proof of that." Then they danced.

With Hetty's beauty and bank account, she could have left provincial New England behind and reigned in the upper echelons of Manhattan, with summers spent in a Newport mansion, a life straight out of an Edith Wharton novel. But Hetty was not hungry for the *trappings* of wealth; what interested her was wealth itself. Worried that her increasingly frail Aunt Sylvia was falling under the influence of strangers, Hetty boarded a steamer for Massachusetts.

Visits with her aunt proved contentious because Sylvia spent her money in a manner her niece found frivolous. One afternoon, acting on the belief her aunt's maid Fally was muscling in on her employer's money, Hetty pushed her, a move that resulted in the maid tumbling down the stairs. Sylvia paid $1,000 in compensation, a small fortune in the mid-1800s; Hetty begged for forgiveness and departed to rejoin her father.

For most of her thirty years, Hetty's lexicon had revolved around the words stocks, bonds, bulls, and bears; now a new one—romance—entered her life. On an 1864 trip to Boston, Hetty was in the Parker House Hotel and chanced to see Solon Goodridge, a business acquaintance of her father. Goodridge introduced her to his friend Edward Green. The Vermont-born Edward had worked in the Far East for twenty years, where he had faced pirates and storms at sea. What interested Hetty more than his past was that Edward Green was a millionaire—and it's likely green was Hetty's favorite color. A further credential of Edward's was that like Henry Grinnell, he was a member of the prestigious Union Club. But a shadow was cast over their courtship when her father suddenly fell ill. In between acting as his nurse, Hetty helped manage his business portfolio.

When Edward Green asked permission to wed thirty-year-old Hetty, her father agreed. He was dying, and though his daughter had amply proved her financial brilliance, even serving as the family bookkeeper starting at the age of thirteen, he harbored the belief that a woman could not handle money. To protect his daughter, he made a stipulation in his will that her husband would not be able to access her funds without her approval. When Edward Robinson passed away in 1865, he left behind a six-million-dollar fortune. He bequeathed Hetty a million dollars in cash plus the ownership of a San Francisco waterfront warehouse. The rest was left in trust for businessmen to invest; Hetty was furious, knowing that she had more monetary acumen than those who would control the vast majority of her inheritance.

Less than three weeks later, Sylvia Howland passed away, and Hetty rushed to New Bedford to be present for the reading of her aunt's will. To her fury, her aunt had left her a million dollars rather than her entire estate, and once more, trustees would manage the funds. Hetty felt she was the biblical Esau who had lost her birthright for "a mess of pottage." Her bitterness over the fact that others were in charge of her wealth is evident in her words: "I am able to manage my affairs better than any man could manage them, and what man has done, women do. It is the duty of every woman, I believe, to learn to take care of her own business affairs." To rectify the injustice, Hetty hired an attorney, claiming beneficiary Dr. William Gordon had drugged her aunt with laudanum, an opiate medication, and had substituted a fake will for the original. In a trial that garnered headlines, celebrated attorney Oliver Wendell Holmes sided with Hetty, testifying on her behalf.

In the midst of the lengthy trial turmoil, in 1867, the thirty-four-year-old Hetty and Edward Green married at the Grinnell home. As the couple took their vows, the newly minted Mrs. Green made her own: While her Aunt Sylvia had been the richest woman in New Bedford, Hetty was determined to be the richest woman in America. As rumors ran rampant that Hetty had been the one to forge the will, the newlyweds boarded the Cunard Line ship the SS *Russia* and set sail for England.

The couple moved into the Langham Hotel, the most luxurious in London, where fellow guests included Henry Wadsworth Longfellow, Andrew Carnegie, and Sir Henry Stanley. In an echo of her debutante days, due to her large-scale British investments, Hetty received an engraved invitation for presentation to Queen Victoria. At this juncture, Hetty's investments increased by $1.25 million—and so did her family. In 1868 she gave birth to her son, Edward Howland Robinson Green, nicknamed 'Ned' and 'the

Colonel.' Bad news dampened the joyous occasion; despite her high-powered attorneys, Judge Nathan Clifford dismissed her American court case. Soon after, Hetty took out a license to carry a pistol. In her variation of William Shakespeare's words in Henry VI, "The first thing we do is, let's kill all the lawyers," Hetty explained she had acquired the firearm, "Mostly to protect myself against lawyers. I'm not much afraid of burglars or highwaymen." Three years later, the Greens welcomed their daughter, Harriet Sylvia Ann Howland Green, nicknamed 'Sylvie.' In 1873, with the dismissal of legal proceedings, the family returned to New England on the *SS Russia*.

The Greens settled in Bellow Falls, Vermont, where they moved in with Edward's mother, Anna, who had received the house as a gift from her son. Excitement mounted in Bellow Falls as they awaited the arrival of the woman rumored to be a millionaire. Speculation was she would arrive draped in furs and jewels and would spread her wealth in her adopted town. The reality was far different. In her early forties, with her former beauty gone, fashion and hygiene were not a priority. Taking over grocery shopping duty, she haggled over every purchase; in another penny-pinching ritual, she made soap herself from animal fat. After examining an old sled, she found "some perfectly good nails" that she pulled out by hand.

Part of the year, the Greens lived in Manhattan, where Hetty spent time on Wall Street. The street derived its name from a wall the Dutch settlers erected in the 1650s to keep the British out. In Hetty's era, Wall Street was the provenance of men. A 1909 article in *The New York Times* stated, "It is difficult to reason about money and business with an angry or weeping woman. Her view of Wall Street and all its works suddenly becomes entirely emotional, and only a broker with infinite patience can calm her." Hetty Green punctured the stereotype. On one afternoon, she journeyed to the financial center with a satchel filled with $200,000 in bonds. Her broker John Cisco warned her of the danger of carrying such a huge sum on public transportation and suggested she take a carriage the next time. Hetty responded, "A carriage, indeed! Perhaps you can afford to ride in a carriage—I cannot."

Even workaholic Hetty sometimes took time off, and the Greens visited Central Park, where leisure offerings included goat cart rides, carousels with painted horses, and sail boating. One afternoon, Ned injured his foot while sledding, which then ended up causing a knee injury. A few years later, he fell while playing in a tree, resulting in further knee damage. At home, Hetty bathed and dressed his wound. When the doctor arrived, she sent him away in the belief she had provided as good a treatment as a professional. She explained that if the physician had stepped off his buggy, she would have had to pay his fee. When the injury did not heal, Hetty dressed in shabby clothes so she would be charged a reduced rate and sought help in New York and Baltimore. The medical prognosis was that Ned needed his leg amputated below his knee. With no other options, his bereft parents agreed, and Edward paid for the procedure. Hetty buried her son's leg in the family plot, where Ned would be reunited with his appendage forty-seven years later.

Cracks in the Greens' marriage appeared. While Edward had been able to stare down pirates and storms, his wife left him cowering. Hetty had turned a blind eye to his philandering and drinking; however, his one unforgivable sin was he had used her money to fund businesses that went south. She paid $700,000 to his creditors, but their relationship had run its course. Due to her Quaker religion, they never divorced. When Edward passed away, Hetty, who wore black for the remainder of her life, arranged his interment in the Immanuel Episcopal Church.

Other than the Edwards in her life—her father, husband, and son—and her Skye terrier, Dewey, she cared the most for her children. She was extremely proud of Ned, whom she installed as the president of her Texas railroad. To keep him focused on business—and keep a wife's claws from his staggering fortune—she urged him to remain single. He agreed but lived with his former girlfriend. The woman, who rumor held had been a former chorus girl or call girl, was named Mabel Harlow; Hetty referred to her as "Miss Harlot." After his mother's passing, Ned dissipated his mother's fortune by spending $5 million a year on his collection of jewels, rare stamps, and coins. Sylvia, at age thirty-seven, married Matthew Astor Wilks, age fifty-six, the great-grandson of John Jacob Astor. When asked if she approved of the marriage, Hetty replied, "I am happy if my daughter is happy." Like her brother, Sylvia never had children. Upon her 1951 passing, she gave away $100 million; one of her beneficiaries was Wellesley College, whose administration building bears the name Green Hall.

Money remained Hetty's concern: She spent her seventy-seventh birthday clipping coupons. O. Henry alluded to her in a short story when a girl settled on a cheaper room: "I'm not Hetty if I do look green." Vilified for her appearance and her anti-consumerism, Hetty was delivered a raw deal by history. Though she was merciless in business, she never set out to harm anyone. Her reputation as a miser can be laid at the door of prejudice against her gender. She stated, "I go my own way, take no partners, risk nobody else's fortunes, [and] therefore I am Madame Ishmael, set against every man." Rather than behaving like an actual villain, in the Panic of 1909, Hetty bailed out New York City when the bank refused assistance.

The richest woman in America passed away in 1916 at age eighty-one, with a fortune estimated at between $100–$200 million—$2.5 billion in contemporary currency. In comparison, J. Pierpont

Morgan, (the model for Uncle Pennybags, the Monopoly Man), passed away with $80 million; John D. Rockefeller with $900 million. For muscling in on the billionaire boys' club, Hetty had earned the epithet "The Witch of Wall Street." However, as one of history's greatest financial geniuses who made it in a man's world, Hetty should be hailed as "The Wizard of Wall Street."

CHAPTER 2

Madame C. J. Walker: Much Will Be Required (1867)

"I got my start by giving myself a start."

—MADAME C. J. WALKER

Sarah in her seven-passenger Cole limited edition touring car

In William Shakespeare's "Sonnet 29," the speaker bemoans, "I all alone beweep my outcast state." By contrast, rather than indulge in a pity party, Sarah Walker turned her misfortune into a fortune, and in the process, she became America's first self-made female millionaire.

Hair—comprised of lifeless keratin protein—has long been equated with female pulchritude. Corinthians states, "If a woman have long hair, it is a glory to her; for her hair is given her for a covering." Lady Godiva achieved immortality when she rode naked on her horse through the streets of Coventry, her modesty preserved by her flowing tresses. Irish poet W. B. Yeats wrote of his lover, "Only God, my dear/Could love you for yourself alone/And not your golden hair." Women's crowning glory led in Sarah's case to renown and fortune.

This future millionaire's story began on a plantation by the Mississippi River in Delta, Louisiana, where one Robert W. Burney owned sixty enslaved people, including Owen and Minerva Breedlove. Arriving two days before Christmas, 1867, due to grueling poverty, Sarah was the only present her parents received. Unlike her siblings, Louvenia, Owen Jr., Alexander, and James, she was born into freedom. Nevertheless, the family was still enchained in their role as sharecroppers. They also had to contend with white supremacist groups: the Knights of the White Camellia and the White League, groups associated and allied with the now-better-known KKK.

Owen and Minerva had likely "jumped the broom," a ritual for the enslaved to legitimize their unions. With $100 they realized from an abundant 1868 cotton harvest, they were able to marry in a Christian ceremony; two-year-old Sarah, her baby brother Solomon, and their four older children attended.

When Sarah was old enough, she worked alongside her family in the fields under the suffocating Southern sun. Aware cotton field work translated to survival, Sarah was heard to declare that no one could beat her at harvesting and processing cotton bolls. Because Mississippi was averse to providing knowledge that would enable Blacks to raise their station in life, her formal schooling spanned only three months. Tragedy entered the Breedlove cabin with the death of first Sarah's mother and then her father, possibly from disease borne from the bayous. At age seven, Sarah went to live with her sister Louvenia and her husband Jesse Powell in Vicksburg. Four years later, her foster father found work for Sarah as a caregiver for white children. When little Sarah walked past the town's shop windows, she would look longingly at their displays. Later, Sarah described Jesse Powell as "cruel;" her comment stemmed from either emotional and/or sexual abuse.

Escape arrived at age fourteen through a common-law marriage with Moses McWilliams, undertaken "in order to get a home of my own." She was delighted at the birth of her daughter, Lelia; but by age twenty, Sarah was a widow. Moses' cause of death is unknown, though he may have been a victim of lynching.

In 1888, Sarah headed north with three-year-old Lelia to escape violence and poverty. Her destination was St. Louis, where her brothers were barbers. Her first residence was the venue of stabbings, murders, and a brothel. She worked as a washerwoman for $1.50 per diem, a job she held for a decade. Because of her long shifts, Sarah had to leave Lelia at an orphan's home a few days a week. On one occasion, reality hit home, "I was at my washtub one morning with a heavy wash before me. As I bent over the washboard and looked at my arms buried in soapsuds, I said to myself: 'What are you going to do when you grow old and your back gets stiff? Who is going to take care of your little girl?' " Another weight was the Breedlove family tragedies: Her brother,

Alexander, died from an intestinal illness, and Louvenia's son, William, ended up in Mississippi's notorious Parchman Prison convicted of manslaughter.

In a bid to ease her hardships and provide her daughter with a father figure, Sarah married John Davis, a decision she soon regretted. They fought over his lack of motivation, his girlfriend Susie, and his drinking. Their marriage ended when John chose his mistress over his wife.

During their embattled relationship, Sarah had experienced a significant amount of hair loss. The affliction was common for woman of the era, caused by infrequent washing, illness, scalp disease, lice, and poor diet. Stress from her husband might also have exasperated her condition. What increased her self-consciousness was the vogue for long hair. Women with luxuriant locks looked out from newspapers and magazine covers. Jazz singer Helen Humes' 1923 song, "Nappy Headed Blues," illustrated Black women's hair issues: "Bought myself some hot irons, gonna start to fryin' hair/Straighten it or burn it, makes no difference, I don't care... Got to smooth these knots out, got to be an Indian queen." Sensing a niche market, Kinkilla, Kink-No-More, and Straightime appeared. The Boston Chemical Company sponsored Ozono, a product that claimed to "take the Kinks out of Knotty, Kinky, Harsh, Curly, Refractory, Troublesome Hair."

Often Sarah recounted the genesis of her hair elixir: "For one night I had a dream, and in that dream a big Black man appeared to me and told me what to mix for my hair. Some of the remedy was from Africa, but I sent for it, mixed it, put it on my scalp, and in a few weeks, my hair was coming in faster than it had ever fallen out." The actual origin story was not as visionary. Sarah started her career working for the Black businesswoman Annie Turnbo Pope Malone, the proprietor of the Poro School of Beauty

Culture. Annie's product had helped Sarah reclaim healthy hair. When Sarah wanted to strike out on her own, she experimented with Annie's mixture until she came up with her own, a recipe comprised of coconut oil, beeswax, and violet extract that she called Wonderful Hair Grower. The formula, in conjunction with the hot metal comb invented by a Frenchman in 1870, helped smooth hair, allowing Black women to adopt the popular Gibson Girl style.

Armed with Poro products, Sarah Breedlove headed to Denver to try her luck. She believed that the city's soil—and thus water—contained alkali and was hard on hair, making the city a receptive market. She arrived with $1.50 and a heart full of hope. Two days before her thirty-eighth birthday, Reverend William Dyett officiated at the wedding ceremony of Sarah to Charles Joseph (C. J.) Walker. Deciding to open her own business, she founded the C. J. Walker Company. Although her husband later claimed that he was the brains behind their enterprise, he had told his wife that he "could see nothing ahead but failure." Her friends also warned her about the pitfalls of striking out on her own. She said of the naysayers, "Everybody told me I was making a mistake by going into this business, but I know how to grow hair as well as I know how to grow cotton."

A marketing maven, Sarah advertised in the growing number of Black newspapers. Several ads focused on before and after photos featuring Sarah's own transformation. Her confidence proved to be justified when the party line in the Walker's rooming house rang with orders. Fifty-five years before Mary Kay Ash had trained women to work as "independent beauty consultants," Sarah hired "Walker agents," allowing her female labor force to share in the profits and thereby providing thousands of Black women an alternative to livelihoods as farm laborers, domestics, and washerwomen.

Because Denver had a limited Black population, Sarah traversed the country selling her Wonderful Hair Grower. By 1907, the former washerwoman, who had once earned $300 a year, was earning the same amount per month. At the time, most Black women earned $20 a month as domestics, and white male factory workers' monthly incomes ranged from $40 to $60 per month. A lyric from the song "Nappy Headed Blues" reflected Sarah's success, "Run to Madame Walker, send a fifty-dollar bill/Then send me some pomade, help a poor girl if you will." Her Walker agents also increased in number; at her company's zenith, she had a sales staff of 20,000 in America and the Caribbean. Her directive to her female employees was one she herself followed: help those who need help. With preachers praising the Walker System of Beauty from their pulpits to encourage the development of a Black aesthetic, Madam's coffers overflowed.

However, while her finances flourished, her five-year marriage floundered. C. J. had been on the road promoting their company for several months, and Sarah was not miserable over his absence. Standing in the shadow of his successful wife, C. J. might have engaged in extramarital relations in a bid at self-affirmation: his affair with Dora Larrie proved the death knell to his marriage. Post separation, he wrote to his former wife, begging her to take him back, "I am tired of Louisville and am writing these lines with tears dripping from my eyes." His entreaties fell on deaf ears. A further family fracture occurred when Lelia's one-year marriage to John Robinson, a man of whom her mother had not approved, ended when he took off after an argument. The newly single mother and daughter drew strength, both personal and professional, from one another.

While working in Indianapolis, Sarah diversified her assets in case her present business suffered a setback. She purchased real estate in several cities, including five lots in Indianapolis, twenty in Gary, Indiana, and individual properties in Los Angeles and New York. One reward of her success was a seven-passenger Cole touring car, a limited edition model. Due to her metamorphosis from sharecropper to business tycoon, Black leaders took note, and when they didn't, she refused to be sidelined; Sarah disrupted Booker T. Washington's National Negro Business League Convention after he ignored her. Indignant, she took the floor, declaring, "Surely you are not going to shut the door in my face. I am a woman who came from the cotton fields of the South. I was promoted from there to the washtub. Then I was promoted to the kitchen cook. And from there, I promoted myself into the business of manufacturing hair goods and preparations. I have built my own factory on my own ground." She received their attention. Sarah also refused to be silent when confronted with social injustice; when the Isis Theater charged Blacks twenty-five cents for admission while whites paid a dime, Sarah commissioned the Walker Theater, where an evening of entertainment was not sullied by racism.

The Walker women's lives changed when they met Fairy Mae Bryant, the middle of eight children of Sarah Bryant, a widowed washerwoman. Because Fairy Mae had long hair cascading to her waist, she became a model for Madame Walker's Wonderful Hair Grower. Since Lelia did not have children, and since the twelve-year-old was living in poverty, Lelia offered to adopt Fairy Mae and promised Mother Bryant that she would provide Fairy Mae education, a share in the business, and contact with her biological family. Preferring a lavishly furnished twelve-room house to her impoverished home, the child was thrilled with the idea. In 1912, the adoption took place, and Fairy Mae Bryant legally became Mae Walker Robinson.

A peripatetic journey ended when Sarah joined Lelia in her luxurious Harlem residence, part home, part beauty salon. Vertner

Tandy, a Cornell graduate who was likely New York State's first Black licensed architect, built Lelia a Harlem townhouse that combined two townhouses into an elegant red-brick façade. Mother and daughter joined Harlem's community of influential and high-profile residents; Lelia changed her first name to A'Lelia in 1922. They were a fixture in Manhattan's theater, art, and music communities. Shopping sprees included Madame's purchase of a 3.8-carat solitaire diamond from Tiffany encircled with "sixty-six tiny diamonds" and a pair of matching earrings.

After a lifetime of frenetic activity, Sarah wanted a home in a secluded and scenic spot. The woman who had been born in a cabin found her forever home in upstate New York, in a 1916 Italianate Renaissance mansion in Irvington-on-Hudson (named after writer Washington Irving) that consisted of thirty rooms on three floors connected by marble staircases. The estate included a Louis XVI suite of mahogany furniture, an $8,000 Estey organ, and Rodin sculptures. Decorating touches included bronze and marble statues, candelabras, tapestries, and paintings. The showplace served as an artistic salon frequented by notables from artistic, political, and business circles. The neighborhood was none too shabby as fellow residents carried the names Rockefeller, Astor, Vanderbilt, Tiffany, and Morgan. Opera great Enrico Caruso, a family friend who provided entertainment at Walker soirees, christened the estate Villa Lewaro, an acronym formed from the two leading letters of Lelia Walker Robinson's names. Sarah used her mansion as a site for balls whose attendees included Langston Hughes and photographer James Van Der Zee. When critics sniped that her mansion was a monument to "undue extravagance," Sarah countered that Villa Lewaro was "a Negro institution built to show the race what a lone woman accomplished and to inspire them to do big things."

Sarah Breedlove Walker's life is an against-all-odds story: the daughter of formerly enslaved parents who was born in a cabin on a plantation yet died a millionaire despite the tyranny of Jim Crow. What is even more inspiring is she earmarked her wealth for the betterment of others. Every year, she donated $10,000 to Southern colleges and sent six students to Tuskegee Institute. Her philanthropy included founding a Black YMCA, restoring Frederick Douglass' home, and donating $5,000 to the NAACP. A fierce fighter for justice, Sarah gave $5,000 to the National Conference on Lynching. Through her activism, she rubbed shoulders with Booker T. Washington, Ida B. Wells, and Mary McLeod Bethune. In 1917, Sarah attempted to meet with President Woodrow Wilson regarding making lynching a federal crime, but he did not grant her an interview. In Dr. Martin Luther King Jr.'s "I Have a Dream" speech on the 1963 March on Washington, he claimed that the United States had given Black people a "bad check" and had defaulted on their promissory note. The FBI branded him the most dangerous Negro in the nation. Forty-four years earlier, the Military Intelligence Division had put Sarah Walker's name on the list of "Negro subversives" for her involvement in the 1919 International Paris Peace Conference.

Villa Lewaro remained Sarah's residence until her death brought on by a heart attack in 1919. Her *New York Times* obituary carried the headline, "Wealthiest Negress Dead." At her passing, her fortune ranged from $600,000 to $700,000, a sum equivalent to $9 million in contemporary currency. After A'Lelia died, she bequeathed the mansion to the NAACP. In 1998, the US Postal Service issued a thirty-two-cent commemorative stamp of Madame Walker. She was the third in the postal service's Black Heritage series; those previously honored were the abolitionist Harriet Tubman and star athlete Jackie Robinson.

Madame C. J. Walker's last words were to Dr. Ward, "I want to live to help my race." Her true legacy is she followed the admonition of Luke, "For of those to whom much is given, much is required."

CHAPTER 3

Helena Rubinstein: Chutzpah (1872)

"There are no ugly women, only lazy ones."

—HELENA RUBINSTEIN

Women CEOs are no longer an oxymoron; Sheryl Sandberg helped expand Google and Facebook into titans of the Internet. In contrast, when Helena Rubinstein established her brand built on lipstick and lotion, female head honchos were as rare as sunburn on the cosmetic czar's porcelain complexion.

By coating eyelashes with mascara, painting lips, and drawing on brows, cosmetic devotees are paying homage to a mogul who died over half a century ago. Chaja, later anglicized to Helena, was the eldest of eight girls born in Podgórze, Poland. The Rubinsteins later moved to Kraków, where they lived in the Jewish Quarter of Kazimierz, a suburb immortalized by Steven Spielberg's movie *Schindler's List.* Her father, Hertzel, preferred studying the Torah to eking out a living as a kerosene dealer. Her mother, Gitel, insisted that her daughters, who were devoid of dowries, use her cream concoction, as their looks were their marital lifelines.

As the eldest, Helena was expected to be the first to obey a paternal demand by taking a husband. Refusing to endure a loveless marriage, she left home with her mother's parting gift: twelve jars of cold cream that would prove to be her version of Aladdin's lamp. Helena moved first to her aunt's house in Kraków, and then to live with another who lived in Austria. In Vienna, her relatives initiated her into the intricacies of their fur business. At age twenty-four, Helena, armed with a parasol and her jars, landed in Coleraine in western Victoria, Australia, where she lived with her uncle, Louis Silberfeld, in the sheep-farming outback. She shed the name Chaja for Helena—likely an allusion to the ancient world's femme fatale who, according to playwright Christopher Marlowe, had a face that had "launched a thousand ships." When asked about her past, Helena painted a portrait of her childhood "country estate, her monied past, her medical studies at the University of Kraków."

For two years, Helena worked for Louis as a housekeeper and clerk in his store without remuneration. To better her chances in life, she enrolled in English classes, where she asked her teacher "What does "bugger" mean? My uncle calls me that." As soon as she had achieved basic proficiency in English (although she always spoke her adopted language with a strong Yiddish accent), she left behind the family-style economic exploitation.

Helena moved from one poorly paid job to another, such as a stint as a waitress at Melbourne's Café Dore. Her dream was to start a business, an endeavor that would prove a Sisyphean struggle since she would have to come up with the funds as well as overcome the prejudices against self-employed women. Her fate seemed as grim as the one she would have endured had she remained in Kraków.

Women of the outback, whose faces bore the ravages of the broiling Australian sun, constantly complimented Helena on her milky complexion. The female fortune-seeker, rather than pointing out that Poland had less fiercely sunny weather, attributed this blessing to her mother's cold cream. She dropped hints her jars held an old family recipe that contained secret ingredients sourced from herbs found only in the Carpathian Mountains. She cooked up vats of the product she named Crème Valaze ("gift from heaven" in Hungarian), incorporating her "secret ingredient" into the cream: lanolin, an oil produced by sheep—and in the outback, there were thousands of them.

The girl from the shtetl was on the road to becoming the high priestess of beauty as well as an entrepreneurial heavyweight. Helena brought cosmetics, which formerly were only associated with prostitutes and actresses, into the vanity tables of millions. Interested in the scientific aspect of beauty, Helena paid to study with Marcellin Berthelot, the brilliant chemist who had invented bleach-based disinfectant. To promote herself as more than a beautician, Helena posed in a white lab coat and billed herself as "The First Lady of Beauty and Science."

There had been no time in the workaholic's life for romance until Helena met Edward William Titus, with whom she shared several commonalities. He had started life as Arthur Ameisen in Kraków; but as a respected journalist in Australia, he had anglicized his name due to anti-Semitism. Edward became her marketing and publicity manager; the professional relationship soon surpassed the solely platonic. For their 1908 wedding, Helena presented Edward with her greatest treasure: not her virginity, but rather equal shares in Helena Rubinstein Cosmetics. Edward always referred to his wife as Madame, a name that stuck. A rude awakening occurred when, as she descended the ornate staircase of her honeymoon hotel in Nice, she observed her husband kissing the hand of a younger, red-haired woman. Bordering on the stout and self-conscious over her height, her husband's roving eye fueled Helena's insecurity.

Desirous of other worlds to beautify, Helena sailed to Europe. In 1908, she established her Maison de Beauté Valaze at 24 Grafton Street in Mayfair, London. The salon, located in the former home of Robert Cecil, the Marquess of Salisbury who had served twice as Britain's prime minister, bore colors inspired by the Ballets Russes. When Prime Minister Herbert Asquith's wife, Margot, left the salon in full regalia of lipstick, rouge, and powder, women ranging from society doyennes to shop girls beat a path to Madame's door.

With the storm clouds of war hovering, Helena left her European establishments in the hands of a trio of her sisters that she brought from Poland. In heavily accented English, she recalled first stepping foot in New York in 1914, "It vas a cold day. All the American vomen had purple noses and gray lips, and their faces vere chalk vhite from terrible powder. I recognized that the US could be my life's vork." The following year, Madame opened a salon in Manhattan which she micromanaged while wearing a tomato-colored dress and eight strands of pearls. Her assistant was her sister Manka—

another sister summoned from Poland. Unlike others of her era who believed a woman's vocation was motherhood, Helena felt at home in her entrepreneurial emporium. She explained, "Work has been my best beauty treatment! It keeps the wrinkles out of the mind and the spirit. It helps to keep a woman young. It certainly keeps a woman alive!" Helena became the archrival of a fellow cosmetic queen: Elizabeth Arden, who she only referred to as "that voman." Helena, who was a force to be reckoned with during board meetings, sat on a cushion to appear taller and deflect attention from her petite stature.

After the war, Helena and her family returned to Paris, where she bankrolled her husband in establishing the Black Manikin bookstore in Montparnasse, an emporium that rivaled Sylvia Beach's Shakespeare and Company. He also founded the Black Manikin Press, which went on to publish D. H. Lawrence, Gertrude Stein, Ernest Hemingway, Aldous Huxley, and Samuel Beckett. Salon member Jean Cocteau christened Madame "The Byzantine Empress of Beauty." In a less flattering description, he also described her as "an old Polish frog...with a huge casket of jewels." Helena rubbed shoulders with Colette, Pierre-Auguste Renoir, Amedeo Modigliani, Ernest Hemingway, and James Joyce. The press also led to Helena's husband's affair with writer Anaïs Nin. While Madame's wealth brought her entry into rarefied circles, her background made her a fish out of the proverbial water. Hoping to furnish verisimilitude for his work-in-progress novel, Marcel Proust asked Helena whether demimondaines lined their eyes with kohl. She recalled Proust wore a full-length, fur-lined coat and smelt of mothballs, and she dismissed him as "nebbish-looking." She further remarked with her trademark directness, "But then, how could I have known he was going to be so famous?" Her long-suffering assistant, Patrick O'Higgins, recalled her remarking, "How was I to know those writers were worth a *sou*? I never had a moment to read their books. To me, they were *meshuga*—and I always had to pay for their meals!"

At age thirty-seven, Helena had her first son, Roy, followed three years later by Horace. She worked almost up to her delivery date and did not curtail her twelve-hour workdays. At the apogee of her career, she owned fourteen factories, had established her brand in more than thirty countries, and had a staff of 32,000.

Despite their transition from penniless Polish immigrants to fame and wealth, as well as their sons, the Titus marriage was developing serious crack lines. He was a man of letters; she was at a loss in a highbrow milieu. While Edward collected a who's who of the 1920s intelligentsia, Madame collected possessions: homes, jewelry, art, and clothes. Although Helena blamed their 1938 divorce on serial adultery, she admitted she was also culpable when she confessed, "My heart has always been divided between the people I loved and my ambition." Armed with a substantial settlement, Edward discreetly departed Manhattan for Paris. While Dr. Faustus had sold his soul for knowledge, Helena had sold hers for wealth, power, and acclaim.

In 1928, the makeup mogul sold the American branch of her company to the Lehman Brothers for $7.3 million ($84 million in contemporary currency). Over the following year, the Depression, coupled with mismanagement, lowered the price of the company's stock from sixty to three dollars. Regretting she had sold her birthright, Helena regained control of her company in a move that netted her a $5.8 million profit.

The cosmetics colossus made up in jewels what she lacked in inches. She mixed pieces from her collection of eye-popping gems—including antique pieces once owned by Catherine the Great—with dime store baubles. Madame kept her legendary collection of gems in a filing cabinet: "A" for amethysts, "D" for diamonds, "E" for emeralds... She draped herself in haute couture from designers Balenciaga, Chanel, and Schiaparelli. Paradoxically, Helena padded around her twenty-six-room Manhattan penthouse turning off lights, became upset if a maid broke a teacup, and indulged in Bloomingdale's basement sales.

Another of Madame's passions was art, and she obtained pieces from Christian Dior, a youthful antiques dealer. Her residences in Manhattan, Connecticut, Paris, the French Riviera, and London held priceless paintings. A room in her Park Avenue triplex displayed seven Renoirs, a still life by Frida Kahlo, whom Helena had met on a trip to Mexico, and a drawing by Andy Warhol. The cosmetic queen gifted the pop artist a ruby and silver ring inlaid with the initials "H. R." With the tenacity of a pit bull when it came to getting what she wanted, Helena showed up at Pablo Picasso's home on the Riviera, announcing she would not leave until he painted her portrait. Picasso drew a series of pencil sketches he referred to as "a few police notes." Twenty-seven portraits of Madame portrayed her as a Polish princess, dripping with jewels.

Unsurprisingly, the woman who had shared her childhood home with eight sisters, followed by a stint as the poor relative in her uncle's home, took great pride in her palatial homes. Her consultant was Salvador Dali; interior designer David Hicks decorated her British duplex with violet walls and magenta chairs. Her Manhattan suite displayed a green carpet designed by Miro, twenty Victorian carved chairs with seats swathed in purple and magenta velvet, Oriental pearl-inlaid coffee tables, gold Turkish floor lamps, and six-foot-tall blue vases. Caring more about her taste than what was in vogue, life-sized Easter Island sculptures and African masks stood in proximity to venerable pieces of art. Magazines featured her residences as backdrops for fashion shoots, such as in a 1935 *Vogue* photograph taken at her

New York home in which actress Merle Oberon posed by a Fang reliquary head sculpture from Africa. For an outdoor party held at her property on the Cote d'Azur, she hung her Chagalls, Monets, Renoirs, and Modiglianis from the trees.

Although she was a woman wedded to her work, at a 1938 party hosted by the Comtesse de Polignac, Helena met her second husband. In her sixties, Helena wed the forty-three-year-old Russian émigré Artchil Gourielli-Tchkonia, an impoverished prince. She married for love as well as for a title—though the royal title might not have borne too much scrutiny. Being referred to as princess proved the ultimate coup for the girl from the Kraków Ghetto. A bonus for having her name preceded by "princess" was that it conferred bragging rights, something she lorded over the recently divorced Elizabeth Arden. Artchil said of his wife, "Beside Helena, every other woman is uninteresting"—not to mention poor. Artchil passed away in 1955; three years later, her son Horace died in a car crash. Helena found solace in work, explaining she had squeezed three hundred years of work into a single lifetime: "I did it not for money but because I love work. I will never retire."

While commanding an international corporation, Helena was unlikely to have indulged in that "nebbish" Marcel Prout's "remembrance of things past." As much as Helena tried to draw a curtain over her biography, every time she spoke, her Yiddish accent revealed her roots. Despite her Orthodox upbringing, Helena did not attend synagogue. However, she helped spirit several Polish Jews away from Europe and gave them jobs in her salons. Helena also demonstrated solidarity to Judaism by keeping the surname Rubinstein in an era rife with anti-Semitism. Her decision kept her flagship storefront relegated to Fifth Avenue's side streets. The diminutive dragoness also used her money to fight discrimination. When she attempted to upgrade from one posh Park Avenue apartment to one with a bigger balcony, the owner refused, since he did not rent to Jews. Helena then directed her accountant to buy the entire building.

In 1964, thieves posing as florists delivering roses broke into her Park Avenue apartment and surprised the ninety-two-year-old as she lay in bed. Due to a pile of papers strewn on her sheets, the intruders did not notice her purse—which held the keys to her safe that contained a million dollars in jewelry. Surreptitiously, she extracted her key and dropped it into her cleavage. When the thieves discovered the purse, they found a HR powder compact and five twenty-dollar bills. The purse also held a pair of diamond earrings valued at $40,000 that slipped away as the thieves dumped out its contents. After tying Helena to a chair, they fled with $100. When her butler freed her, she instructed him to put the roses in the icebox; after paying for the roses, the thieves had only netted sixty dollars! Not long after the horror of the home invasion, Helena departed for Paris, Tangier, and Normandy.

When she passed away at age ninety-four from a stroke, Helena left her empire to her son Roy, as well as to several charitable organizations. Charles Revson, the founder of Revlon, whom she referred to only as "that nail man," took over her Park Avenue triplex. Her art, real estate, haute couture, and jewelry fell under the hammer of auction houses. The cosmetics empire eventually came under the ownership of L'Oréal, a concern that had originated with Eugène Schueller, who had been in league with the Nazis in Occupied France.

Before her 1955 passing, Helena had showed her secretary a paper. She explained, "This is a piece of history. The famous magic formula for my original cream." The paper, yellow with age, held the words: "vegetable oil, mineral oil, wax." The overriding question remains: How did she transition from Chaja to Helena, to Madame, to princess? The answer: Chaja had chutzpah.

CHAPTER 4

Diane von Fürstenberg: It's a Wrap (1946)

"I created the dress, but really the dress created me."

—DIANE VON FÜRSTENBERG

If we could eavesdrop on Cinderella, we would overhear her tell her granddaughters about her hardscrabble youth: named after cinders, dressed by anthropomorphic mice, forced to rely on a gourd as transportation. She would likely end by explaining how a pair of shoes can alter their destiny. For Belgium-born billionaire Diane von Fürstenberg, life changed, not through footwear, but through an item of clothing.

France's Coco Chanel found fame and fortune through her little black dress, and Diane von Fürstenberg found hers through the wrap dress. Diane Simone Michelle Halfin was born in 1946 in Brussels, Belgium, the daughter of Jewish immigrants Leon, from Russia, and Lily, from Greece. Their hope for a better life ended when the Nazis goosestepped into their adopted country. With gold coins hidden in his socks, Leon fled to Switzerland. To protect their youngest daughter, Lily's parents sent her to live with a Christian family, unaware they were members of the Resistance. While she was riding her bicycle throughout Brussels to deliver false identity papers to Jews, police arrested the undercover emissary. Lily spent eighteen months in the Auschwitz and Ravensbrück concentration camps.

The twenty-one-year-old Lily Nahmias returned to Belgium. Ill and weighing only forty-nine pounds, she wed Leon, her fiancé prior to her internment. Eighteen months post liberation, on New Year's Eve, Lily welcomed her daughter. In 1952, Diane's brother Philippe completed the family.

Although the Halfins enjoyed an upper middle-class lifestyle, tensions ricocheted throughout their home because Leon was unable to grasp Lily's psychological fragility stemming from her Holocaust horror. As a child, Diane did not understand why her mother had two lines of blue tattooed numbers on her left arm. Another source of distress was that with her dark, frizzy hair and brown eyes, Diane felt like the ugly duckling compared to the Belgian girls, who had blonde straight hair and blue eyes. In her teens, however, Diane transformed into a swan.

Despite Leon's objections, Lily sent Diane to Pensionnat Cuche, a private boarding school next to Lake Sauvabelin in Lausanne, Switzerland. Two years later, she returned home at her father's insistence. Her parents argued nonstop in an escalating series of fights that ended with their divorce. The following year, at age sixteen, Diane left for Stroud Court, a girls' boarding school in Oxfordshire, England. Excursions to swinging London of the sixties introduced the teen to mod fashion; she felt wearing go-go boots and miniskirts was a step away from dating Paul McCartney. Stroud Court was where she surrendered her virginity: first to Sohrab, an Iranian architecture student and her first swain, and then to her French friend, Deanna. After graduation, Diane and Deanna enrolled in the University of Madrid; anti-Franco protests resulted in sporadic classes.

In Lausanne, a friend from her Swiss boarding school days introduced Diane to the blonde Prince Edouard Egon von und zu Fürstenberg (known as Egon), also an adherent of sexual fluidity. What they did not have in common was their backgrounds: While Diane was the daughter of a mother who was a Jewish Holocaust survivor, Egon's mother, Clara Agnelli, was the heiress to the Fiat fortune. Her father had been a Russian refugee; by contrast, his father, Prince Tassilo Egon Maximilian Fürstenberg, hailed from the Austro-German nobility, whose family tree traced back to Charlemagne, the ninth-century king of the Holy Roman Empire. Egon whisked Diane away to the Far East, where they toured Hong Kong, Cambodia, India, and Thailand. In the south of France, she sailed on a yacht belonging to Egon's uncle, Gianni Agnelli, and watched the Grand Prix in Monaco. Her prince took her to a costume ball in Venice, where she moved in the firmament of stars including Elizabeth Taylor and Richard Burton.

At age twenty-two, draped in a Christian Dior wedding gown, Diane married her Prince Disarming in the medieval city of Montfort-l'Amaury, France, in front of five hundred guests. The reception was at Auberge, owned by Maxim's of Paris. The one cloud over the occasion was that Prince Tassilo expressed his horror that his son, whom Pope John XXIII had baptized, was marrying "this dark little Jewish girl." One reason—although she had not shared the news—was because she was three months pregnant. Displeased with his new daughter-in-law, he attended the ceremony but bowed out of the reception. The newlyweds spent their honeymoon sailing the fjords of Norway, followed by a month with friends on Sardinia's Costa Smeralda.

The couple's Manhattan base was 1250 Park Avenue, an abode they shared with their children, Alexandre and Tatiana Desirée, as well as their retinue. Other places to hang their hats were an apartment in Paris and a beach house in Sardinia, the latter a wedding present from Egon's mother. Known as the European Park Avenue prince and princess, they threw cocktail parties whose guests included Andy Warhol, Yves St. Laurent, and Paloma Picasso. Egon and Diane dined with Jackie Kennedy Onassis and Aristotle, her shipping tycoon husband, at Manhattan's El Morocco. Jackie and Diane shared a hairdresser, Edgar Montalvo; the designer called him "the best blower in town." In those days, Diane ironed her hair as she hated her natural wild locks. Since Egon was related to Monaco's royals, they received invitations to parties hosted by Prince Rainier III and Princess Grace.

While most women would have felt their plates were full enough with an active night life, international travel, and two children, Diane explained her desire for a career, "I had to be someone of my own, and not just a plain little girl who got married beyond her desserts." In 1972, she opened a store on Seventh Avenue. *Vogue* editor Dianna Vreeland helped boost sales, as did her royal title. Egon shared her love of fashion, having seen his first couture collection at the age of two while in his mother's arms.

The Belgium bombshell's eureka moment arrived when she saw Julie Nixon Eisenhower on television defending her father, President Richard M. Nixon, during Watergate. Flattered that the First Daughter was wearing a Diane von Fürstenberg top, the designing woman created a one-piece wrap dress. The garment, crafted without hooks, buttons, and zippers, appealed to the feminist zeitgeist of the era and proved a welcome contrast to the unisex suits of women in the workforce. Wedding feminism and femininity, the garment consisted of a soft fabric adorned with patterns running the gamut from the world of nature to geometric prints, thereby providing customers an array of visual themes. The $86 dress, which is the subject of exhibits in the Costume Institute of the Metropolitan Museum of Art and the Smithsonian, became an iconic fashion statement, catapulting the twenty-eight-year-old to fashion superstardom. Within the first year of the dress' debut, DVF was producing 25,000 of them per week. Four years later, she had sold a million and appeared on the cover of *Newsweek*. The accompanying article stated that Diane von Fürstenberg was "the most marketable woman since Coco Chanel." (Although Diane kept her married name, she dropped the umlaut over the U. Gloria Steinem convinced her to forego the title of "Princess" for Ms.) At a White House dinner, seated next to President Ford, the First Lady of fashion exchanged light-hearted banter with the nation's chief executive regarding how she had supplanted the president for that month's issue of *Newsweek*. Secretary of State Henry Kissinger eagerly made her acquaintance. On a 1976 flight to Cleveland, a man seated next to her asked, "What's a pretty girl like you doing reading the *Wall Street Journal*?" She refrained from showing him her picture on the front page.

DVF, begun with a $30,000 investment, had grown into a $100 million dollar enterprise. The garment became so intricately bound with its designer that Diane joked, "It will probably be on my tombstone: Here Lies the Woman Who Designed the Wrap Dress."

In contrast to her thriving business, the Fürstenberg marriage was faltering. A strong believer that promiscuity did not end in marriage, Egon slept with anything—man, woman, or mineral—and was open to threesomes with various anatomical combinations. Due to his promiscuity, he received the epithet, "Egon von First-in-bed." Unhappy with her relationship, she stated, "I was in charge of my children, I was in charge of my life, I was in charge of my business, I was a woman in charge." In a variation of wearing her heart on her sleeve, Diane wears a gold and diamond necklace bearing the words "In Charge;" her New York office displays the exhortation on numerous signs. Egon and Diane separated and finalized their divorce in 1983. Diane kept her title and custody of their two children. They continued to deeply care for one another, and Diane was with Egon in Rome when he passed away, purportedly from AIDS.

As a sanctuary from Manhattan, at age twenty-six, Diane purchased a 'room of her own,' and then some: Cloudwalk, a seventy-five-acre, eighteenth-century farm in Litchfield County, Connecticut. The estate's former owner, Johnson & Johnson heiress Evangeline Johnson, had christened the property. The estate holds an apple orchard, gardens, a stream, swimming pool, waterfall, and five ancillary structures. As she is always working, Diane converted a barn into a studio with soaring ceilings. The most interesting outdoor touch is a giant lipstick sculpture carved from a tree trunk. Neighbor Henry Kissinger and his wife often came for dinner. She purchased a second room of her own as her thirtieth birthday gift to herself: a Fifth Avenue apartment whose former owner was Rodman Rockefeller. Her friend Françoise, Oscar de la Renta's wife, decorated it in an expensive bohemia theme.

The Merrie Divorcée, feeling free to bed and not wed, had a long list of lovers. Of her custom-made neo-deco bed (a present from her mother for her thirtieth birthday), Diane reminisced, "In my wild days...that bed can tell all the stories." In between designing clothes and caring for her son and daughter, nights were mainly spent partying at Studio 54 with the likes of Bianca Jagger and Mick Jagger, David Bowie, Richard Gere, Warren Beatty, and Ryan O'Neal. Another habitué was Andy Warhol, who immortalized her on canvas. The Belgian Diane, like the Greek Diana, was a huntress whose catches were Richard Gere (she described him as "cute"). She pronounced Omar Sharif "the worst lay she ever had." A proponent of women being able to take the same sexual laissez-faire attitude as men, Diane recalled how she was intimate with both Ryan O'Neal and Warren Beatty in a single weekend. Who else can claim the same? In contrast, she turned down David Bowie and Mick Jagger after they approached her with the offer of a ménage à trois.

While Diane had any number of men in her life, she only loved two of them: Egon and Barry Diller. At age twenty-eight, when she first met Barry, she had no idea what a significant role the prince of Paramount Studio would play in her life. The list of the director's eventual blockbuster movies included *Marathon Man, Saturday Night Fever*, *Grease*, and *Urban Cowboy*. His friends were astounded when he started seeing Diane, as he had always been open about his homosexuality. Andy Warhol's observation was, "I guess the reason why Diller and Diane are a couple is because she gives him straightness and he gives her powerfulness." An irate Barry Diller countered the pop artist's pronouncement saying, "Diane and I were actually motiveless when we came together. It was a *coup de foudre*." This expressive French phrase refers to an unexpected love-at-first-sight wonder. The designer brought out the soft side of the man who had the moniker "killer Diller." In the seventies, when they first started seeing each other, for Mother's Day, he bought her a speedboat so Alexandre and Tatiana could waterski in the lake near Cloudwalk. For their Fourth of July party, they had a get together with actress Candice Bergen, writer

Jerzy Kosinski, and socialite Slim Keith, who brought along film star Claudette Colbert. New Year's Eve was spent at Woody Allen's party, where Barry gave Diane twenty-nine loose diamonds in a Band-Aid box. For her forty-ninth birthday, he gifted her forty-nine diamonds; with his $4.2 billion fortune, he could afford grand gifts.

At this point, Diane was living on cloud nine until a series of events upended her life. In 1980, after a Caribbean cruise where Barry was the captain, she received a phone call informing her that Lily was in dire distress. Her mother had gone to Germany on a business trip with her partner. In the hotel, hearing men conversing loudly in German sent her into a panic; terror-stricken, she hid under the concierge's desk. Diane immediately flew to Switzerland to spend time with her mother, who was in an asylum. Deeply shaken, along with her children, Diane took off for Bali, where she fell in love with a Brazilian named Paulo, staying in his bamboo house. Even during their idylls, she could not turn off her entrepreneurial button, and she created a perfume inspired by her exotic/erotic locale: Volcan d'Amour. The relationship lasted four years, as did her wardrobe of sarongs.

When Diane bid farewell to her tropical idyll, she turned to Barry Diller, with whom she had weathered many storms: the crash of her first business, tongue cancer, her mother's nervous breakdown, and car and skiing accidents. After years of turning down his proposals, for his birthday, she offered to at last tie the knot. The venue for the ceremony was New York's City Hall, where the only guests were her brother and children Tatiana and Alexandre. Celebrity photographer and friend of the bride Annie Leibovitz captured the memory. In tribute to her recently deceased mother, her bouquet held lilies. The delighted groom gave his wife twenty-six wedding bands to symbolize the twenty-six fallow years when they had not been an official couple. A party with 350 guests in attendance took place later that evening in Diane's Greenwich Village loft.

The couple own several places to hang their hats, wrap dresses, and Warhol paintings. Diane's European refuge is her apartment in the Parisian suburb of Saint-Germain-des-Prés, an area redolent of former residents Josephine Baker and Ernest Hemingway. Her self-described "tree house" in Manhattan's Meatpacking District is a glass structure overlooking the Empire State Building. When a romantic getaway is needed, their $45 million oceanfront property in Miami Beach on Biscayne Bay serves; Bee Gees star Barry Gibb is among their neighbors. For West Coast living, there is the Beverly Hills home where Diane and Barry threw an engagement party for Jeff Bezos and Lauren Sanchez, welcoming guests Oprah Winfrey, Selma Hayek Pinault, Barbra Streisand, and Kris Jenner, among others. Her first home in Connecticut will be her final resting place, specifically near a bridge over a stream. As Diane pointed out, "At Cloudwalk I will become a mushroom." Their floating palace is their yacht, *Eos* (Greek for goddess of the dawn), whose prow is a nine-foot figurehead modeled after Diane. Until Jeff Bezos' $500 million yacht, the *Eos* was the world's most expensive.

Due to multiple addresses and with one floating, it is as difficult to locate the legendary designer as it is Waldo. However, a journalist tracked her down to Italy. The interview took place in a palazzo overlooking the Grand Canal, a palace owned by Egon's aunt, the ninety-seven-year-old Christiana Brandolini d'Adda. Diane von Fürstenberg remarked of her new residence, "Venice is a nice stage for the winter of my life." However, for the woman who has rivaled cats in the number of lives they purportedly possess, no one is likely to hear her pronounce, "It's a wrap."

CHAPTER 5

Dolly Parton: Brave Enough to Try (1946)

"It takes a lot of money to look this cheap."

—DOLLY PARTON

◇◇◇◇◇◇◇◇◇◇◇◇◇◇◇◇

In 1809, Canadian author Edmund Vance Cooke wrote a poem that described a squalid village in which Nance Lincoln had just given birth. A local groused of the newborn Abe Lincoln, "Poor young'un born without a chance!" Another baby "born without a chance," Dolly Parton, made the transition from cabin to mansion. In her meteoric rise, she never lost her homespun roots or her humility.

Her 1994 memoir, *Dolly: My Life and Other Unfinished Business*, opened with a self-mythologizing sentence, "Once upon a time and far, far away, back in the hollers at the foothills of the Great Smoky Mountains..." Dolly was the fourth of twelve children of her mother, Avie Lee Owens, who was married at age fifteen to the seventeen-year-old Robert Lee Parton. The teenaged couple rented a ramshackle lodging in the Tennessee woods. To supplement his sharecropper wages, Robert brought home wild game that Avie Lee served as meals: rabbit, squirrel, groundhog, turtle, and bear. After the birth of their first three children, Willadeene, David, and Denver, the family relocated to a one-room cabin on the banks of the Little Pigeon River in East Tennessee, a home without electricity, without an indoor bathroom. Dolly reminisced they had "two rooms and a path and running water, if you were willing to run to get it." For Dolly's birth, Doc Thomas arrived on horseback; Robert paid him in cornmeal. To entertain her daughters, Avie Lee fashioned dolls that consisted of a corncob body for which Robert created a mouth with a fire poker. Dolly's became her prize possession; she christened the toy 'Tiny Tassel Top.'

An indelible childhood experience occurred when Avie Lee sewed Dolly a winter coat made from scraps of discarded clothing. Dolly thought she looked like Joseph; her classmates thought she looked like white trash. Years later, Dolly composed *The Coat of Many Colors*, singing, "Now I know we had no money/But I was rich as I could be/In my coat of many colors/My momma made for me..."

When Dolly was five, Avie Lee wrote down the lyrics to her daughter's song "Life Doesn't Mean that Much to Me." Her grandfather Jake declared that Dolly "started singing as soon as she quit crying." A natural-born performer, Dolly placed a tin can on a stick as a makeshift microphone. Standing on her porch, her audience was "whatever was in the front yard—human, animal, or dirt."

The key to Dolly's lavish looks began with her perception she was homely. She recalled, "I was an ugly little ol' young-un." I used to overhear people saying, 'Look at that little ugly tabby-headed young-un. She don't even look like one of Robert and Avie Lee's kids." To compensate for her perceived shortcomings, Dolly used purple pokeberries to darken her lips, burnt matches to apply eyeliner, and mashed-up honeysuckle for perfume. In her memoir, she wrote that she would only leave the house without her hair and makeup done at gunpoint. She also sleeps with her makeup on in case of an earthquake. Growing up in a Pentecostal household, the sisters drew what they called "Jesus sandals" on their feet and pretended to be biblical characters. Dolly dearly coveted a pair of red high heels that arrived in a charity box. She recalled, "I loved high heels even before I knew I was gonna be short!" She never outgrew her youthful love of stilettos: She wears them around her mansion, and even her golf shoes have heels.

At age ten, her Uncle Bill arranged for her to perform on the *Cas Walker Radio Show* in Knoxville, Tennessee. Bill recalled, "She caused some clamor. She was an instant hit. The engineers came a-runnin' to find out who that young-un was, a-singin' so growed-up-like." Cas gave her airtime on his television show; but because her family did not own a TV, they were unable to tune in. Before one episode, Cas organized a publicity stunt where participants had to climb a greased fifty-foot pole; the first to reach the top would receive $50. The enterprising Dolly immersed herself first in water, then rolled herself in sand to provide friction. Her winnings led to the purchase of the Partons' first television. A lucky break arrived when she performed on the *Grand Ole Opry*. Johnny Cash introduced the ten-year-old, who sang, "You Gotta Be My Baby." The four thousand spectators gave the singing sensation three encores.

Determined to be the first in her family to graduate high school, Dolly returned home. Still self-conscious over her looks, Dolly began to wear heavy makeup, a look she modeled on the woman she referred to as the town tramp. While the town denigrated the "fallen woman," Dolly felt the lady of the night was "the prettiest thing she had ever seen" with her peroxide blonde hair piled on the top of her head, red lips and fingernails, high heels, and tight shirt. She aspired to a "cheap and gawdy" look that she actualized when she donned the façade of a Backwoods Barbie. To add height to her five-foot frame, she teased her hair into a towering bouffant. When her metaphoric ship arrived, Dolly took to buying hundreds of wigs teased into towering heights. A fan of stars Marilyn Monroe, Jayne Mansfield, and Mae West, she used her money to buy peroxide. Local mean girls pronounced her "trashy." The first glimpse Dolly had of the world beyond the mountains occurred in 1964 with Sevier County High School's senior class field trip to New York City. The outing coincided with the Broadway musical hit *Hello, Dolly!*—leading the girl from the 'holler' to exclaim, "They must have been waitin' for me!" Tired of the poverty, pettiness, and patriarchy, Dolly desired a life far beyond East Tennessee: "I used to see relatives marrying one ol' s**tty guy after another, and their teeth would rot out, and I'd think, 'That is not what I'm a-gonna do with my life.' "

Six years after her field trip, Dolly returned to New York City, but there was no warm greeting of "Hello, Dolly" this time. She reminisced, "We came here, and we stayed down on, what is it, Forty-Second Street, where all the whores run? We went out walking, and we saw there were all these porno movies, and we were thinking, 'Oh, my God, this don't look like a good place.' And we were overdressed—lookin' like I do now, we did look like trash, and so we looked the part." When a man "started grabbing me in places I reserve for grabbers of my own choosing," she threatened that if he touched her one more time, she would shoot him. As she was carrying a gun, she could well have—in a phrase from her film *9 to 5*—transformed him from a rooster to a hen.

On a Greyhound bus, Dolly left for Nashville, picking up some barter side work at a diner where she refilled the salt and pepper shakers in exchange for food. Other means of urban survival included eating off trays left in hotel hallways. On her first day in Nashville, Dolly was outside the Wishy-Washy Laundromat when a stranger remarked, "Y'all gonna get sunburnt out there, little lady." Carl Thomas Dean and Dolly started dating; she was distraught when he joined the army for a two-year stint.

A year later, Dolly had her first recording with Monument Records, whose executives told her, "Nobody's ever going to take you serious as a songwriter or a singer if you look like that, because you look more like a hooker than you do a singer." Not only did fans get used to her appearance, they expected Dolly would wear outfits that only Marilyn Monroe, Mae West, Barbie dolls, and King Louis XIV could have pulled off. Her first album, *Dumb Blonde*, proved prescient as she declared, "Cause this dumb blonde ain't nobody's fool." Dolly hitched her wagon to Porter Wagoner, who hired her for his eponymous television show. By the early 1970s, Dolly had her hit single "Coat of Many Colors."

Three years after she left small-town Tennessee, Sevierville designated a Dolly Parton Day, and several thousand people participated in a parade in her honor. In 2010, the University of Tennessee bestowed an honorary doctorate on the state's famous daughter. Dolly remarked, "Just think, I am Dr. Dolly. When people say something about 'double D,' they will be talking of something entirely different!"

With her soaring popularity, Dolly bought a Cadillac; a terrible driver, she crashed her car into the brick wall of the studio parking lot. With finances no longer an obstacle, Carl Dean and Dolly wed in a secret ceremony in Ringgold, Georgia, in 1966. Seven years later, Dolly penned her signature song "Jolene" based on a woman who had flirted with Carl. Comeuppance came to the flirtatious "Jolene" when Dolly ran into her after a span of years and made a discovery: "As she was as broad as a barn, I didn't feel threatened anymore. That's my revenge!" Dolly and Carl acquired Willow Lake Plantation, a twenty-three-room mansion situated on sixty-five acres near Nashville in the town of Brentwood, complete with a swimming pool, tennis court, and chapel. The estate provides ample space for Dolly's sentimental treasures, including Porter Wagoner's dry cleaning receipt with the scrawled lyrics to her 1971 classic "Coat of Many Colors" and her first song royalty check, for which she received $1.02. Her book *Behind the Seams: My Life in Rhinestones* details her voluminous closets that hold everything from her childhood coat of many colors to the disco-ball suit she wore to the Academy of Country Music Awards.

Childless, Dolly took in her five younger siblings, who called her 'Aunt Granny' while Carl was 'Peepaw.' Due to Carl's reclusive nature, rumors have always dogged their relationship. The couple has an open marriage, about which Dolly pronounced, "It's very healthy for both of us." Dolly dresses to the nines even while in the privacy of her mansion. She quipped that when she sees Carl snoring in his La-Z-Boy chair, she asks herself, "Where is Jolene when I need her? Come on, you can have him now!"

Porter Wagoner, a decade her senior, served as Dolly's musical father figure, and together they cranked out lucrative duets until Dolly succumbed to the seven-year itch. No longer willing to play the role of the dutiful lil' lady, Dolly decided to branch out on her own. As a parting gift to him, Dolly composed, "I Will Always Love You." The song soared to number one on the country music charts. Elvis Presley approached her hoping to record her song—but his request came with the stipulation he would receive half the publishing rights. She turned down his offer; with the money she made on royalties, she could have bought Elvis' home, Graceland, many times over. For the 1992 film *The Bodyguard*, Whitney Houston sang a soul-stirring rendition of "I Will Always Love You." Porter sued Dolly for breach of contract for deciding to go solo and won a $1 million award. Despite the stress of the lawsuit, Dolly felt she had made the right move.

The small-town girl moved to Los Angeles, where she added to her country repertoire with pop music, including the duet with Kenny Rogers, "Islands in the Stream." Dolly had her first million-selling record with "Here You Come Again." In addition to winning a Grammy, Dolly appeared on *The Tonight Show*, *Cher*, and *Hollywood Squares*, and she had her own program, *Dolly*. In 1977, along with family members, she formed a band called the Gypsy Fever Band. The exterior of her tour bus, dubbed "The Coach of Many Colors," was a mixture of pink, purple, and silver; inside, it held hues of yellow, pink, and orange.

Hollywood beckoned in 1980 when Dolly shared the silver screen with heavy hitters Jane Fonda and Lily Tomlin in the movie *9 to 5*, a fantasy of revenge against a chauvinist male boss. Not only did she excel in her role, Dolly also wrote the theme song, which made it to the number one slot on pop and country charts. Another breakout performance was in a film whose title described Dolly Parton herself: *Steel Magnolias*. Leaving Tennessee in her rear-view mirror, Dolly toured London, Sweden, Alaska, and Hawaii. In England, Dolly performed for Queen Elizabeth II. Dolly said that the queen wore "just as much jewelry as I did, though maybe she was a little tastier with it."

In a world far away from the Tennessee woods, Dolly's superstar status opened the doors to rarefied zip codes. In the 1970s, she hung out at celebrity hot spot Studio 54, whose owner, Steve Rubell, threw a party in her honor where he filled his nightclub with hay bales, along with a backdrop that showcased cows and a white horse. The guests wore country-western outfits; ironically, that evening, Dolly herself arrived in a sparkly black chiffon. She partied with Andy Warhol, who immortalized her in all her blonde glory on his canvas. During that era, Dolly also met designers Calvin Klein and Diane von Fürstenberg. When Dolly, clad in a red miniskirt and matching red jacket, entered the Manhattan eatery Le Madri, she became the focus of all eyes. Ivana Trump sent the singer a bottle of wine.

Dolly Parton's appearance is an indelible part of her repertoire: gravity defying breasts (often the butt of her own jokes), wind-defying platinum wigs, and her age-defying face. But although she occupies a hallowed niche in pop culture, and despite having written three memoirs, she remains elusive. How did this product of a poor, white, Southern Christian milieu turn into a media sensation mogul? How did she pull off the metamorphosis from rags to rhinestones? Deeply religious, Dolly ascribes her higher power as the source of her success. In *Songteller: My Life in Lyrics*, Dolly wrote, "A great line will just come to me, and I'll go, 'Hey, thank you, Lord. I know I didn't think of that.' " She also credits her success to her work ethic: while most people work nine to five, Dolly works from three in the morning on, too busy to spend time on sleep. In Dolly-speak, "I may look like a show pony, but I'm a workhorse."

She has written that her three passions are "God, music, and sex," but she has a fourth: money, motivated by her hardscrabble youth; the tireless Dolly manages her $650 million fortune. *The Wall Street Journal* described her as "one of the most important women in the world for business and in industry." Capitalizing on her fame and fortune, the singer founded Dolly Parton Enterprises; she has her own record label, movie production company, and music publishing company, the latter of which brings in $150 million annually. She has investments in real estate, restaurants, radio stations, macadamia nuts, and Williams Sonoma bakeware—just for starters. The crown jewel in her multipronged empire is her theme park, Dollywood, located on seven hundred acres in Pigeon Forge, Tennessee, with an annual revenue of $30 million. There is a replica of her childhood mountain homestead and one of the Southern Gospel Hall of Fame. Nearby is Dollywood's Splash Mountain, the state's largest water park.

In recognition of her having given so much back to Pigeon Forge, the region raised $60,000 for a life-size bronze Dolly Parton statue that stands in the courthouse square, an honor generally reserved for soldiers who fought for the Confederacy. The monument depicts a young, barefoot Dolly in rolled-up jeans, sitting on a rock and holding a guitar. Of the honor, Dolly stated, "I'm prouder of that statue than almost anything in my life." Not all superheroes wear capes; some are clad in corsets. Dolly has put more than 200 million free books in the hands of children through her Imagination Library organization. During the pandemic, Dolly donated $1 million to develop a Covid-19 vaccine. With her astronomical fortune, Dolly can afford to buy any number of islands in the stream.

The rhinestone cowgirl says her wish is to die onstage in the middle of a song...at age 120. The rags-to-riches life of this funny, feisty, fabulous (and self-made) performer has proved her courage. As she herself has said, “You’ll never do a whole lot unless you’re brave enough to try.”

CHAPTER 6

Donatella Versace: The Modern Medusa (1955)

"I don't mind not being tall. I think tall."

—DONATELLA VERSACE

The Medusa flag flies above the Versace boutique, Milan, Italy

World-renowned fashionista Donatella Versace is the fabulous, formidable, and unforgettable force behind a world acclaimed label. The family that commandeered a billion-dollar industry hailed from the rugged region situated on the toe of Italy's geographical boot. When Donatella was born a decade after the end of World War II, the town of Reggio di Calabria still bore the scars of heavy Allied bombings. Antonio Versace, after his obligatory two years of military service in Mussolini's fascist army, married Francesca, who owned a clothing store. The couple had children Fortunata (called Tina), Santo, and Giovanni Maria, (called Gianni). The Versaces visited a carnival where twelve-year-old Fortunata sustained an injury that resulted in her death. Partial healing arrived a year later with the birth of Donatella.

The nine-year age difference between Donatella and Gianni did not prove an impediment to their extremely affectionate sibling relationship. Known for her glow-in-the-dark platinum locks, at Gianni's urging, a hairdresser gave her highlights when she was ten years old. After classes, she often headed for the beaches to roast under the sun that turned her skin the color of Milan's rooftops. Of the sibling dynamic, Donatella recalled, "There was always Santo, the calm one, Gianni, [who was] the *enfant terrible*, and me." From an early age, Gianni longed for escape: In his hometown, he was disparaged as the boy who preferred sewing to soccer and boys to girls.

Donatella attended the University of Florence, where she studied literature and languages. Compliments of her brother, rather than the torn jeans and fringed vests of the hippie era, she wore clothes by Kenzo, a Paris-based Japanese designer. When Gianni bought them a pair of matching full-length leather coats, they stood out in backwater Calabria like the idiomatic sore thumb. On the weekends, the diva-in-training headed for Milan, where she worked alongside her brother. After their mother Francesca's death, a distraught Donatella dropped out of university, and the siblings turned to one another for solace.

In 1978, Gianni opened his own label and boutique, whose logo was the snake-haired Medusa of ancient Greek myth. When he acquired a 45,000-square-foot baroque palazzo on Via Gesù, the palazzo's door knocker bore the image of the Greek Gorgon. The establishment sports leather chairs embossed with oversized Medusas; espresso cups have mini ones. The bad girl of Greek mythology appears on doors, etched in glass, and on employees' belt buckles. One bathroom has no fewer than fourteen.

Gianni and Donatella ran Versace as their sibling fiefdom, in which they cooperated and clashed in equal measure. Not a fan of his sister's skintight pants or her ever-present heels, he told her to lay off those "damn stilettos." Desirous of hiding her five-foot-two stature, which made her feel dwarfed by statuesque models, Donatella clung to her high heels. Despite their spats, Gianni stated of his sister, "We can fight at six o'clock and have a nice dinner at eight." Gianni treated his sister to a twenty-carat diamond ring.

Gianni had remarked, "If I was to marry, I would look for a girl like Donatella." Whether or not his sister shared this sentiment, in 1985, Donatella wed Paul Beck, a model from Long Island, New York. The venue was a tiny church in Moltrasio on Lake Como; Italian pop star Ornello Vanoni was the maid of honor, and the bride wore a gown designed by her brother. Gianni's wedding gift was a lavish apartment in the exclusive zip code of Viale Majno that had two kitchens, several dressing rooms, and vast closets. Her bedroom's bathroom, one that a friend dubbed "the eighth wonder of the world," held python-skin-covered chairs as well as tiles that depicted massive Magritte pink and red lips. Her bathtub was made of marble. Eventually, Gianni acquired two more adjacent apartments as add-ons, leaving Donatella with a twenty-one-room home.

With that many rooms, there were more than enough for a nursery. During her pregnancy, Donatella continued to puff on the ever-present Marlboro Reds that left her with a hoarse voice. Her Milan staff covered the warning-label words "Smoking Kills" on her cigarette packs with stickers bearing a DV monogram in medieval script. Her lighter carried pink crystals; her ashtray bore the Medusa logo. Pregnancy did not entail putting her sky-high heels in storage. Gianni christened his niece Allegra Donata; his term of endearment for her was *principessa*. Not an adherent of the maxim "All things in moderation," Donatella threw her daughter over-the-top parties. For one birthday, fifty children attended the celebration at Via Gesù. Gianni fashioned Allegra's dress; but as he was not fond of rambunctious kids, he was a no-show. Before leaving, each guest received a party favor parcel of Versace perfumes, T-shirts, and purses. Daniel, who arrived four years later, received his name from the Elton John song. In Gianni's book *Do Not Disturb*, in which he described his magnificent estates, the dedication was a tribute to his niece and nephew: "to my little princess" and "my little teddy-boy." When Donatella took Allegra ice skating at the elegant Swiss resort at St. Moritz, Donatella wore a black catsuit, a gold ski jacket, and a diamond bracelet. She has admitted that on ski vacations, she never hit the slopes, but added, "I have gorgeous clothes." Several muscular bodyguards and a personal assistant that bears a striking resemblance to Fabio trailed after them. *Mamma mia*!

The 1990s were the golden years for the king and First Lady of fashion. The decade saw the world's greatest supermodels strutting down the Versace catwalk: Liz Hurley made her splash in *that* safety-pin dress, on which each pin bore the Medusa logo.

After Gianni purchased his Miami mansion (whose original owners had named it Casa Casuarina after a Somerset Maugham story), Donatella became a part of the celebrity culture and partied with rock stars. In 1994, she attended Madonna's thirty-sixth birthday party, where the material girl bared her breasts before jumping into her pool. Donatella made her own variation of a splash with her gold dress covered with Medusa heads. In a kaleidoscopic blur, she was in Milan with Tupac and in Paris with Lisa Marie Presley, who worked as a Versace advertising model. Her frenetic pace could be attributed to squeezing every drop life offered from each day: "To go to sleep is the last thing I want to do." Her lack of sleep may also have stemmed from her daily eight cups of espresso. Nights were a tapestry of champagne and coke—the latter not of the soft drink variety. Shrugging off rumors about Donatella's addiction, Gianni replied, "My sister's crazy." At the height of her hedonism, her drug paraphernalia consisted of a tiny gold spoon with a Medusa head. (For any wanting a "regular" spoon, Versace sells a Medusa Gilded Coffee Spoon for $425.)

As she aged, Donatella has become a goddess with a campy personal style. Due to decades of bleaching and hot ironing, a top Manhattan hairdresser flies to wherever Donatella is staying to style her extensions. She has them redone every six weeks at an annual expenditure of $150,000 per year. A commando at dieting, her toned arms are the size of Twizzlers. Donatella's makeup routine entails black eyeliner and layers of false eyelashes, some made of mink. Actor Rupert Everett, a friend of Donatella, has described her as "a kamikaze blonde in black leather and stilettos, more like a character from *Blade Runner* than the stately doyenne of a Milanese fashion house." Per her instructions, her chef uses low-fat ingredients *sans* salt and with a mere drizzle of oil. Her accessories are golf-ball sized diamonds and a gold watch that would look oversized on Shrek. Her towering heels add six inches to her height, and her sexy attire accentuates her toned body. She owns outfits in every color found in a Crayola box except red—the color of the house of Valentino.

On *Saturday Night Live*, comedian Maya Rudolph performed a recurring sketch of the Italian socialite. After watching the skit, Donatella phoned Rudolph and complained, “I can tell from a mile away that your jewelry is fake. You can’t do that to me, darling...I’m allergic to it. I get a rash all over my body.”

When staying at the Ritz in Paris—along with her bodyguards—Donatella flew in her own florist from Milan, deeming the hotel’s flowers not up to her standard. When the manager showed Gianni the Imperial Suite, he turned it down as too expensive, remarking, “Give it to my sister. She likes grand things.” Other favored hotels were the pricey Waldorf Towers in Manhattan and the bungalows at the Beverly Hills Hotel. When notified she would be their guest, the Dorchester Hotel in London sprayed her suite with her favorite floral perfume. Once, after renting a palatial villa in St. Tropez, she brought in her own furniture to replace the Native American style décor. If her expenses exceeded her generous salary, Santo and Gianni picked up the tab. When the blues intruded, Donatella visited Cartier and Harry Winston.

After returning from the United States in 1997, Gianni developed inner ear cancer, and in his absence, Donatella became the face of Versace. A *Vanity Fair* article entitled “La Bella Donatella” showcased a photograph of her in which she was nude—except for the diamond that her brother had bought her as a gift. As she took on more responsibilities, however, Gianni began to consider his sister as more his rival than his partner. Under a cloud of sibling discord, with the awareness of impending mortality, Gianni wrote his will.

After six months, with his cancer in remission, the sibling iceberg melted. In mid-1997, Gianni was at his oceanfront Miami mansion, looking forward to joining Elton John at his French villa in Nice. As he walked up the marble stairs of his estate to unlock its iron gate, Andrew Cunanan shot Gianni in the neck and face.

While Cunanan fired his fateful shots, eighteen fashion houses were organizing a fashion show complete with catwalk on Rome's Spanish Steps in honor of Gianni Versace. Donatella was staying at the Hotel de la Ville, a seventeenth-century palazzo-hotel whose terrace offered views of the Vatican and the Colosseum. The suite had a white baby grand piano, compliments of composer Leonard Bernstein.

During preparations, hearing of his brother's assassination, Santo cried out, "Donatella, *vieni qua subito*!" ("Come with me!") When Donatella learned their brother had passed away, her primal scream stopped the models in their tracks. At this time, eleven-year-old Allegra and six-year-old Daniel watched as the news of their uncle's murder interrupted their cartoon. The throng of reporters was so dense that thirty bodyguards had to escort Santo, Donatella, and the children into their Mercedes. A private jet flew the siblings to Florida. Feeling that they would not want to stay at Gianni's mansion, Madonna extended an invitation to stay at her home, one they refused. They were unable to grieve in peace since Casa Casuarina was under media siege. Absorbed with preparations for the funeral, Donatella retained her composure. However, at dinner, when the chef served vanilla *budino*, her brother's favorite, she broke down. The following day, the siblings returned to Italy; Santo held the gold box that contained Gianni's ashes. Donatella had the key to the gate of the Miami mansion, the last thing her brother had held.

Of her desire to stage a fitting funeral for her brother, Donatella stated, "Gianni was killed like a stray dog, I want him to have a funeral fit for a prince." The venue was the Duomo, the world's third largest Catholic church. The Versace siblings convinced Milan to close off the Via dell'Arcivescovado, a concession not even granted Pope John Paul II. A who's who of celebrities bid *arrivederci* to the designer. In the sea of two thousand mourners sat Princess Diana; six weeks later, Santo and Donatella attended Diana's funeral. Sitting in a pew with faces etched with grief and heads covered with black veils sat Donatella and Allegra.

When the attorney read the will, Santo and Donatella sat in stunned silence: Gianni had excluded them. He had bequeathed his 50 percent share of Versace, a company valued at $805 million, to his *principessa* Allegra. He bequeathed his $47 million art collection, one that held two Picassos, to Daniel. Gianni's multimillion-dollar homes in Italy, Lake Como, Manhattan, and Miami became the property of the shareholders: Santo held 30 percent, Donatella 20 percent, and Allegra 50 percent. Because the art collection was in the company's name, it became the property of the company.

After the funeral, Donatella, Paul, and their children fled the media frenzy and flew to Necker Island, the British Virgin Island resort owned by English magnate Richard Branson. The cost of their stay was $12,000 per night. Despite her devastation, she had to look after two minor children; Allegra was traumatized and had practically stopped eating—the shock triggered the onset of her chronic anorexia. Marital troubles led to Donatella's divorce shortly after her daughter's thirteenth birthday. Her second marriage, to Manuel Dallori, lasted a year. Afterwards, dating was low on her hierarchy of goals. She explained, "I have an interest, of course, but I'm too busy. And then I think, 'Oh my God, who wants to date me.' I'm so complicated. People have a low perception of me, men especially. They think, 'This woman, she's a nightmare.' " To top off the tension, Donatella was in the throes of a cocaine addiction. Partially as an antidote to her anxiety, Donatella indulged in expenditures such as a $2 million diamond ring, which she charged to the business. Despite her exacting attention to her appearance, Donatella landed on Blackwell's worst-dressed list, along with Anna Nicole Smith and Princess Anne. Of the diminutive diva, he wrote that she "resembles a flash-fried Venus, stuck in a Miami strip mall. Time to toss the peroxide once and for all."

Under these weighty burdens, Donatella was apprehensive about taking the reins of Versace. She knew the eyes of the world would look with cynicism on the kid sister daring to follow in her genius brother's footsteps. Her responsibilities entailed designing male and female clothing lines for the brands Versace, Versace Atelier, Versace Collection, and Versace Jeans Couture. In addition, she was also in charge of perfume, watches, eyeglasses, shoes, purses, and scarves. Of her debilitating doubt, she said, "I realized that all the eyes of the world were on top of me, and really, people didn't believe I was going to pull through. All these people depending on me, their jobs on my shoulders, to live up to Gianni's dream. I'm going to f*** up everything Gianni did?" Her worst fears were actualized: Versace posted losses of $7.1 million in 2002.

Two years later, at a gathering at Via Gesù for Allegra's eighteenth birthday, Santo, Allegra, and Daniel, along with Elton John, staged an intervention where they persuaded Donatella to enter rehab. Although she was filled with consternation the facility would not adhere to her diet of low-fat ingredients, her main concern was relinquishing her heels. On her private plane to the Arizona rehab known as the Meadows, she sobbed. The stint proved successful, and she emerged equipped to assume control of Versace.

Ultimately, Donatella proved that the harsh landscape of her Calabrian roots had given her a steel backbone. She stated, "I had been listening to everyone else, and then I realized, who was the person my brother listened to? Me." In 2018, Michael Kors purchased Versace in a $2.1-billion-dollar deal.

PART TWO

Heiresses

CHAPTER 7

Evalyn Walsh McLean: Sita's Curse (1886)

"But we had the money, or rather, it had us. We were held fast in its clutches."

—EVALYN WALSH MCLEAN IN HER MEMOIR, QUEEN OF DIAMONDS.

◇◇◇◇◇◇◇◇◇◇◇◇◇

It is said that things one wears don't make the man, or the woman, for that matter—but Evalyn Walsh McLean would have been a forgotten footnote of a fabulous fortune had her path not crossed that of the fabled Hope Diamond. The story of this society queen began when nineteen-year-old Thomas Walsh traveled steerage from Tipperary, Ireland, to America. He built bridges for the Colorado Central Railroad until he heeded the clarion call, "There's gold in them thar hills!" Rumor ran rife that miners had located gold in the Black Hills of South Dakota. Infected with mining fever, he headed for Deadwood. As the wagon convey was full, he took the next one; he later discovered Native Americans had scalped and killed all the passengers from the first transport. When Thomas failed to find his motherlode, he opened a hotel in Leadville, Colorado.

In Leadville, Thomas struck romantic gold. Although a Roman Catholic, he wandered into a Protestant Church, where he fell for a woman in the choir. He married Carrie Bell Reed in 1879. Thomas moved to a mining camp in Sowbelly Gulch, where he and his bride lived in a converted railroad boxcar. After losing their firstborn, they doted on children Evalyn and Vinson.

While living in Ouray, Colorado, with Carrie Bell out of town and son Vinson only toddler age, Thomas confided in ten-year-old Evalyn, "Daughter, I've struck it rich." After two decades, Thomas had discovered a gold mine. Thomas' Camp Bird Mine churned out $5,000 a day in precious metal. He eventually sold Camp Bird Mine for $5.2 million and a share of future proceeds. The wealthy Walshes left for Washington, DC, where the press referred to Thomas as the "Colorado Monte Cristo." Thomas scooped up real estate near the White House. In gratitude for the millionaire's endorsement, President McKinley invited the Walshes to a White House reception and appointed Thomas as a commissioner to the Paris Exposition of 1900. Riding on that wave, the Walsh family set sail on the White Star Line ship SS *Majestic* and spent a year at the

Elysée Palace Hotel in Paris. The couple hosted a party aboard a Seine River steamer, transforming it into a floating pleasure dome.

For a tour of the continent, Thomas arranged for a private train replete with five cars. The days the family spent in Ireland were emotional stopovers for the expatriate *paterfamilias*, and as a devout Catholic, he was deeply moved when the Walshes had a private audience with Pope Pius. They visited the resort town of Ostend for a meeting with Belgium's King Leopold II; the royal met with Thomas hoping he would invest in Leopold's copper and silver mines in the Belgium Congo. Despite the lure of further riches, Thomas refused; Leopold's colonialism had claimed ten million lives, producing inhumanity about which Joseph Conrad wrote his famed novel "Heart of Darkness." The King visited the family in the States when he attended the St. Louis World's Fair.

The prospect of the royal visit was partially the impetus for Thomas to build a four-story Beaux Arts mansion located at 2020 Massachusetts Avenue, Washington, DC, in the center of what is currently Embassy Row. (The Indonesian embassy occupies the site of the former Walsh residence.) The vast estate required the work of twenty-three servants to maintain it. The home's architectural jewel was a three-story reception hall with a stained glass dome. The top floor held a ballroom and a theater, while a pipe organ delivered music to the dining room. The central staircase was reminiscent of an ocean liner made of mahogany. At the conclusion of one dinner party, a giant flower balloon opened and songbirds flew out, serenading the guests. Another gala was held for Alice Roosevelt, President Theodore Roosevelt's daughter.

When Evalyn was nineteen, the Walshes rented Beaulieu, a "cottage" in Newport, from Cornelius Vanderbilt III. The siblings spent the summer attending balls, lawn parties, and the beach, which they drove to in Evalyn's red Mercedes. In Rome, Evalyn had met the Italian Prince Altieri, who possessed matinee idol looks. He had proposed, and Evalyn was considering the prospect of becoming a princess and living in a palace. Sensing her father was distraught at the thought of leaving his daughter behind in Europe, she offered to break up with the prince in exchange for a red Mercedes—which she then drove around in Paris and Monte Carlo. The question that directed Evalyn's days was, "What amusing thing can I do next?"

On an August afternoon in 1905, brother and sister went to the Clambake Club for a luncheon. On the return to Beaulieu, the Mercedes, which Vinson was driving, careened out of control and struck a wooden bridge. Evalyn ended up in the water, trapped under the car. In her terror, all she could think of was her brother. Rescuers brought her to Alfred G. Vanderbilt's nearby mansion; she had sustained a broken leg, while the impact had resulted in Vinson's death. To help her through the physical and emotional grief, Evalyn became addicted to morphine.

Edward Beale "Ned" McLean, a man she had known since age nine, kept her company, bringing her records for her gramophone. Ned's grandfather, Washington McLean, owned the *Cincinnati Enquirer, The Washington Post,* and a railroad line. His family home, Friendship, located two blocks from the White House, was a Florentine villa designed by John Russell Pope, who had also been behind the Jefferson Memorial and the National Gallery of Art. His alcoholism led to Evalyn's observation, "He got drinking so frightfully he used to have to tie a handkerchief around his arm to get the drink up."

On a 1908 July afternoon, while on a drive in Denver with the chauffeur in the front, Ned and Evalyn discussed their plans for their future. Evalyn decided against a wedding because she figured they would both be too drunk and scared to walk down the aisle. They eloped the next day; the Walshes and McLeans both gave the newlyweds a gift of $100,000. The couple took a three-month honeymoon in Europe and the Mideast. They purchased a two-seater Mercedes in Paris, and it awaited the McLeans when they docked in Amsterdam. Evalyn always kept the car as a souvenir from this happy time, the way other women would a champagne cork, faded violets, or a ticket stub. Other purchases were a chinchilla coat and a traveling case made of gold that held toiletries, which was a replica of one made for the Crown Princess of Germany. In Constantinople, Evalyn told the American ambassador, John G. A. Leishmann, of her desire to visit the Yildiz Palace to meet with the Turkish Sultan, the Caliph of all Mohammedan faithful. Before they returned home, they visited Cartier's in Paris and left with the ninety-five-carat diamond known as "The Star of the East," acquired for $120,000.

In 1909, Evalyn gave birth at home at 2020 Massachusetts to her son Vinson, whom the press heralded as "the hundred-million-dollar baby." The doting family purchased a golden crib and a golden tub; King Leopold sent a quilted canopy. One of the first to welcome the baby was President Taft. Her father Thomas was diagnosed with cancer soon thereafter, and Evalyn and Ned rushed to San Antonio, Texas. When Thomas died in 1910, President Taft was among the mourners; Carrie Bell and Evalyn were too distraught to attend the interment. The McLeans remained in Texas to help Carrie Bell in her bereavement. They felt horrible at their separation from baby Vinson; moreover, when their baby was two months old, they received kidnapping threats.

When Evalyn and Ned vacationed in Paris, jeweler Pierre Cartier visited the mining and newspaper heirs at the Hotel Bristol. He carried a package containing a magnificent jewel that Evalyn had seen on the Sultan's favorite concubine. Cartier shared that during the Turkish Revolution, the woman had died from stab wounds. Making a full disclosure, he explained the notoriously cursed Hope Diamond's history began in seventeenth-century India when Jean-Baptiste Tavernier, a French adventurer, plucked it from the eye of a Hindu idol. In revenge, the temple's priests placed a curse on all who owned the blue diamond. Perhaps the first victim of the curse was Tavernier; a pack of wild dogs mauled him to death in Constantinople. Louis XIV, a subsequent owner, died from smallpox. The Sun King passed the jewel to his heir, Louis XVI, who, along with his queen, lost his head to Madame Guillotine. After forty years, the stone showed up in England in the possession of banker Henry Thomas Hope—whose surname gave the gem its deceiving moniker. Following his death, Abdul Hamid II, the Sultan of Turkey, presented it to Subaya, his favorite; she died of stab wounds when an uprising deposed the Sultan.

Evalyn pooh-poohed the curse—she felt her fortune made her immune to bad luck; however, the setting was not to her liking. Realizing few people could afford the jewel, Cartier reset it on a chain of diamonds and encircled the blue stone with even more diamonds. Cartier left for America aboard the Lusitania along with the Hope Diamond. Knowing Evalyn remained the most probable buyer, he set a course for Washington, DC, and paid a visit to 2020 Massachusetts Avenue. This time proved a charm as Evalyn decided she had to possess the beautiful blue diamond. Mike, Evalyn's Great Dane, sometimes walked the mansion with the fabled gem affixed to his collar. Although she did not believe in the curse, Evalyn still asked Monsignor Russel to bless the blue diamond.

Evalyn recalled with fondness those heady days when "the dining room tables were seventy-five feet long with a hundred people at each table" and two thousand guests filled their home and gardens. Vinson's birthday parties were elaborate: For party favors, each boy received an electric railroad train, and each girl received an expensive doll. The doting mother recalled she never spent less than $150,000 for each of her son's big days. They also treated their son to a private showing of the circus. One day, Ned said that three-year-old Vinson needed a companion, since he was mainly in the company of bodyguards, governesses, and other adults. He suggested bringing a Black child into their home to serve as his son's friend, who could later serve as his valet. The parents of five-year-old Julian agreed to this scheme. When the Walshes and Julian—dressed in the same fashionable attire as Vinson—traveled to the South, the Black Pullman porters were shocked at the sight of a Black child in the company of the "hundred-million-dollar baby." But the plan fizzled, and the couple returned Julian, along with money. After the arrival of siblings John, (nicknamed Jock), Edward Jr. (Neddie), and Emily—who later changed her named to Evalyn, Vinson gained nonreturnable playmates. President Harding and First Lady Florence served as Emily's godparents.

The family spent weekends at Friendship, where Ned added an eighteen-hole golf course on which Presidents Harding and Coolidge played. (Harding also used the home for his extramarital liaisons.) First Lady Florence Harding and Evalyn were both adherents of a fortune-teller known as Madame Marcia; the superstitious Florence was fearful of the Hope Diamond. A llama purchased from the Ringling Brothers Circus wandered the grounds, as did a donkey and goats. A madcap monkey spilled alcohol on Harding's white suit, and a parrot cried out multilingual curses learned from a diplomat. The McLean children rode on miniature horses and a brightly painted buggy that had once belonged to P. T. Barnum's star, General Tom Thumb. The last soiree at Friendship took place on New Year's Eve, 1936, on Jock's twenty-first birthday; 325 dinner guests attended, with an additional 325 for dancing. As she did for most galas, Evalyn wore the Hope Diamond, the Star of the East, and six diamond bracelets. Fifteen private detectives guarded the walking Fort Knox. Cole

Porter wrote of the heiress in his lyrics for "Anything Goes." Idaho senator William Edgar Borah said of the wealth-laden ballroom, "This is what brings on revolutions."

In 1919, Ned decided to go to the Kentucky Derby; to keep an eye on his drinking, Evalyn came along. Before leaving, they hired two security guards, and they left instructions there were to be no outings. Disregarding the directive, Ned's valet, Meggett, took Vinson for a stroll. A Ford, going eight miles per hour, hit Vinson as he ran across the road. Before he passed away, Vinson asked his grandmother, "Is it wicked for me to love Mother more than God?" In her newfound understanding of the unbearable grief of losing a son, Evalyn contributed $100,000 for the hoped-for return of the kidnapped Charles Lindbergh Jr.

By the end of the 1920s, the Walsh-McLean marriage was collapsing. The political elite ostracized Ned for his involvement in President Harding's Teapot Dome Scandal; Ned accused his wife of marital meandering, and they separated in 1929. At a Santa Monica party, Ned fell for Rose Davies, the sister of Marion Davies, the actress and mistress of publishing tycoon William Randolph Hearst. To live with Rose, Ned moved to Beverly Hills, where he leased a house from cowboy star Tom Mix. He procured a divorce and served it to Evalyn wrapped as a 1932 Christmas present. With his escalating mental instability, Evalyn committed her husband to Baltimore's Sheppard and Enoch Pratt sanatorium. Doctors diagnosed him with amnesia caused by alcoholism. In the hospital, he met fellow patient Zelda Fitzgerald, who later recalled Ned went by the name Mr. Orlo, and that together they danced the hokey pokey. Ned died in his hospital room, convinced he was a German spy. When *The Washington Post* faced bankruptcy, Evalyn relinquished ownership of it to Eugène Meyer for $825,000. His daughter, Katharine Graham, later ran the paper.

The last home of Washington, DC's hostess with the mostest was situated in Georgetown perched on a hill. The estate held an oversized portrait of President Harding. The mansion held the remnants of her former six estates, all of which she had lost due to her dwindling of her fortune, a misfortune caused by Ned's financial mismanagement and her over-the-top spending. Arranged around the swimming pool were larger-than-life statues of Molière, Rembrandt, Beethoven, and Louis XIV.

Friends headed to the Georgetown home in 1947 to bid farewell to Evalyn, who had passed away from pneumonia. On her deathbed, she wore the Hope Diamond and other prized jewels. Many suspected the reason behind her decline was she had lost her will to live after her daughter Evalyn had died at age twenty-four from an overdose of sleeping pills, leaving behind a four-year-old child, Mamie Spears Reynolds. Evalyn's great-grandson Joseph Gregory said his grandmother Mamie had teethed on the blue diamond.

The Walsh heirs sold the Hope Diamond to acclaimed jeweler Harry Winston. Ronald Winston, CEO of Harry Winston, who valued the Hope Diamond at $200 million, stated it was "the most expensive object that can be held in one hand." Nine years later, Winston donated the diamond to the Smithsonian. Rather than deliver the priceless gem to the museum via armored car, Winston sent it through the US Mail. James Todd, the postal worker who delivered the gem, faced a series of unfortunate events: a truck crushed his leg, he injured his head in a car accident, his house burned down, and he lost his wife and dog. An estimated seven million visitors view the fabled jewel each year. After gracing the necks of the wealthy and the damned for three centuries, the Hope Diamond had found its final home, ending the goddess Sita's curse.

CHAPTER 8

Marjorie Merriweather Post: Elijah's Manna (1887)

"My father once said that if I were cast ashore on a desert island, I'd organize the grains of sand."

—MARJORIE MERRIWEATHER POST

In 1871, Emperor Wilhelm I of Germany was a guest at Baron James de Rothschild's Château de Ferrières just outside Paris. After being mistaken for the estate's owner, the royal responded, "No king could afford to live here. It could only belong to a Rothschild." Marjorie Merriweather Post was the American Christian scientist version of the European Jewish Rothschilds.

What madeleine pastries did for the French Marcel Proust, cereal does for Americans: It calls back nostalgia for yesterday. The catchphrases of breakfast mascots remain indelible: "They're Gr-r-reat!" "Trix are for kids!" "Snap. Crackle. Pop." Because millions were "Cuckoo for Cocoa Puffs," cereal heiress Marjorie Merriweather Post wore the tiara of an American royal. Her floating palace, a 316-foot yacht called the *Sea Cloud*, was the world's largest privately owned vessel, one that could hold four hundred passengers. The Duke and Duchess of Windsor were among the ship's glitterati guests. Upon viewing the *Sea Cloud*'s Louis XVI master suite, Queen Maud of Norway remarked, "Why, you live like a queen, don't you?"

The woman whose life was, for the most part, as sweet as the sugary concoctions behind her stratospheric wealth was born in Springfield, Illinois, to Charles William Post (better known as C. W. Post) and Ella Post, née Merriweather. Seeking a cure for his physical and mental breakdown, Charles checked into Dr. Kellogg's sanatorium in Battle Creek, Michigan, and the family relocated to the town. Experimenting on his two-burner stove in his white barn, Charles concocted a cereal he named after a biblical prophet and the food God sent to the Israelites. After an outcry from religious groups, Charles renamed his product Post Toasties. Another of his bestsellers was Grape-Nuts.

Eight-year-old Marjorie would sit on a hayloft where she glued labels on cereal boxes; sixty years later, she could still recall the taste of the glue. After the wheat flakes turned to gold, the Midwestern Midas kept his daughter grounded: When Marjorie wanted a moleskin coat for her doll, her father made her set traps to catch the moles. Afterwards, she had to skin, tan, cure, and sew their fur. At age ten, Marjorie accompanied her father to board meetings and family factories. Another parental lesson was self-defense. On her way to school, Marjorie passed a hangout for boys. Charles taught her how to box, and a right hook to a bully's stomach ended the catcalls.

During her childhood, Charles gifted his only child shares of Postum that were worth $3 million by the time she was sixteen. Despite her wealth, Charles was concerned over her extravagant spending on clothing. In 1904, when Marjorie insisted on buying new furs, he wrote to his daughter, who was a student at Washington, DC's elite Mount Vernon Seminary for Girls, saying, "You have more than double the clothes, shoes, and stuff that any girl, no matter how rich, should have at seventeen. Now make some of the furs you have do and don't order more dresses or clothes before you return... Dad wants you *sensible,* so go slow." His daughter, however, did not think he was sensible when he divorced her mother Ella to marry his secretary, Leila Young, who was twenty years his junior.

Although Marjorie adored her father, she did not follow his directives on eschewing extravagance; the heiress spent a quarter of a million dollars a year on her wardrobe. And when she found shoes she liked, she bought the 'glass slippers' in a rainbow of colors. Her spending philosophy: 'If you've got it, flaunt it'—and flaunt it she did.

With the heiresses' beauty, brains, and beaucoup bucks, the world was her oyster, one she wanted to share with a man she loved. A year later, eighteen-year-old Marjorie married Edward Bennett

Close, a New York lawyer from a prominent family. The bride, who had taken annual European trips with her father, included Papa Post on her honeymoon to Egypt and Italy. As a wedding gift, Charles presented the newlyweds with a sizable check and built them 'The Boulders,' an eleven-room estate in Greenwich, Connecticut. The marriage soon eroded: Edward loved the cocktail hour; Christian scientist Marjorie hated it. Further tension arose when Charles realized that his son-in-law had no interest in running the Postum Cereal Company.

Along with her marital problems, Marjorie suffered a major setback in 1914 when Charles ended his life with a shotgun blast in his mouth. Speculation was he had come to the proverbial end of his rope due to ill health and depression. Another contributing factor was Leila's affair with Lawrence Montgomery, whom she subsequently wed. His death left his only child with a $20 million inheritance that she went on to parlay into a billion dollars in contemporary currency. At a time when women could not vote, the intrepid Marjorie ran the Postum Cereal Company, which eventually became Post Cereal, now known as Post Consumer Brands. When asked the reason behind her business acumen, Marjorie responded, "My father."

Although Edward spent $5,000 decorating his wife's private Pullman car with orchids, his wandering eye had wandered to the French maid. The suspicious wife ordered their valet to dust the floor of Edward's bedroom with talcum powder to check how many footprints appeared. After fourteen years and the arrival of children Adelaide and Eleanor, the couple divorced. Edward's remarriage produced his granddaughter actress Glenn Close. Despite the marital discord, Edward was—after her father—the man she loved most.

In 1919, Marjorie married Manhattan stockbroker E. F. Hutton (Edward), with whom she had a third daughter, Nedenia, who later went by the name Dina Merrill in her career as an actress. The family of three lived in a fifty-four-room Manhattan apartment. At Edward's urging, Postum (with cereal boxes bearing the brand name 'Post' in white letters on a red backdrop) became a public corporation with 200,000 shares on the New York Stock Exchange. However, a literal goose laid the golden egg for the Huttons. As they dined on their yacht, a waiter served the couple a goose that had been frozen. Intrigued, Marjorie visited Clarence Birdseye, who had discovered the quick-freezing process. She bought his plant for $20 million and changed her company's name to General Foods Corporation.

The Huttons spent the winter months in Palm Beach, Florida, where Marjorie built a 115-room pink palazzo massive enough that she could entertain in a grandiose style. She purchased seventeen acres between Lake Worth and the Atlantic, which led to her christening her new home "Mar-a-Lago," Spanish for "from sea to lake." On the recommendation of showman Florenz Ziegfeld (better known as 'Flo' Ziegfeld) and his wife, actress Billie Burke—who starred as Glinda the Good Witch in *The Wizard of Oz*—she hired Joseph Urban, a Viennese architect who had designed New York's Metropolitan Opera House. The living room had a thirty-four-foot ceiling, and its walls displayed silk needlework tapestries that had once graced a Venetian palace. A 4,000-pound ballroom length marble table, inlaid with semiprecious stones, bore a likeness to one in Florence's Uffizi gallery. Other decorating flourishes included golden faucets. When guests' jaws dropped upon visiting the palatial estate, husband Edward's stock response was, "You know Marjorie said she was going to build a little cottage by the sea. Look what we got!" And what their guests got on one occasion was a private performance by the Barnum & Bailey Circus.

Unlike Marjorie's first husband, the second Edward was active in the Post family business, and under his directive the company acquired Jell-O, Baker's Chocolate, and Log Cabin Maple Syrup. Despite her father C. W. Post's aversion to coffee—a beverage he equated with taking dope—Edward purchased coffee corporations Maxwell House and Sanka. Six years later, Marjorie froze out her second spouse.

Her third trip down the aisle was with diplomat Joseph E. Davies. When President Roosevelt appointed Joseph ambassador to the Soviet Union, fearful of shortages under Stalin, Marjorie used her yacht to transport twelve lockers of Birds Eye frozen foods, two thousand pints of pasteurized cream, and twenty-five refrigerators to Moscow. With the communists selling off royal remnants, the consummate collector acquired priceless relics. Her penchant for acquisitions had begun as a child, when she started accumulating silver teaspoons. Later in life, imperial possessions were her passion. The heiress owned pear-shaped diamond earrings that Marie Antoinette had sewn into her pocket before her arrest at Varennes, a diamond necklace Napoleon had presented to the Empress Marie Louise, and the diamond wedding crown Empress Alexandra wore the day she wed Tsar Nicholas II. When Joseph's next appointment was as the US ambassador to Belgium, Marjorie embraced the move, declaring with a sense of relief concerning that nation, "Thank God. It's got a king." After two decades of wedded bliss, the couple divorced in 1955.

Before tying the knot with husband number four, Herbert A. Mays, the seventy-one-year-old bride remarked she was "walking on fluffy pink clouds." The pink clouds transformed to gray ones after Marjorie saw nude photographs of Herb cavorting with young men at Mar-a-Lago's oceanside swimming pool. The incriminating pictures clarified a dinner in Montmartre where Herbert had "seemed unduly interested in the waiters." Referring to her string of bad marriages, "Eleanor's like me," she said of her second daughter, who had wed six times, "she always married stinkers." (Her other two daughters married three times each.) When Marjorie asked her lawyer why her forays into matrimony always failed, he responded, "The reason is you try to make them all Mr. Post." After the fourth fiasco had not led to "merry weather," Marjorie resumed her maiden name. In summing up her life, she told her friends that she had enjoyed many lovely things but had no luck with husbands. With a shrug of her shoulders, she asked, "Ain't it hell?" Perhaps it was not hell enough; as she lay dying in 1973 at age eighty-six, she proposed to her doctor.

Along with acquiring men, art, and jewels, Marjorie accumulated real estate as other women did charms on their bracelets. While taking a bite out of the Big Apple, in addition to Mar-a-Lago, Marjorie owned a fifty-four-room triplex. Her Adirondacks summer home, Camp Topridge, housed Marjorie's American Indian collection, comprised of totem poles, stuffed animals, and war bonnets worn by Geronimo and Sitting Bull. Two servants spent four hours a day dusting the collection. She flew guests in on her plane, the *Merriweather*; once they arrived, their accommodations were a private cabin that included a maid and a footman. As with all her properties, Topridge had a golf course.

Perhaps the home closest to the heiress' heart was Hillwood, currently a museum, whose catalogue states of its founder, "In her lifelong pursuit of beautiful and finely made objects, she shared a common taste with the royalty and nobility of eighteenth- and nineteenth-century Europe and Russia." Indeed, Hillwood possesses the greatest collection of Russian imperial art outside the Soviet Union. The marbled entrance hall showcases a painting of Catherine the Great in royal regalia, and the estate houses prized Fabergé eggs. The walls of the staircase feature portraits of various Romanovs.

Whatever the venue, Marjorie was the consummate hostess to guests who bore surnames like Vanderbilt and Kennedy. Butlers used yardsticks to determine the precise placement of dinner plates, napkins, and candleholders. At Hillwood, liveried servants served dinner on plates that had once graced the dining room table of Emperor Franz Joseph I of Austria and Empress Elisabeth. The Post pet schnauzer slept in a dog bed that had once belonged to Belgian royals. While the champagne flowed, Marjorie stuck with fruit and vegetable juice; breakfast was Grape-Nuts. In a nod to her modern Midwestern roots, sometimes the dinner menu held General Food products such as Maxwell House coffee and Jell-O.

Demonstrating the true spirit of *noblesse oblige*, the heiress provided two thousand beds to the Red Cross hospital at Savenay, France, during World War I. Half a century later, Marjorie gave receptions in Washington for veterans wounded in Vietnam. She personally oversaw a Salvation Army feeding station in New York that served a thousand per day. Her largesse included a $100,000 grant to the National Cultural Center in Washington, now known as the John F. Kennedy Center for the Performing Arts. The National Symphony received a donation of $1.5 million.

Marjorie had enjoyed big houses, big jewels, and big art, along with great heartaches. The tragedies that shadowed her life were her parents' divorce, her father's suicide, and her four divorces. In her final days, she was kept in the dark about the drowning of her twenty-four-year-old grandson, David Post Rumbough, in a Long Island boating accident. She predeceased her great-granddaughter, Nedenia Post Dye, heiress to a $35 million dollar fortune, whose murder in Honduras at the hands of a local entertainer known as "The Canary" made international headlines.

If one of Marjorie's staff had been a fortune-teller who could have envisioned her life unfolding in a crystal ball, would she have feared her fabulous fortune? Or perhaps she would have seen in the globe's depths a rarefied destiny, one that she could have described with the original name of Post Toasties: Elijah's Manna.

CHAPTER 9

Bunny Mellon: The Halitosis Heiress (1910)

"Nothing should be noticed."

—BUNNY MELLON

◇◇◇◇◇◇◇◇◇◇◇◇◇◇◇◇◇

The great American financial dynasties originated with railroads (Vanderbilt), oil (Rockefeller), and steel (Carnegie).

But there was only one scion of these dynasties whose wealth was predicated on bad breath: Rachel (Bunny) Mellon.

Entering the Listerine "Stink lab" in New Jersey is equivalent to stepping into a human mouth—one with terrible breath. The purpose of the "stink lab" is for the mouthwash manufacturer to test its various products. The company produces, for example, Listerine Zero, a nonalcoholic brand for distribution in Muslim countries where spirits are prohibited; Green Tea Listerine targets the Asian market; Listerine Naturals courts Americans who desire a holistic formula.

In 1879, Dr. Joseph Lawrence created an antiseptic for use in surgical procedures. Two years later, Dr. Lawrence sold the formula to Jordan Wheat Lambert, who founded the St. Louis-based Lambert Pharmaceutical Co. To promote his product, Jordan traveled to London to meet Dr. Joseph Lister, who had first used the treatment when performing operations. Since fewer patients then died, Queen Victoria rewarded him with a knighthood. Jordan received permission from the newly minted Sir Lister to license his name, which resulted in the brand Listerine. With his newfound prestige and wealth, Jordan was among the local leaders who visited the White House to persuade President Grover Cleveland to come to St. Louis for the 1888 Democratic Convention. As an adult, Jordan Lambert's fifth child, Gerald Barnes Lambert, later came up with catchy ads such as the now-cliched expression, "Always a bridesmaid but never a bride," one that associated the bridesmaid's single status to her failure to gargle. Another caption—alongside a married couple—held the slogan, "Till breath do us part." In 1928, Gerald took his company public and presciently sold its shares for $25 million—in contemporary currency $340 million—before the Stock Market Crash of 1929.

In tribute to the Lamberts' donation of land for the St. Louis Airport and their financing Charles Lindbergh's historic flight, the pilot christened his plane *The Spirit of St. Louis*. The liquid golden goose made Gerald's daughter Rachel a woman of means. A nanny called her 'Bunny,' which became a lifelong nickname even though she grew to a height of five-foot-nine. Her father served as the president of the Gillette Safety Razor Company and managed the family pharmaceutical firm. In the 1920s, after the company repurposed an old Latin word to coin the term 'halitosis,' sales skyrocketed. In 2000, Pfizer purchased the pharmaceutical firm for $110 billion.

The Lamberts' main residence was the fifty-two-room Albemarle estate in Princeton, New Jersey, which was equipped with a ballroom and a large staff. With the advent of automobiles and airplanes, the family purchased the latest models. Bunny and her sister Lily attended Miss Fine's private school, whose former students included the daughters of Presidents Woodrow Wilson and Grover Cleveland.

Mary Lennox, the protagonist of Frances Hodgson's 1911 novel, *The Secret Garden*, shared similarities with Bunny Lambert; the novel's heroine was born in British India to wealthy, emotionally cold parents. After moving to England, the fictional Mary found her purpose in gardening. Bunny felt overshadowed by her brother, Gerald Jr. (nicknamed Sonny), who was the cherished only son, and by her younger sister Lily, praised as the most beautiful daughter. When Bunny was eleven, her maternal grandfather, Arthur Lowe, presented her with a children's wildflower guide that whetted her love of nature. As a child, her first garden epiphany had occurred upon spying a clump of garden phlox, a moment of which she later said, "Like a magic carpet, it has carried me through life's experiences."

After graduating from high school at Foxcroft, Bunny wanted to attend college to study stage design. Gerald vetoed the notion, insisting her vocation lay with marriage and motherhood. As compensation, her father took her on a trip to the Bahamas on his yacht, once the property of Cornelius Vanderbilt.

In October, 1929—the date and the month that coincided with the stock market crash—the Lamberts threw Bunny a coming-out ball at Albemarle. She was a regular at the debutante parties, such as the one for Woolworth heiress Barbara Hutton held at the Ritz-Carlton. The cost for roses was $50,000, a staggering amount as Depression-era families survived on fifty cents a day. One of Bunny's beaus was Stacy Barcroft Lloyd, Jr., scion of a banking and brewing fortune. They shared mutual interests in sailing, horseback riding, and golf, and both hailed from upper-class Episcopalian and Republican backgrounds. At age twenty-two, the couple married at Trinity Episcopalian Church in Princeton. Bunny's maid of honor was Leila Delano, whose cousin, Franklin Delano Roosevelt, had just won the presidential election. One of Bunny's cherished gifts from Stacy was a horseshoe-shaped gold and sapphire pinkie ring. In 1939, Bunny and Stacy attended a Christmas dinner at the White House hosted by the president and First Lady Eleanor Roosevelt. The evening's entertainment was the newly released film *Gone with the Wind.*

Following the Pearl Harbor bombing, Stacy informed his wife that he was to be stationed in England for his new role in the Office of Strategic Services, the predecessor of the CIA, a revelation that led her to blurt out, "You can't, we just got new lampshades." When Bunny wrote to him of the birth of their baby, Eliza Winn, Stacy replied in a letter addressed to his "Dearest Hun Bun." What helped ease Stacy's homesickness was that his Virginia neighbor and friend, Paul Mellon, was also serving in the same OSS unit and they shared a London lodging. During his service, Stacy interviewed a foreign news correspondent, the writer Ernest Hemingway. Trouble loomed in the Lloyd marriage when Bunny heard rumors her husband was seeing Rose Greville; however, she chalked them up to rumor. Upon his return to the States, Lloyd had a joyful reunion with Bunny, daughter Eliza, and son Stacy Bancroft Lloyd III (nicknamed Tuffy). Stacy senior gave Bunny a gift of a gold compact with her initials spelled out in rubies.

At age thirty-six, Bunny took stock of her life: she was a mother of two with a rocky marriage. As an exit route, she set her sights on the recently widowed Paul Mellon, father of two, who was assuaging his grief with the time-honored crutches of drinking, smoking, and womanizing. Bunny set out to ensnare the fifth richest man in America, who had an estimated fortune of $400–$700 million—$3.3 billion to $5.9 billion in contemporary currency. Although reeling from the double betrayal of Paul and Bunny, when his former brother-in-law, Sonny, died on a United Airlines crash, Bunny's ex Stacy Lloyd attended the Princeton funeral.

The Mellons traveled on their DC-3 plane, whose accoutrements included sleeping quarters and a décor of French paintings. They spent time in Manhattan in a townhouse on the Upper East Side; on trips to Paris, they stayed in a penthouse in the Hotel de Crillon. Although Paul and his father Andrew did not see eye to eye, they shared a love of art. Upon his death, Andrew only willed his son an 1882 John Singer Sargent portrait of Miss Beatrice Townshead holding a terrier (Paul's favorite breed); the remainder of the canvases went to the National Gallery. During European sojourns, they searched for paintings. She favored canvases with scenes of flowers and fruit, and they purchased Vincent van Gogh landscapes: *Flower Beds in Holland* and *Green Wheat Fields, Auvers*. Other masterpieces they acquired: a Renoir featuring flowers in a vase; a Cézanne with three green pears; a Manet of a melon on a wooden, paint-spattered table; and a

Picasso of a woman in a garden. In Switzerland, Paul, interested in psychotherapy, introduced her to Carl Jung. While on a walk, the famed therapist told her, "You're the wise one. Keep picking flowers." Bunny, however, preferred psychics over psychologists.

When not picking flowers or working in her magnificent gardens, Bunny made the best-dressed list, knocking off her sister-in-law, Ailsa Mellon Bruce. Her designer handbags had eighteen-karat gold zippers; interiors bore the intertwined initials B. M. She accessorized with a diamond bracelet and a necklace made of emeralds. Her blue pendant diamonds, when put up for auction, were expected to sell for between $10 million to $15 million. Her preferred jeweler was Fulco di Verdura, a Sicilian duke whose Manhattan store enjoyed the patronage of Wallis Simpson, the Duchess of Windsor. Mrs. Simpson's love of nature inspired creations such as a sapphire-and-emerald flower with a canary diamond center. The duke collaborated with Salvador Dali for his surrealistic line. Katharine Hepburn wore his pieces in the film *The Philadelphia Story*. In 1950, Paul commissioned a brooch for his wife that consisted of a gold tree, embellished with twenty-six ruby apples with diamond leaves.

The Mellons' main residence was a nineteenth-century Virginia farmhouse called Oak Springs, a 5,000-acre spread complete with a retinue of two hundred employees that consisted of horse trainers, gardeners, and chauffeurs. On the walls hung museum-worthy paintings such as a Rothko whose estimated value was $150 million. A bronze statue of Paul's Kentucky Derby winning horse, Sea Hero, stands on its grounds. They turned another residence, Brick House, into a repository of treasures which held their collection of first editions, including hand-painted manuscripts by the British poet and artist William Blake. Bunny purchased a 1486 volume by Parisian miniaturist Antoine Vérard and a Thomas Jefferson letter where he wrote of his garden. Floral works of art gracing the walls bore the names of Pablo Picasso and Andy Warhol. A four-volume set of John James Audubon's guide, "Birds of America," was found in the library; Sotheby's sold a similar set for $11.5 million. On her privately owned Cape Cod island, Oyster Harbors, nine gardeners tended the vegetable garden. Paul's joke with the gardeners was, "Is this one of my $1,000 tomatoes?"

As they were passionate philanthropists, Paul's Bollinger Foundation, underwritten with $20 million, distributed poetry awards. In a controversial move, the foundation awarded the 1949 prize to Ezra Pound, who had been indicted for treason for his pro-Mussolini propaganda broadcasts and who was in a psychiatric hospital. The same year, Bunny turned her attention to the $2.5 million restoration of Virginia's Trinity Episcopal Church, built in 1895. Her architect renovated the structure to resemble a medieval Norman French church. The stained-glass windows originated in Holland, made from glass fragments salvaged from bombed European churches and greenhouses; its ancient door came from France. The blue stones that lined the walls were from boulders in the nearby Blue Ridge Mountains. Bunny mentioned to the rector, "I'm a different sort of Christian. I don't really come to pray. I come in to talk with God because he's a dear, dear friend of mine."

A generous friend to her earthly associates, Bunny sent her pilot around the country to deliver fresh flowers and vegetables from her Virginia farm. She scoured the beach at her Cape Cod estate for the perfect clamshell in which to encase a gift of pearl earrings as she frowned upon Tiffany's blue boxes, which she considered "déclassé."

In the mid-1950s, fault lines appeared in the Mellon marriage. Bunny believed that Paul had rekindled his affair with British paramour Valerie Churchill Longman, with whom he had cheated on his first wife when stationed in England. Although Bunny likely never went beyond emotional adultery, she shared she was not sitting home knitting while hubby had affairs. Despite marital roadblocks, however, they stayed together.

When Queen Elizabeth II and Prince Philip planned their first official trip to the States, the queen, an avid horsewoman, decided to visit the Mellons' prized horses, followed by tea at their estate. London's *Daily Herald* pointed out that the royals were sidestepping protocol by visited the home of a divorcée. The paper added, "Dozens of America's top hostesses would give their minks and jewels to change places with Mrs. Mellon." Bunny shrugged off the media frenzy, "We are tremendously honored and thrilled that the queen and Prince Phillip should visit us. But why in the world are so many people interested in knowing about us? We live a plain ordinary sort of country life down here." Three decades later, she entertained royals Charles and Diana.

Bunny had an abiding friendship with First Lady Jacqueline Kennedy. After visiting Oak Spring, Jacqueline told Bunny, "Jack is going to ask you something tonight, and you better goddamn say yes." The request: the president wanted Bunny's assistance in sprucing up the White House Rose Garden. The reason the grounds required beautification was because President Dwight D. Eisenhower had cut down the roses and turned the area into a putting green. Bunny's green thumb also left its mark on the Kennedys' summer home in Martha's Vineyard, as well as the John F. Kennedy Presidential Library and Museum overlooking Boston Harbor. Bunny presided over the floral arrangements for President Kennedy's funeral bier.

Tragedy arrived in 2000 when a truck hit Bunny's daughter Eliza Winn as she crossed a Manhattan Street. She suffered a brain injury that left her a paraplegic and unable to speak. She received round-the-clock care at Oak Springs, where she passed away after eight years. Six years after the loss of her daughter, Paul died at age ninety-one. His widow auctioned off many of her possessions in Sotheby's sale of the century. So great were her treasures that the catalogue for the estate filled four volumes. The auction garnered $218 million that Bunny donated to a horticultural research center located on her Virginia farm.

Traditionally, well-bred ladies' names only appeared in the headlines on three occasions: their birth, marriage, and death notices. Although fiercely private, Bunny was often media fodder. After John Edwards' presidential bid ended through a sex-and-money scandal, news leaked that the 101-year-old widow had forked over $3 million in "Bunny money." Another $725,000 went to the candidate's personal bank account that he used to keep his mistress, Rielle Hunter, and their baby a secret from his terminally ill wife. Of her contribution, Bunny stated, "Well, I suppose it's my own damn fault. He was so attractive. And you know I'm weak on good looks." After the trial, Bunny remarked to her friend who had introduced her to John, "Didn't we have fun?"

When Bunny passed away at age 103, her beloved Oak Spring Farms was put on the market for $70 million. Bunny's interment was in the Mellon family plot on the grounds of the Trinity Episcopal Church. Among the famous who paid their final respects were Bette Midler and former senator John Edwards. Her grandson, Stacy Lloyd IV, said his "Granbunny" had taught him how to appreciate nature's beauty. Jackie once teased her, "Bunny, you think all your ducks are swans." A tenor sang "Shenandoah;" Bette Midler performed "The Rose."

In the closing scene of *Citizen Kane,* media mogul Charles Foster Kane's dying word is "Rosebud"—the name of his cherished childhood sled found item amongst his priceless collections. Tucked amongst Bunny's treasures were two objects her staff had been told not to touch: an old bottle of Listerine with a rusty cap, and a children's book, *Flower Guide: Wild Flowers East of the Rockies*. The scent of the roses in the White House garden offers no hint they came from the hand of the Halitosis Heiress.

CHAPTER 10

Zsa Zsa Gabor: My Close-up (1917)

"He taught me housekeeping. When I divorce, I keep the house."

—ZSA ZSA GABOR ON HER FIFTH HUSBAND, NED SHERRIN

◇◇◇◇◇◇◇◇◇◇◇◇

Zsa Zsa Gabor was a femme fatale who feasted on public adulation her entire life, even in her sunset years. The blonde siren traversed the road from Europe to America in a story that could have sprung from the pages of a Hollywood film script.

Zsa Zsa hailed from the aptly named Hungary, as she was voracious in her appetite for the good—or rather, the *grand* life. Born in Budapest in 1917, her parents christened her Sari, after opera prima donna Sari Fedak; she became known by the singer's nickname, Zsa Zsa. She was the middle of three daughters of Jewish parents, Vilmos Gabor and his twenty-year-younger wife, Jancsi "Jolie" Gabor. Vilmos was in the diamond business and told Zsa Zsa never to accept one of less than ten carats. Zsa Zsa later quipped, "Diamonds are a girl's best friend and dogs are a man's best friend. Now you know which sex has more sense." Sisters Magdolna (Magda), Zsa Zsa, and Eva attended Madame Subilia's School for Young Ladies in Lausanne, Switzerland. In Budapest, a chauffeur transported the girls to acting and dance classes.

After falsifying her daughter's age, Jolie entered Zsa Zsa in the Miss Hungary beauty pageant. Although mother and daughter claimed she had won, the judges disqualified her as she had not submitted her application in time. The teenaged Zsa Zsa met the fifty-year-old Turkish diplomat, Burhan Belge, who joked that if she had been older, he would have made her a member of his harem. A few months later, she showed up at his Ankara home with her terrier, Mishka. During their marriage, she accompanied her husband on a lecture tour of London, where she captivated writers H. G. Wells and George Bernard Shaw. The marriage collapsed after six months; Zsa Zsa laid the blame at her own door since she had embarked on an affair with Kemal Atatürk, the founder of modern Turkey. With her diplomatic passport, on the eve of World War II, Zsa Zsa decamped from Ankara with twenty-one trunks of clothes—minus her husband. With their beauty and talent—well, their beauty—the Gabor sisters cut a wide swath. Jolie said of her girls' allure, "My daughters know how to ride, to play tennis, ice skate, and all the sports. Not too much can they do these things—not too much to make big muscles—but enough to be a charming companion to a man."

Zsa Zsa made Jolie proud when she bagged a billionaire ten months after immigrating to the States. Hotel czar Conrad Hilton was having a drink at Ciro's on Sunset Boulevard when the blonde beauty made a grand entrance on the arm of Lana Turner's former fiancé. Despite his conflicted feelings over the Catholic church's refusal to recognize his divorce, Conrad presented Zsa Zsa with a twenty-five-carat diamond engagement ring. In 1942, the fifty-five-year-old groom and his twenty-five-year-old bride wed at the Santa Fe Hotel. What put the damper on the diamonds was how Conrad, in a nod to his Catholic guilt, insisted on separate bedrooms. Zsa Zsa decorated hers in the décor mode of the film *Gone with the Wind*. Although she was able to bring the divorced Jolie to the States, her grandmother and her son, Sebastian Tilleman, perished in the Holocaust. Zsa Zsa relinquished her Judaism and was a practicing, lifelong Catholic.

The Hilton-Gabor marriage sagged under the weight of other crosses in addition to Conrad's Catholic guilt: Zsa Zsa's horror over her grandmother's murder, and Zsa Zsa's affair with her seventeen-year-old stepson, Nicky. Despite her bubbly persona, Zsa Zsa suffered from bipolar depression. Her family sent her to a sanatorium that subjected her to shock treatments she likened to torture. Of the nightmare experience, she recalled, "How shall I describe the nightmare of the next weeks, days, and nights and horrors that might have been invented by Dante? No one came to visit me: Not Conrad...not Eva...no one."

When the Hilton-Gabor marriage imploded, Zsa Zsa confessed, "How could I separate him from his money? Would I have been interested in a man twice my age if he wasn't rich? I don't think so."

At the time of their break-up, Zsa Zsa was pregnant with daughter Francesca—Jolie's only grandchild. In the belief her paternity would not bear too much scrutiny, Conrad never developed a close relationship with Francesca. Of his billion-dollar fortune, he left her $100,000—that she mainly used to contest his will. Zsa Zsa, in comic crowing regarding her divorce from the hotelier, satirically stated, "Conrad Hilton was very generous to me in the divorce settlement. He gave me five thousand Gideon Bibles."

She took her third walk down the aisle with actor George Sanders. While Conrad had put Zsa Zsa on the financial map, George helped bring her further into the world of entertainment. While waiting for her husband to return from London, she accepted a last-minute slot on *Bachelor Haven,* a television show that offered advice to the lovelorn. When asked about her jewelry, she answered, "Dahling, oh zese! Zeese are just my vorking diamonds." A star was born. The kryptonite in their marriage was George's paranoia his wife was dabbling in infidelity. Sixteen years later, in a nod to keeping it in the family, George married Zsa Zsa's sister Magda. That marriage lasted six months; George died by suicide.

A magnet for men, after Zsa Zsa threw a Hollywood party for the son of the Dominican dictator, General Rafael Trujillo, the party's honoree sent her a $17,000 chinchilla coat and a Mercedes-Benz. Mother Dahlink's response to the lavish gift, "So, what do you expect—for him to send flowers to a girl like Zsa Zsa?" A US Congressman had a different take and called Zsa Zsa "the most expensive courtesan since Madame de Pompadour."

Additional trophy husbands kept Zsa Zsa dripping in diamonds. She became engaged to her fourth husband, investment banker Herbert Hutner, on their third date, a decision influenced by a $3 million ring. Hutner lasted a year more than the number of carats. The next ring came via oil heir Joshua Cosden Jr., whom she left as "he bored me interminably." Hubby number six lowered the bar on the bizarre. In 1975, she married her neighbor, the five-time-married Jack Ryan, the engineer behind the Barbie doll. His mansion, dubbed 'the Castle,' was home to flesh-and-blood Barbies who charged by the hour. When Jack did not prove to be her Ken, he responded, "That marriage cost me $260,000 a bang." Her eighth spouse, Michael O'Hara, was the lawyer who handled her divorce from Jack. The wedding ceremony to Felipe de Alba was of a single day's duration. She explained her ill-advised nuptial as a "momentary craziness."

With an estimated fortune of $40 million accumulated through beddings, weddings, and entertainment earnings, Zsa Zsa purchased a palatial Los Angeles villa located at 1001 Bel Air Road, Bel Air, that Howard Hughes had built and Elvis Presley had once owned. She shared the estate with her nine shih tzus—including three bearing the names Pasha Effendi, Genghis Khan, and Macho Man. Her love of her canine companions was evident by the bell at her front gate that bore a bas-relief of St. Francis stroking a dog. A diva in the air as well as on the ground, Delta Air Lines security officials removed her from a flight for her refusal to keep her retinue of dogs in their travel kennels. The mid-century material girl's hangar-sized closet held five thousand garments; red carpets covered the floors. The estate had a cushion embroidered with her favorite quotation: "Never complain, never explain." Zsa Zsa's real estate portfolio also contained a Palm Springs home formerly owned by Magda that sported a bright pink exterior and a front yard pool. A third property was a thirty-acre California ranch where she housed her nineteen racehorses as well as her prized white Arabian, Silver Fox. An accomplished horsewoman, she once rode in the Rose Parade.

Her final spouse—the ninth—was the twenty-seven-years younger, six-time-married Prince Frédéric von Anhalt, Duke of Saxony, who had started life as Hans Robert Lichtenberg, the son of a German police officer. He had gained his title after Princess Marie Auguste of Anhalt, the Duchess of Saxony, Kaiser Wilhelm's daughter-in-law, had adopted him as an adult. To meet the woman who could provide the lifestyle to which he aspired, he rented a white Rolls-Royce Corniche convertible and hired two students to act as his driver and bodyguard for the night. He crashed a black-tie party at the Holmby Hills estate of writer Sidney Sheldon where he "ran into" Zsa Zsa. Smitten, she invited her prince to move into her $10-million-dollar mansion. On their wedding day, Jolie staged a heart attack, but her ruse failed to stop the nuptials. They took their vows in Zsa Zsa's stable so Silver Fox could serve as best man.

The couple weathered many storms; one was financial as they lost a reported $10 million through Ponzi financier Bernie Madoff. Another issue was infidelity. The aristocrat observed, "The secret to a long marriage is infidelity." Reflecting on her multitude of romances, she declared her philosophy on how to keep men from straying: "Shoot them in the legs."

Although Zsa Zsa shared she disliked living in sin, she had liaisons with entertainers Frank Sinatra; Richard Burton, who she said liked to talk dirty in bed; Sean Connery; and the spectacularly endowed Dominican playboy husband to heiresses Barbara Hutton and Doris Duke, Porfirio Rubirosa. Another horizontal conquest Zsa Zsa laid claim to was President Richard M. Nixon, of whom she reminisced, "A great mind. A big brain," and she insinuated that was not the biggest thing about "Tricky Dicky." In her memoir, *One Lifetime is Not Enough*, she wrote that Nixon had set her up with Henry Kissinger "but clothes never came off." Journalist Dan Zak of *The Washington Post* imagined their hypothetical flirtation with their German and Hungarian accents, "Vut do you vunna do?" "I dunno, dahling, vhatever you vant." Kissinger had to beg off a second date, as he had to invade Cambodia. Other purported paramours were John Paul Getty and Prince Aly Khan. Gabor's romantic dalliances also included a flirtation with the actress Greta Garbo. The men spurned were John F. Kennedy, Elvis Presley, Henry Fonda, and John Huston. Zsa Zsa philosophized, "There is nothing wrong with a woman encouraging a man's advances, as long as they are in cash."

While the Gabor sisters were of the ilk of those who are "famous for being famous," they appeared in movies and television. In her glory days, Zsa Zsa acted for director Orson Welles in *Touch of Evil* and for John Houston in *Moulin Rouge*. On *The Late Show with David Letterman*, in her heavily accented Hungarian accent, she peppered her conversations with her ubiquitous use of "Dahlink;" she claimed she used the term because she had trouble remembering names. She also charmed audiences with her Zsa-isms: "Husbands are like fires. They go out if unattended;" and "I want a man who is kind and understanding. Is that too much to ask of a millionaire?" In later years, she had cameos on *Gilligan's Island*, *The Beverly Hillbillies*, and *Hollywood Squares*. As a guest on *Laugh-In*, she spouted her philosophy, "I always said that marriage should be a fifty-fifty proposition—he should be at least fifty years older and have at least fifty million dollars."

Age did not diminish Zsa Zsa's unabashed nature. In 1989, she was driving her $215,000 Rolls-Royce Corniche in Beverly Hills when police officer Paul Kramer stopped her for expiration tags and possessing an open bottle of vodka. Bored with the procedure, the actress drove off. When he pulled her over again, she shouted, "I'm bringing the Reagans in on this!" and then accosted him in a slap heard around the world. For her day in court, a hundred reporters, including some from Europe, were present. When asked if she was prepared for a long trial, she cooed, "I have enough outfits to last a year." Talking to the cameras that had followed her for decades, she announced, "I am a horsewoman. I am a princess. I am Zsa

Zsa." Fans and foes wore T-shirts that expressed their perspective: either "Hang Zsa Zsa" or "Free Zsa Zsa."

The diva wronged pled her case thus, "When he was chasing me, I thought of the Gestapo. I can't help it. I wasn't scared in Europe. We had the Nazis, the Russian tanks. But I was here scared on Olympic and La Cienega. I didn't believe that an American taxpayer could be treated like this." She spent seventy-two hours in jail.

The golden years were devoid of luster. Ninth husband Frédéric sued her daughter Francesca, claiming she had forged her mother's signature with the purpose of taking out a $2 million loan against her mother's $14 million home. Francesca countered that her mother was the victim of elder abuse perpetrated by her husband. The court threw out the lawsuit when Zsa Zsa failed to show up for court. The countless photographs featuring Zsa Zsa could serve as her visual diary; a 2016 mug shot contrasted with her early ones where she wore pink mink and designer dresses, dripping with diamonds. Perhaps to prove he was still vital and virile, Frédéric leaked the tidbit to the *Daily Express* that he had conducted a decade-long affair with Playboy centerfold Anna Nicole Smith and had fathered her baby Dannielynn, a claim without merit. He also alleged lesbian robbers had tied him, naked, to the steering wheel of his Rolls-Royce. In an astute observation, Zsa Zsa admitted, "You know, the moment a man is bad, I fall in love with him. I always marry bad men. It's a sickness, my sickness. The worse they tell me they are, the more I am attracted. That's my tragedy."

In 2002, Zsa Zsa, then in her eighties, was hospitalized for a month after a car driven by her hairdresser, Jared Millard, struck a utility pole in West Hollywood. She sued him for $108 million. The accident left her in a wheelchair, and she retreated from the spotlight. Further physical afflictions followed: a leg infection, a stroke, and a hip replacement. The most devastating health horror was when surgeons amputated her right leg above her knee after an infection proved resistant to antibiotics. Her penchant for tying the knot and clinging to her sex symbol status had led to Bob Hope's joke, "You can calculate Zsa Zsa Gabor's age by the rings on her fingers." The Prince had his own health scare; in 2010, mistaking his wife's nail glue for eye drops, he glued his eye shut.

The Grim Reaper at last paid a visit to the ninety-nine-year-old force of nature. The world did not remember her for her unforgettable film roles, only for the one she played to perfection: being Zsa Zsa Gabor. According to her will, she expressed her wish that she be buried in her homeland, the former Austrian-Hungarian empire. Five years after his wife's passing, Frédéric carried an urn with three quarters of Zsa Zsa's ashes (with the rest remaining in Los Angeles) to London, then Germany, and lastly to Hungary. He interred his late wife in a prominent Budapest cemetery, the final resting place of famous Hungarian actors and writers. A white satin ribbon over her grave bore a single word, emblazoned in gold: "Dahlink."

During her final interview at age ninety, dressed in Chanel, her eyes curtained by false eyelashes, her hair a silver cloud, the star reigned from her wheelchair.

CHAPTER 11

Betsy Bloomingdale: The Big Brown Bag (1922)

"Real style comes from within."

—BETSY BLOOMINGDALE

The Bloomingdale brothers might have christened their store after their surname because of the positive connotation of the word "blooming." The adjective also applied to queen bee

Betsy Bloomingdale, who did not wilt even when a treacherous thorn protruded.

In the 1970s, after an introduction to Andy Warhol at the April in Paris Ball, Betsy exclaimed, "I didn't really think there was an Andy Warhol!" to which he replied, "I didn't really think there was a Betsy Bloomingdale." Betsy not only existed—she was larger than life.

An only child, Betty Lee (called Betsy) was born in Beverly Hills to Australian émigré parents Vera and Dr. Russell Lee Newling; her father was a Harvard-educated orthodontist. Due to Dr. Newling's prominence, Betsy moved amongst the firmament of Hollywood stars, such as Merle Oberon, Cary Grant, and James Stewart. She attended the exclusive Marlborough School in Hancock Park in Los Angeles and then Bennett College in Millbrook, New York. After graduation, Betsy was a bridesmaid at Gloria Vanderbilt's wedding to Pat di Cicco, a Hollywood agent and alleged mobster. Betsy's aspiration was to marry a doctor.

Instead of a physician, Betsy landed one of America's biggest fish: Alfred Bloomingdale, who had arrived on the West Coast to produce movies. Hell-bent handsome, Alfred had also inherited a fortune as the grandson of a founder of Bloomingdale's—Bloomie's to its fans. If his coffers were not overflowing enough, in 1950, he came up with Dine and Sign, one of the first credit card companies. A year later, his business merged with the Diners Club, where he served as chairman. The Bloomingdales' 1946 marriage conferred on Betsy an alliterative name, a fabulous fortune, and a niche in high society. She also carried clout with her husband, who claimed his wife had converted him "from a Jewish Democrat to a Catholic Republican." They had children Geoffrey, the owner of an exotic fruit ranch, Lisa Bell, an artist, and Robert, a film producer, who gave them eight grandchildren. Neighbors throughout the years included Barbara Stanwyck, Jack Benny, Bing Crosby, Frank Sinatra, Michael Jackson, and Barbra Streisand. As America's aristocracy, the Bloomingdales were known as "Queen Betts" and "King Alfred."

The couple's Holmby Hills estate, situated near Sunset Boulevard, included an outdoor atrium living room, a swimming pool, and a garden of cypress trees. Their entrance courtyard had a nineteenth-century sundial that carried the inscription, "Let others tell of storms and showers—I'll only count your sunny hours."

Not only did Alfred provide *carte blanche* at Bloomingdales, he also encouraged Betsy to visit Parisian fashion houses Chanel, Dior, and Givenchy, where she shelled out $20,000 for haute couture gowns. The women from Betsy's old Beverly Hills zip code rued they had not snared Alfred Schiffer Bloomingdale.

In 1964, Betsy Bloomingdale's name was on *Vanity Fair's* International Best-Dressed List; fortunately, the Holmby Hills home had eleven closets to hold her fabulous finery. Betsy kept meticulous notes as to when she had worn each gown and with which earrings, bags, and hosiery so as not to repeat a look. Betsy donated sixty of her outfits to the Fashion Institute of Design & Merchandising. For inspiration, she kept a journal of the menus and furnishings of the Rothschilds and of Princess Ghislaine de Polignac.

For five decades, Betsy traveled extensively, leading to a 1966 *Women's Wear Daily* column that gushed, "Betsy Bloomingdale's black-and-white tweed luggage never seems to cool off. She's always off to New York, Honolulu, Europe..." She was part of a rarefied jet set on Rupert Murdoch's yacht, moored in Morocco along with the Kissingers, the Cronkites, and Malcolm Forbes. Other travel companions included Elizabeth Taylor, Princess

Caroline, Ivana Trump, Kirk Douglass, and Karl Lagerfeld. The hostess with the mostest threw dinner parties with glitterati guests Prince Rupert Lowenstein, Joan Collins, Merv Griffin, Katherine Ross, and Walter and Lee Annenberg. Betsy recorded seating arrangements, menus, wines, and flowers to prevent any déjà vu dinners. As presentation was a pressing concern, centerpieces of dahlias and zinnias came from the Bloomingdale garden. When taking coffee and cordials, the dinner party retired to the dining room, where white orchids in Chinese vases were displayed on the baby grand piano. To share entertaining tips, in 1994, the arbiter of "the best of everything" collaborated on the publication of *Entertaining with Betsy Bloomingdale: A Collection of Culinary Tips and Treasures from the World's Best Hosts and Hostesses*. Along with recipes, Betsy philosophized, "It's not what you put on the table, it's what you put in the chairs." Of the art of entertaining, she wrote, "Giving a party or hosting a dinner is in many ways like a performance. You are the producer, director, stage manager, and finally the actor." There were also chapters dedicated to theme parties, such as one that centered on the dance craze for the Twist.

While the 1968 film *Guess Who's Coming for Dinner?* revolved around a daughter bringing her Black boyfriend to meet her parents, the Bloomingdales' 1980s dinners centered on entertaining the powerful. Alfred had been one of the "kitchen cabinet," a group of wealthy Californian businessmen who had helped propel Ronald Reagan to the White House. Their impeccably turned-out wives, known as The Group, had befriended Nancy Reagan. Each summer, the two power couples drove to the Reagan ranch in the Santa Ynez mountains north of Los Angeles to help Nancy celebrate another birthday. The Bloomingdales were present in 1980 when Reagan won the White House and joined in the triumphant drive to a victory party at the Century Plaza Hotel in Los Angeles' Century City.

During the Inauguration, the Bloomingdales enjoyed ringside seats. When the Reagans left Washington, DC, to attend a Bloomingdale dinner, Betsy laid out the red carpet. As word leaked of the special guests, neighbors lined the street, waving American flags. The whirring of helicopters signaled the Reagans' arrival. The considerate hostess served refreshments to thirty Secret Service men; the doctor's daughter said, "I'd never be blasé about the president coming for dinner." In turn, the Bloomingdales were regular guests at the White House. As Betsy and Nancy were always celery thin, it is highly unlikely they indulged in the President's jellybean jar. The women shared such a strong bond the press dubbed Mrs. Bloomingdale the "First Friend." Both held black belts in shopping and subscribed to the Duchess of Winsor's observation, "You can never be too rich or too thin." Together, they flew to the wedding of Prince Charles and Lady Diana Spencer. To facilitate their friendships, the Bloomingdales stayed in an apartment at the Watergate complex in Washington, DC.

In her husband's final days, when Reagan battled Alzheimer's disease, Nancy leaned on her first friend more than ever. After the presidential funeral, Betsy remarked of the grief-stricken Nancy, "Like any widow, she adjusted. But Nancy missed Ronnie terribly and always." A staunch philanthropist, Betsy fundraised for the Ronald Reagan Presidential Library. Betsy's last public appearance was at Nancy's funeral on the library's grounds, where her burial plot was beside Ronald's. At age ninety-three, Betsy attended in a wheelchair in the front row, impeccably attired in a black pants suit, bearing witness as one of the few remaining members of the Reagans' inner circle.

While fashion was one of Betsy's claims to fame, it also paved the way for scandal. In the 1970s, an official at customs caught Mrs. Bloomingdale bringing two Dior garments from France into the States. Upon inspection, it became apparent she had altered the price for the garments to make them appear less expensive. The following year, Betsy pleaded guilty to one count of tampering with an invoice. The result was a hefty fine, as well as mud on her face. However, what Alfred was doing in his spare time made her offense amateur hour.

As Betsy was aghast at a wrinkle in a tablecloth, one can only imagine her consternation when she discovered her husband's double life. Although Betsy had been able to convert Alfred from a Jewish Democrat to a Catholic Republican, she had not been able to convert him to vanilla sex. Alfred had met seventeen-year-old Vicki Morgan in 1970 when she worked as an usher at Grauman's Chinese Theater in Hollywood. He had wooed her with the promise that he would make her a movie star. Although he did not put her on the silver screen, he paid her $18,000 a month for her services. She was married with a son who she had conceived out of wedlock. He saw her through her divorce and two other weddings and sheddings when her husbands proved problematic. But while Alfred was hospitalized with cancer, Betsy, now in charge of finances, discovered Vicky's existence and terminated payments. After Alfred's 1982 death, Betsy was forced to adjust to further revelations.

The widow was horrified when her name appeared in the papers—and not for spearheading a charitable event or attending a society soiree. Headlines trumpeted, "Bloomie was a sex monster!" While typically the wife cites the other woman, in Alfred Bloomingdale's sordid saga, the other woman was the one pointing the finger. A superstar palimony attorney represented Vicki in her $10 million suit claiming her lover had promised her lifetime support and a house for services rendered. She claimed Alfred had considered her his "other wife" and that she had accompanied him on overseas trips. The suit argued Miss Morgan had been Alfred's "confidante, companion, and therapist who helped him get over his Marquis de

Sade complex." There is no mention of how Betsy described Vicki. The "storms and showers" mentioned in the inscription on the sundial had arrived.

Just as it seemed the fallout could not get worse—it did. The deposition brought lurid details of Vicki's sadomasochistic relationship with her thirty-seven-years-older married lover. One of the tantalizing tidbits was that Alfred had a "Jekyll and Hyde" personality, and Vicki testified she had watched as women stripped, let Alfred bind them with neckties, and rode on their backs as he beat them. Marvin Mitchelson, the celebrity divorce lawyer who filed Morgan's palimony suit, recalled of his client, "She said she knew political and sexual secrets about this administration that would make Watergate look like a play school." The trial proved so sensational that White House aide Morgan Mason asked Mitchelson to tone it down out of respect for the widowed Mrs. Bloomingdale. Vicki's court confession also embarrassed the White House when she said pillow talk with Alfred included details of campaign contributions for his buddy Ronnie. Other salacious tidbits that were outed: Vicki had also had affairs with actor Cary Grant, Morocco's King Hassad—who showered her with jewels—and an exiled Saudi princess. *Time* magazine reported that fifteen years earlier, Alfred had doled out $5,000 in a blackmail payment because of his habit of beating up prostitutes. Despite his record, President Reagan had appointed him to the Foreign Intelligence Advisory Board. Shortly afterwards, Alfred had become ill.

Betsy contended that the other woman had used sex as a credit card and was thus not entitled to further payment as her services were no longer relevant. Los Angeles Superior Court Judge Christian Markey dismissed most of Vicki's suit, claiming that her relationship with Bloomingdale was "no more than that of a wealthy, older, married paramour and young, well-paid mistress...

and was...explicitly founded on paid sexual services." Ms. Morgan, painted claws still pointing, filed another $1 million suit citing contracts Alfred had signed in which he had promised her half his interest in various Show-Biz Pizza franchises.

If the salacious story had not served up enough spicy details to the paparazzi, further revelations reared their heads. Vicki had ended up in rehab where she met Marvin Pancoast, a mentally disturbed cocaine addict with whom she shared an apartment after they checked out of their facility. As Vicki slept on a hot July night, he bludgeoned her to death with a baseball bat. He said his motive was her narcissism, her shallowness, and an argument over finances. Marvin said of his victim, "Vicki was special. She had this quality. You just couldn't get enough of her." A jury awarded Vicky's estate $200,000 to be held in trust for her fifteen-year-old son, who had been visiting his grandmother at the time of his mother's murder. Mitchelson said, "She took a lot of secrets to her grave," referring to his client's claim that she had procured "entertainment" for high-placed government officials. At the time of her death, Vicki was allegedly negotiating a TV docudrama and a film based on her life.

Another torturous twist in the society soap opera occurred during Marvin's trial when he recounted his confession. His attorney, Arthur Barens, charged that "persons unknown" had committed the murder to suppress videos of Vicki engaging in sex with Alfred and several prominent government officials.

Dominick Dunne based his 1990 *roman à clef*, *An Inconvenient Woman*, on the affair, a cautionary tale of the excessively privileged. The White House residents no doubt turned green at their ties to the tabloid tales of kink, greed, and murder.

Betsy Bloomingdale weathered the fallout by attending Mass every morning. She reigned as the doyenne of high society until her death at age ninety-three from a heart condition. Her final hours were in her beloved Holmby Hills estate; its proximity to Sunset Boulevard proved an apt connection as Betsy's passing marked the demise of the country's Grande Dame. Though the media had feted the supreme hostess for years, perhaps the greatest compliment appeared in a column in *Town & Country* asserting that Queen Betts embodied Rudyard Kipling's ideal, though his pronoun was paraphrased: "Though she walked with kings, she has never lost the common touch."

While Tiffany's is associated with blue bags, Bloomingdale's, though a more subdued color, are similarly iconic. Celebrities who have clutched the bag include Jacqueline Kennedy Onassis, Diane von Fürstenberg, Sarah Jessica Parker, Calvin Klein, and Andy Warhol. The classic has made cameos in *Friends* and *Gossip Girl* and has appeared in the likeness of a cake, a Limoges porcelain box, and a diamond pendant. The store has used the image on a pickleball paddle, a Ralph Lauren sweatshirt, and chocolate boxes.

The Bloomingdale totes come in three sizes: the Little Brown Bag for jewelry, the Medium Brown Bag for clothes, and the bag that would be best to hold Betsy Bloomingdale's biography: the Big Brown Bag.

CHAPTER 12

Marella Agnelli: In Sunshine and In Storm (1927)

"He knows how to make boredom disappear, more than anybody else I ever met."

—MARELLA AGNELLI ON GIANNI AGNELLI

The birth of the woman who became known as Marella Agnelli, heiress to the Fiat fortune, was the result of the joining of two worlds: that of an aristocratic Neapolitan diplomat and an American whiskey heiress. Princess Marella Caracciolo di Castagneto was born in 1927 at Villa Cancelli, a sixteenth-century manse perched on a hilltop overlooking Florence. Her mother, the former Margaret Clark of Peoria, Illinois, had purchased the estate with the wealth from her family's whiskey distillery, Clarke Bros & Co. Marella's father, Filippo, the eighth Duke of Melito and the third Prince of Castagneto, was a descendant of Neapolitan nobles. She had an older brother, Carlo, and a younger one, Nicola, as well as a half-brother, Ettore, born from her father's affair with a young widow. (Ettore's daughter eventually married into Belgium's royal family.) Marella later reminisced that one nocturnal activity was to sneak into her garden, where she listened to the invisible creatures hiding in the darkness. The Wall Street Crash of 1929 had eroded their fortune, and Filippo was the first of his relatives to seek employment. In his position as a diplomat, he moved to Ankara, Turkey, along with his wife and three children. With the advent of World War II, the embassy sent him to Lugano, Switzerland, where he participated in the anti-fascist resistance.

Marella attended school in Paris, where she studied art and design at the Académie des Beaux-Arts and Académie Julian. On the romantic front, she ended her relationship with Charles de Ganay, a French aristocrat and the owner of a castle, after he postponed their wedding for a week to go grouse hunting. Marella's life would have been far different had it not been for the grouse. At age eighteen, Marella befriended the Agnelli sisters, who painted such a wonderful portrait of their brother, Gianni, who had fought in the war, that Marella was enraptured even before they met. After their first encounter, she described Gianni as "magnificent." However, as he paid Marella scant attention, she licked her wounds and moved on.

The car czar and his siblings were the heirs of the fifty-billion-dollar Fiat fortune. The name 'Fiat' was an acronym for Fabbrica Italiana di Automobili Torino, the company their grandfather, Giovanni, had founded in Turin in 1899. When Mussolini assumed power, the car company aligned itself with the dictator.

After his parents' passing, Gianni, the eldest of seven, assumed a paternal role. The billionaire-about-town had the nickname "*l'Avvocato*" ('the lawyer'), as he had studied law, a profession he never practiced. With his good looks and astronomical wealth, the playboy of the western world entertained a bevy of beauties at La Leopolda, his magnificent estate on the Riviera. The site was a Pied Piper that drew the likes of Porfirio Rubirosa (husband to heiresses Barbara Hutton and Doris Duke), movie tycoons Jack Warner and Darryl Zanuck, Sicilian Prince Raimondo Lanza, and rising politician John F. Kennedy. The siren of the sea also drew the Greeks, such as shipping magnate Stavros Niarchos, who cruised the Mediterranean in his yacht, the *Eros*, sometimes with Aristotle and Tina Onassis as passengers. Some of Gianni's *amores* included Anita Ekberg and Hedy Lamarr, along with various Italian princesses, international models, and socialites. One he fell for was Jacqueline Kennedy, of whom he confided to his friend Frank Sinatra, "I was in love with Jackie. But we decided to view our relationship as a summer romance." A 1962 telegram arrived from President Kennedy: "*More Caroline, Less Agnelli.*"

Pamela Churchill, the divorced daughter-in-law of Sir Winston Churchill, was a stabilizing influence on Gianni; In the hope of becoming his wife, Pamela converted to Catholicism. Her aspiration was asphyxiated, however, when she entered his magnificent mansion, La Leopolda, at three in the morning and found him in a compromising position with twenty-one-year-old Anne-Marie d'Estainville. Fueled by alcohol, and perhaps cocaine, Gianni jumped in his car; that ended in a collision with a butcher's truck. Gianni suffered a broken jaw and an injured leg, leaving him with a long-term limp that led to his nickname "*le diable boit aux*," or "the lame devil."

In the early 1950s, Marella left for Manhattan where she modeled for *Vogue* contributor Erwin Blumenfeld in exchange for photography lessons. Richard Avedon immortalized Marella in a 1954 black-and-white shot, one in which her strapless gown emphasized her long, graceful neck, earning her the appellation, "The Swan." Truman Capote also dubbed her the swan, his term for each of the well-heeled and elegant women that comprised his inner circle. The photograph, in which Marella resembles a girl from a Modigliani painting, is in the collection of the Modern Museum of Art. Warhol later immortalized her in a portrait. She returned to Italy as a correspondent for publisher Condé Nast.

Upon her arrival, after Gianni's sisters told her of their brother's accident, Marella cancelled a sailing trip to be at his bedside, where she remained and helped with his convalescence. After falling for his caregiver, Gianni traveled from Turin to Rome to ask her parents for their daughter's hand. As he did so, his intended stood behind a door to eavesdrop. Her mother's Puritan streak made her wary of having a son-in-law who was constant paparazzi fodder; however, her husband gave the union his blessing. At the wedding, as news that Marella was three months pregnant had leaked, a guest quipped, "The new Fiat will be ready for delivery in six months." Their nuptials took place in the chapel of the castle known as the Château d'Osthoffen Alsace, just outside of Strasbourg. The bride wore a white satin Balenciaga gown; the groom wore a tailcoat and pinstripe pants. The scene seemed lifted from a fairy tale, with the handsome prince joining his destiny to the beautiful princess. However, in a jarring nod to realism, Gianni was forced to lean on his crutches. The powerful tycoon and his stylish wife were on the threshold of becoming Italy's First Couple, the Kennedys of Italy.

Since the life of a working wife was not in the cards, she bid *arrivederci* to her career with Condé Nast. Noting his young wife did not demonstrate aptitude as a hostess, Gianni contacted Countess Lily Volpi, to whom Marella referred as a "dragoness." The countess called to inform her, "You must come and see me. I hear that you don't know how to run a home," and she gave the newlywed a crash course in how to succeed in the role of billionaire spouse. The dragoness ended her lecture with her brand of wisdom, "To catch a man all one needs is a bed, but it takes a well-run home to keep him." Not only did Marella maintain their dozen homes in an impeccable manner, she dressed in clothes by Valentino and was a fixture on the best-dressed lists while doing it. Similarly, Gianni always looked as if he had stepped from the pages of *Gentlemen's Quarterly:* one of his fashion staples was his gold Cartier watch strapped outside the cuff of his shirts.

As it transpired, being the wife of a high-profile billionaire proved enough to occupy her time. On a trip to Paris for a shopping spree, she booked a berth on a Turin train. When she boarded, she was astounded: There were monogrammed towels, her favorite toiletries, and fresh flowers—compliments of the butler. As Marella recalled of the experience, "This, I soon discovered, was how the Agnellis traveled when they took a night train. This was also when I realized I had entered a very different way of life from the one I was used to." While Gianni was often absent due to his many business ventures, Marella found comfort in religion, gardening, and decorating. Unlike her mother, who had hated domesticity, Marella viewed her multitude of households as canvases awaiting her imprint. The walls of their homes bore fabulous art by Klimt, Matisse, Modigliani, and Renoir, along with modern masterpieces.

In 2002, the couple founded the Pinacoteca Giovanni e Marella Agnelli, a museum in Turin that showcased their paintings.

When Gianni took time off, Marella joined her husband on his sailboat, *Extra Beat*, and on ski slopes—where a helicopter dropped them off on the mountaintops. The new life came with fleets of cars, as well as the use of their company's two helicopters and several private planes. The Agnelli coffers overflowed when Fiat acquired rivals Ferrari, Maserati, and Alfa Romero. Other takeovers included Château Margaux Vineyard, a lion's share of Club Méditerranée, the newspaper *La Stampa*, and the soccer team Juventus.

The Fiat fairy dust extended to their son Eduardo, born in New York in 1954, followed a year later by their daughter Margherita, born in Lausanne, Switzerland. Marella admitted, "Many women have chosen motherhood over marriage. I did the opposite." For Marella, Gianni was the axis on which the Earth revolved.

Parenthood did not dampen their ardor for *la dolce vita*. Gianni would surprise his family with vacations to exotic locales such as the Riviera, where they jumped into the Mediterranean from their low-flying helicopter. The Agnellis sailed on their yacht along the Amalfi Coast in the company of luminaries John and Jackie Kennedy, the Rockefellers, the Kissingers, publisher Katherine Graham, the de la Rentas, and Truman Capote.

Marella's passion was gardening, and she cultivated the acres that graced her seven homes in Turin, Rome, Paris, Manhattan, Corsica, St. Moritz, and the foothills of the Italian Alps. Her love of roses led to a pink variety that bore the name Donna Marella Agnelli. Her landscaping memoir became the basis for two books she co-authored, *Gardens of the Italian Villas* and *The Agnelli Gardens at Villar Perosa: Two Centuries of a Family Retreat*. However, her central preoccupation was with Gianni. In the world according to Marella, love comes in two manifestations: "*amitié amoureuse*" and "*amour passionné.*" The first refers to a loving friendship; the second becomes the center of one's world.

The First Family of Italy seemingly had it all: a billion-dollar fortune, children, grandchildren, and a long-term marriage. However, Gianni was heard to state that while he had always been a devoted husband, he had not been a faithful one. His rationale, "I really loved everything beautiful in life. And a beautiful woman is the most beautiful thing of all. My relationship with *Donna* Marella has always been very good." While many of the other women were merely sex without strings, in the early days of the Agnelli marriage, Giovanni was smitten with Princess Laudomia Hercolani, an affair conducted while Marella was pregnant with their daughter. An Agnelli relative gave her "the talk," explaining that Giovanni "will not only not marry her, he will never leave you." When a journalist questioned Marella about her husband's infidelity, she likened herself to Penelope, who waited steadfastly in Ithaca for her husband while he dallied with Circe.

Serial conquests led to his third nickname: "The Rake of the Riviera." Despite Marella being compelled to overlook adultery, the couple cared deeply for one another and shared a mutual love for art and their adored huskies. One cherished photograph is of Marella in front of the Orvieto Cathedral in Umbria, wearing a necklace that Gianni gave her on a 1955 trip to India. The necklace had come from the Gem Palace in Jaipur, where Gianni had spied several long strands of rubies and emeralds that had served as a decorative piece for the Maharaja of Jaipur. He had them restrung as a necklace that became his wife's signature piece. Photographs show her wearing the cherished jewels at Malcom Forbes' Moroccan birthday party and while standing next to Oscar de la Renta at a party for *The New Yorker.*

Another arena where Giovanni was lacking was in his parental role. Daughter Margherita later revealed, "He was not very interested in being a father." As a teenager, Margherita moved into a storage shed in the grounds of their Rome apartment. Once, when paying a visit to her parents' house, she did so with a shaved head. Gianni's comment was, "She thought she was going to impress me. I absolutely didn't notice at all, didn't say a word. She was disappointed. They always think they can shock you." Son Eduardo, unlike his sister Margherita, did end up shocking. Shy and sensitive, Eduardo suffered from *L'Avvocato*'s verbal grenades and neglect. After dropping out of Princeton, Eduardo tried to find himself and entered an Italian religious community that dabbled in Oriental mysticism. He continued his quest for spiritual enlightenment on a sojourn to India. In 1986, he made a speech where he shared his opposition to materialism. In response, in a move that made Eduardo the equivalent of *The Godfather*'s Fredo Corleone, Gianni bypassed his son as his successor. Eduardo took off for Africa, where he stayed at a beach resort; he ended up in a Kenyan jail for heroin possession. In 2000, he left his home, Villa Sole, a palazzo in the hills above Turin that afforded a view of the ancient city, the Fiat headquarters, and the Alps, and headed to a cliff known as the Bridge of Suicides. Police discovered Eduardo's Fiat Croma abandoned at the side of the road. During their investigation, they saw his body at the base of a 200-foot bridge, lying amidst plastic bags, discarded bottles, and refuse. Arriving by helicopter to the site of the tragedy, Giovanni confirmed that the corpse was that of his son.

While the tragedy was unfolding, Marella was in Manhattan visiting the de la Rentas. Gianni contacted Annette de la Renta, telling her to head to the Agnelli Manhattan apartment so that his wife would not be alone when she heard the devastating news. After learning of the loss of her son, the two women went for a walk in Central Park. Marella related the story her father had told her about Santa Chiara of Assisi, who had lost a loved one in a similar fashion. She elaborated, "And then Santa Chiara heard a voice. It said, 'Chiara, do not despair. Because between the bridge and the water, I was there.' " In resignation she concluded, "Now I know why my father told me that story." Three years later, Marella lost her "*amitié amoureuse*" to cancer.

In a third heartbreak, Marella and Margherita became embroiled in a bitter and public dispute. Gianni had left his only child a $2 billion inheritance that included a huge building adjacent to the presidential palace on the highest hill in Rome, as well as Villa Perosa, the family' s ancestral estate where her ancestors are buried, and houses in Corsica and Paris. Other bequests included paintings by Gustav Klimt, Andy Warhol, and Roy Lichtenstein that collectively carried a billion-dollar price tag. Liquid assets came to $300 million. Nevertheless, Margherita contested her father's will and sued her mother. Marella, cast in the mold of a female King Lear, stated, "I find myself in the unpleasant position of having to defend myself in court, having been accused by my own daughter." A Turin judge dismissed the case. Another cost of the lawsuit was Margherita became *persona non grata* to her mother.

Despite the loss of her husband and son, the estrangement from her daughter, and the effects of Parkinson's, Marella soldiered on. She restored Ain Kassimou, a villa in Marrakesh, Morocco, that Leo Tolstoy's son had built in the 1920s, which she purchased from the estate of the Hermès family.

In 2014, she released *Ho cultivator il mio Giardino*, a book that explored her homes and gardens; its English title was *Marella Agnelli: The Last Swan.* In a *Vanity Fair* article, Marella told the interviewer, "One is never really 'done' with a garden, just as one is never 'done' with life. Day by day and step by step, one just keeps on finding new and clever ways to make them flourish, both in sunshine and in storm."

CHAPTER 13

São Schlumberger: The Portuguese Chameleon (1929)

"I bit of the apple. I did not nibble."

—SÃO SCHLUMBERGER

Portuguese patroness of the arts São Schlumberger is perhaps best known as the woman who graced the canvases of renowned painters Salvador Dali and Andy Warhol despite the independent life she led before serving as their muse. Andy Warhol's famous pronouncement, "In the future, everyone will be world-famous for fifteen minutes," although a hyperbolic statement, applied to the social whirlwind who became a famed hostess on two continents. Ironically, the inauspicious circumstances surrounding her birth had given the appearance that greatness and São would tread divergent roads.

Maria da Diniz Concerçao (nicknamed São) was born in 1929 in Oporto, Portugal. Her father's family earned their livelihood from olive groves whose fruits their factory processed into olive oil. Her mother, Erna Schröeder, was a wealthy German woman. The couple had met as students at the University of Coimbra—the Cambridge of Portugal—where they embarked on a romantic relationship that, although it did not lead to marriage, resulted in the birth of their baby. São's illegitimacy was frowned upon by the ultra-conservative Roman Catholic church of the pre-war era. When São was almost two, Erna left to care for her dying father in Hamburg; World War II prevented her return. Despite the arrival of peace, Erna, who had married another man in the interval, had little interaction with her child. São's father remained single, and his oft-repeated mantra to São was she had ruined his life. He left her in the care of his parents in Beira Baixa, a mountainous province in central Portugal. Of her village, she recalled, "The people are very fierce, independent. Great fighters. They were never conquered. Not by Caesar. Not by Napoleon." His mother was not pleased with raising a child that she had difficulty accepting. She told São, "Your mother is not here, because she doesn't want you." At age ten, São was sent to a Lisbon boarding school run by nuns.

In 1951, São graduated from the University of Lisbon with a degree in history, philosophy, and psychology. As part of her program, she left for Columbia University in New York for a three-month course. Upon her return, São worked for the government as a counselor for troubled teens, a position she detested. She switched her field of study to art and enrolled in the Museu Nacional de Arte Antiga, where she met Pedro Bessone Basto, the scion of an eminent industrial family. An infatuated Pedro followed São when she traveled to New York. Their marriage came with a two-month expiration date when she extricated herself from her wedding vows. The divorce left São mired in misery; she was now a social pariah both due to her illegitimate birth and because she was a divorcée in a country where divorce was illegal.

Another overseas opportunity presented itself when the Lisbon-based Gulbenkian Foundation offered São a fellowship to research children's programs in Manhattan museums. A weekend trip to Houston in the company of Kay Lepercq, a friend from boarding school, and Paul, her bank investor husband, was to lead to an unbelievable destiny. Knowing she would be bored while Paul discussed business with his boss, Kay implored a reluctant São to join them for dinner so she would have a friend with whom she could converse. Kay explained they would be dining with Pierre Schlumberger, who, along with his brother Conrad, had founded one of the world's most lucrative oil companies. In 1940, with the Nazi takeover, the company had moved its headquarters to Houston. Twelve years later, when the company went public, its stock market valuation was $450 million. Twenty years later, the value of Schlumberger Ltd. had increased to $17 billion.

Kay explained that Pierre was a very, very nice man who was deeply depressed over the loss of his wife, Claire Schwob d'Hericourt, a French woman who hailed from a wealthy old Jewish family. The mother of his five children had died from a stroke two years earlier. Kay added that Pierre was extremely reticent; once when a Houston woman seated next to him at a dinner party told him she had bet a friend that she could get him to say more than two words, he responded, "You lose." However, when Pierre saw São, he became loquacious and spoke of racecars, traveling, and art. Although slated to return to New York later that evening, since Paul was still waxing eloquent at two in the morning, São, Kay, and Paul stayed in Houston. Two months later, Pierre proposed to São. The fly in the ointment was that his children, still grieving the loss of their mother, did not welcome a stepmother as replacement. Despite the family opposition, two months after they met, Pierre married São in Houston, Texas. Marriage to a member of the one percent entailed an adjustment period: The first time São prepared a cocktail for her husband, Pierre was not pleased, explaining, "We have butlers to do that." When he saw her in a dress she had worn three weeks earlier, Pierre pronounced, "Never do that again."

As Mrs. Schlumberger, São entered the world of the stratospherically rich. Among the trappings of her wealth was a private jet, and Pierre's art collection, comprised of works by Picasso, Matisse, Monet, and Degas, and the couple purchased an entire floor in Manhattan's One Sutton Place South—a significant change for the woman who had left Portugal in disgrace. After her father's death, São donated his house for use as a community center and presided over the center's opening in her role as the philanthropist—a far cry from that of the illegitimate girl abandoned by her mother.

In a nod to how far she had traveled from her inauspicious past, the Schlumbergers bought Quinta do Vinagre, the 100-acre estate that had been the former summer residence of the bishops of Lisbon; to ornament their garden, they added Henry Moore sculptures. Quinta do Vinagre was the venue for São's 1998 famous "La Dolce Vita" ball that hosted 1,500 guests; among those who attended were Audrey Hepburn, Gina Lollobrigida, the Begum Aly Khan, Loel and Gloria Guinness, the dethroned King Umberto of Italy, the pretender to the Portuguese throne, Dom Duarte de Bragança, and the queen of Holland's daughter. Flower arrangements consisted of two planeloads of gardenias transported from Holland. After the 1974 anti-fascist rebellion, Pierre and São acquired the oldest villa on the French Riviera. Olive trees surrounded the estate, and its stunning seawater pool seemed to flow into the nearby Mediterranean. No wonder São Schlumberger's mantra was, "The sky's the limit."

The couple's main residence was in the Lone Star state until Pierre's mother and sisters ousted him as president of the company. Pierre, feeling his family had stabbed him in the back, severed all relations; when his mother died, he did not attend her funeral. With the loss of his position in the company and of his family, Pierre and São moved to Paris. The power couple made their presence known when, among other lavish expenditures, they donated $1.7 million toward the restoration of the Bourbon king's Versailles bedroom.

A front-row fixture at fashion shows, São wore Givenchy, Saint Laurent, and Chanel and appeared on the International Best-Dressed List's Hall of Fame. As jewels were near and dear to her heart—the bigger the better—she appeared at Studio 54, post black-tie party, dripping diamonds and rubies from Van Cleef & Arpels. Another sparkler arrived when the uxorious husband surprised São with a brown paper bag that held a fifty-one-carat Golconda diamond ring. It was apparent that Pierre was a keeper.

As the girl who had been shuffled from her father to her grandmother and then to boarding school, São collected real estate as other women did charms for their bracelets. The couple bought the seventeenth-century Hôtel de Luzy, a mansion near the Luxembourg Gardens that had once been the home of D'Artagnan, one of the Three Musketeers, and later had housed the mistress of King Louis XVIII's Minister Charles-Maurice de Talleyrand. The palatial property had a mirrored garden, a basement disco, five floors, and seventeen bathrooms.

With the estate's ten bedrooms, there was room for son Paul-Albert and daughter Victoire. To celebrate Paul-Albert's birth, Pierre had presented his wife with a matching emerald earrings, necklace, ring, and bracelet. Victoire's godparents were ex-king Umberto II of Italy and Maria do Espírito Santo, whose family was Portugal's richest. São confessed to a friend that raising children was "not her forte." Of growing up with a mother always immersed in the social vortex, Victoire recalled, "Glamorous figure. Always a new dress. Two chauffeurs—night chauffeur, day chauffeur. Going out to parties. *La femme fatale.* She was the most beautiful woman in Paris for me as a child."

The Schlumbergers became the nucleus of the European elite, and their guests carried the gilded names Rothschild, Thurn und Taxis, and Kennedy. The welcome mat was always out for artists Man Ray and Max Ernst. When not entertaining and gallery hopping, São was a fixture in St. Moritz at Christmas, Venice in September, and Manhattan in the spring. Armed with hubby's fortune, São enhanced Pierre's art collection with purchases of works by Mark Rothko and Roy Lichtenstein. She was the one of the first to commission Andy Warhol to silkscreen her image, and Salvador Dali painted her portrait. The Spanish surrealist designed an elaborate pearl-and-emerald necklace for her that was one of her most cherished jewels.

A long-standing member of the New York Museum of Modern Art, São garnered the admiration of heavyweight patrons of the arts Ronald Lauder (the Estée Lauder heir) and Lilian Auchincloss. São and Pierre were jet-setters whose vacation destinations were in St. Moritz, Venice, and Manhattan. Alas, the "keeper" ultimately developed chinks in his sterling silver knightly armor. A social butterfly, São was saddened when Pierre became more and more reclusive. He explained his reluctance to leave his house by saying, “I don’t want to go outside. I’m afraid I’ll meet some of the family.”

Due to her husband’s withdrawal from the social life São loved, the couple began to lead separate lives. What put a further wedge in their marriage was when Pierre had two strokes. On sidestepping her marital vows, she was heard to say, “It’s such a pity that he was a zero in bed after the stroke.” In the mid-seventies, São embarked on an affair with the Egyptian Prince Naguib Abdallah. She lavished on her lover an apartment and a life-size portrait of him reclining nude except for a lily covering a strategic spot. When São asked Pierre if he wanted a divorce, he adamantly refused and beseeched her, “No matter what you do, I don’t care. The only thing I’m asking you is never to leave me. Please, never, never leave me.” Pierre paid for Naguib’s London-tailored suits and handmade shoes, provided him an allowance of $5,000 a month, and paid his casino debts. For his twenty-seventh birthday, São threw Naguib a party with an Egyptian theme where the centerpieces were ice sculptures of sphinxes, obelisks, and pyramids. Four bare chested men garbed in pharaonic attire, carried a palanquin on their shoulders that displayed a pyramid shaped chocolate cake. Behind it followed São, dressed as Nefertiti, arm in arm with her prince.

After Pierre’s 1986 passing, his will left São embroiled in lawsuits with her children and stepchildren. The most acrimonious tension was with Victoire, a dynamic that deeply distressed Paul-Albert, who died at age thirty-nine from cancer. Although the family feuds put a crimp in her spending, São was still able to live the lifestyle of lifestyles. She rented a house in Tangiers for her and Patrice Calmettes (Naguib’s successor) and had fits of jealousy when Patrice paid too much attention to Diana Ross or the elderly Marlene Dietrich. Another indulgence was her $9 million bachelorette pad in the Seventh Arrondissement, once the home of the oil-rich Romanian Princess Elena Sutu. The pièce de résistance was it overlooked the Eiffel Tower. After dropping a million on renovations, she ordered carpets woven in Bangkok, fabrics from Venice, and craftsmen from London, the latter of whom decorated the walls with feathers. Her baroque consoles once graced a Venetian palazzo, while her mint-green-and-gold library holds Chinese, Russian, and Scottish touches. Salvador Dali's portrait of her was hung in the entrance hall; Andy Warhol's portrait of her was placed in the grand salon. The first-time dress designer Valentino came to call; looking upon touches such as the gold-leaf ceiling, he exclaimed, "Amazing." Another awestruck guest stated of the over-the-top décor, "It's simply hideous. But totally fabulous," words that also applied to the hostess.

During a 1992 dinner, São passed out. A decade before she had been diagnosed with Parkinson's and so relied on medications to prevent her hands from shaking. However, illness did not put the reins on the hostess. In her late seventies, the grand hostess pronounced with pride, "I bit of the apple. I did not nibble." Perhaps this fortitude stemmed from her Portuguese village dwelling ancestors who withstood Caesar and Napoleon. Guests included Sylvester Stallone, Betsy Bloomingdale, Gianni Versace, and the Duke and Duchess of Bedford, who dined on pheasant and venison washed down with Dom Pérignon. When the Duchess of Orleans complimented São on an 1887 bottle of Bordeaux, the following day she received six bottles as a gift. Butlers in white gloves were on hand for serving the delicacies.

In her seventies, her disease confined her to a wheelchair, though she refused to relinquish her position as society doyenne. Many of her staff, including Sebastian, her butler of thirty years, drifted away, as did many of her former friends. However, the Duchess of Orleans and the former UN secretary-general occasionally took her to dine at the Ritz. Another who did not abandon São was

Naguib; but she refused to allow her former lover to see her in her decrepit state. However, in 2003, she had a change of heart and invited him to dinner. During the evening, they reminisced about the heady days of yesteryear when they had beauty, glamour, and clout. Before the evening ended, Naguib shared a Thomas Mann quotation, “For the leaves to touch the sky, the roots must reach to hell.”

Perhaps what becomes a legend most is someone who can seamlessly reinvent herself as did São Schlumberger, the Portuguese chameleon.

CHAPTER 14

Imelda Marcos: Glass Slipper (1929)

"Win or lose, we will go shopping after the election."

—IMELDA MARCOS

The German Grimm Brothers' fairy tale *Cinderella* originated in ancient China, a narrative in which the lady's doll-like feet captured the heart of a prince. The Philippine First Lady, Imelda

Marcos, like her fairy-tale counterpart, understood how a pair of shoes could transform one's life.

If narcissism were a sport, Imelda Remedios Visitacion Romualdez Marcos would excel in every event. Having ascended the pinnacle of Philippine society, she proceeded to pen an autobiography that had only the barest acquaintanceship with the factual circumstances of her life. However, Carmen Navarro Pedrosa's very unauthorized 1970 biography, *The Unknown Story of Imelda Marcos*, lifted the veil on her past. Imelda banished both book and author from the Philippines.

The Steel Butterfly—her moniker derived from her authoritarian manner and over-the-top glamour—had a pockmarked youth. When her father, Vincente Orestes Romualdez, a forty-three-year-old widower, wed his reluctant bride, the twenty-seven-year-old Remedios, their union added six more children to his five. Miserable in her marriage, Remedios only escaped as far as the garage, where she lived with her two sons and three daughters. Imelda's bed was a wooden board propped up by milk cartons. When Imelda was eight, her mother passed away from pneumonia. After squandering his inherited fortune, father Vincente relocated from the capital, Manila, to his hometown of Leyte. While Japanese planes dropped death from the skies during World War II, a barefoot Imelda carried her family's sole asset, a jewel necklace, the beads of which she bartered for food. At age thirteen, she sewed dresses from the fabric of an abandoned parachute. As soon as escape beckoned, Imelda moved to the Manila home of her wealthy relatives.

At five-foot-seven—she appeared taller due to her teased hair and stiletto heels—Imelda towered over most Filipino women (and quite a few men). As a teen, she serenaded homesick American soldiers at GI camps and flirted with them in exchange for chocolate. After appearing in the Miss Philippines Pageant, she earned the moniker "The Rose of Tacloban" (the capital city of Leyte).

Imelda's destiny would have been as a Real Housewife of Manila had it not been for an encounter that changed her destiny, as well as that of her homeland. In 1954, while waiting to see Imelda's cousin, Daniel Romualdez, the Speaker for the House of Representatives, Congressman Ferdinand Marcos spied the brunette beauty. Putting libido over politics, he invited her out for ice cream; she accepted either due to physical attraction, his political position, or desire for dessert. The smitten suitor sent her a diamond for each of the next eleven days, after which time they tied the knot during a congressional recess. Referring to the daily delivery of diamonds, Imelda quipped, "I wish he could have courted me longer." Jeweler Harry Winston estimated the value of her eleven-diamond wedding ring at $300,000. The reception's venue was the park opposite Malacañang Palace where three thousand guests gathered; missing from that number were Ferdinand's common-law-wife Carmen Ortega and their three children. The couple had daughters Imee and Irene and son Ferdinand Jr., nicknamed 'Bongbong.'

Raised as a poor country girl, uncomfortable in her role as the spouse of an up-and-coming politician, and distraught over her husband's infidelities, Imelda suffered a nervous breakdown and sought treatment at a New York psychiatric hospital. Eventually Imelda, like Stella, found her groove and campaigned tirelessly for Ferdinand's presidential bid. Her niche voters were the poor, who worshipped their Cinderella who had risen from their ranks. She arrived in her signature attire of *terno*, the native garment featuring butterfly sleeves (her forever fashion statement), and spike heels tinted to match her purses. She claimed it was her obligation to dress to the nines as "it inspired the poor to dress better."

Upon becoming the tenth president of the Philippines, Ferdinand beamed that his wife was "his secret weapon." *Life Magazine* pronounced the First Lady "the Jackie Kennedy of Asia," a comparison Imelda relished. In contrast, she brushed off comparisons to Evita Peron, the wife of the Argentinean dictator, with the withering comment, "I did not start off in a brothel."

Not cut from the same cloth as Mamie Eisenhower, who had stated, "I had a career. His name was Ike," Imelda thirsted to be more than presidential arm candy. While Ferdinand occupied himself with securing control of the military, Imelda indulged in her "edifice complex." To accommodate the 1981 arrival of Pope John Paul II, Imelda constructed the Coconut Palace, with eight lavish suites. However, preferring a simpler accommodation, the pontiff stayed elsewhere. She also built a cultural, trade, and film center, the latter of which she touted as "the Cannes of Asia," envisioning the new facility as a setting for Miss Universe contests. She also hoped the building would host matches between reigning boxers Muhammad Ali and Joe Frasier. Their heavyweight championship bout, christened the "Thrilla in Manila," was a title that could also describe the reign of Imelda Marcos.

Age did not wither Imelda's lust for lavish buildings. For Irene's 1983 wedding in Sarrat, to ready the town, she spent $10.3 million on a hotel and new airport. She also had local homes remodeled externally so they would resemble residences from seventeenth-century Spain. Imelda also arranged for five hundred first-class cabins on an ocean liner for guests. Ironically, Irene had requested a "quiet affair."

The First Lady of the Philippines sought the spotlight and was in her element when she made the acquaintance of royals Princess Margaret and Prince Charles of England, Princess Firyal of Jordan, the Queen of Thailand, and King Constantine of Greece. She rubbed butterfly-covered shoulders with American presidents Ronald Reagan, Lyndon B. Johnson, Richard M. Nixon, and George Bush. A video captured the party Imelda threw for Nixon where he boogied to Filipino music. Her heart held a special place for international billionaires: the Italian Fiat family, the Agnellis; the Niarchos dynasty of Greek shipping magnates; American real estate baron Donald Trump; and Saudi Arabian arms dealer Adnan Khashoggi. Not one to ostracize those considered villains by the Free World, she met with Chairman Mao, Saddam Hussein, Muammar Qaddafi, and Fidel Castro.

When staying in the Big Apple, Imelda lived at the Waldorf Astoria in a $1,800-a-night suite where she had a daily delivery of $1,000 worth of fresh flowers. One of the crown jewels in their real estate portfolio was their Manhattan mansion, where Persian carpets covered the floors; Picasso, van Gogh, and Brueghel the Younger canvases adorned its walls. According to Andy Warhol, Imelda was the life and soul of every soiree. In his diary, he recorded that the First Lady sang twelve after-dinner songs on Malcolm Forbes' yacht. During the evening, Imelda's assistant invited select guests to an after-dinner party at her Manhattan home, where the party continued at her sixth-floor private discothèque—one that had its own disco ball and live orchestra. As a midnight repast, the guests dined on lobster and steak. A select few stayed behind, so Imelda took them to her private floor of the mansion, where two maids exhibited her jewelry. Gems included a Cartier tiara and a $1.5 million emerald-and-diamond bracelet. The Marcos yacht was an earthly pleasure dome: a guest recalled that two men stood on stepladders with oil drums filled with caviar that they poured into two seven-foot-high Limoges urns.

The possessor of a black belt in conspicuous consumerism beside whom the Kardashians appear miserly, Imelda embarked on multimillion-dollar sprees in Rome, Manhattan, and Copenhagen. One real estate plum she turned down was the Empire State Building, whose $750 million price tag she deemed "too ostentatious." Rumor holds she even tried to purchase Tiffany and Co. The Marcos family's personal art collection held Picassos, Botticellis, and a Michelangelo, the latter of which she had purchased for 3.5 million. Another economic Achilles heel was jewelry; she was the owner of the Star of the South, a gem Ferdinand had given her for their twenty-fifth wedding anniversary. The kite-shaped, 14.37-carat, D color diamond had once graced the finger of Evalyn Walsh McLean, the possessor of the ill-fated Hope Diamond. In the San Francisco airport, Imelda purchased $2,000 worth of gum; another souvenir from a trip abroad was five hundred boxes of macadamia nuts. In 1976, Imelda imported 102 wild animals—including zebras and giraffes—from Kenya to create a private safari on Calauit Island, displacing 254 residents in the process.

President and First Lady Marcos, who had transformed the presidency into a dictatorship, financed their fabulous lifestyles by using the poverty-plagued Philippines as their personal piggybank. The Guinness Book of World Records stated the First Couple were responsible for the greatest theft from a government, which they plundered to the tune of an estimated $5 to $10 billion, with stolen funds hidden away in numerous overseas accounts. For their Swiss bank account, Ferdinand Marcos employed the name William Saunders; Imelda was Jane Ryan. While the Latin Nero fiddled as Rome burned, Imelda shimmied on the floor at Manhattan's Studio 54.

The ambitious Imelda became the governor of greater Manila; she also transformed herself into an islander Lady Macbeth who employed her wifely wiles to further Ferdinand's desertion of democracy. During their two-decade rule, the couple presided over a regime that incarcerated and killed thousands of "enemies of state." The Marcos' regime is associated with the statistics: 3,257 known homicides, 35,000 tortures, 70,000 incarcerations. Against the backdrop of this carnage, Imelda referred to herself as the "Mother of the Philippines."

Amidst the laissez-faire spending on their twenty-nine palatial residences, karma paid a palace house call. As the First Lady presided over a televised award ceremony in 1972, Carlito Dimahilig stabbed her eleven times with a twelve-inch bolo knife. A security guard shot the would-be assassin twice in his back. The attack on Imelda necessitated seventy-five stitches and led to bulletproof bras. She said of the attack, "If somebody's going to kill me, why such an ugly instrument?" Indeed, aestheticism always ruled Imelda's roosts. As she explained, "I love beauty and am allergic to ugliness." President Nixon called with his condolences.

In 1986, the People's Power Revolution forced the Marcos family to flee Malacañang Palace in a helicopter headed for Hawaii. Of their desperate flight, Imelda reminisced, "The slipper was lost. And everything turned into a pumpkin." When the protestors stormed the Philippine Versailles, they stumbled upon art masterpieces, a multimillion-dollar cache of jewelry, 508 floor-length gowns, five shelves of Gucci handbags, sixty-five parasols, seventy-one sunglasses, fifteen mink coats, five hundred black brassieres, and suitcases filled with girdles. On a table was an abandoned meal of caviar. What captured the headlines was the discovery of Imelda's three thousand pairs of shoes; in actuality, there were 1,060. Imelda stated, "They went into my closets looking for skeletons, but thank God all they found were shoes, beautiful shoes." For those who wish to see the beautiful shoes, the Marikina City Footwear Museum in Manila holds 765 pairs and takes up the entire second floor. The media dubbed the former First Lady "Marie Antoinette with Shoes." Despite Ferdinand's $13,500 annual salary, the helicopter carried $15 million in assets. The new government estimated Marcos' "hidden wealth" at $5 billion to $10 billion, in contrast with the Philippines' annual income average per capita at that time of $600. An inkling of the breadth and depth of their financial empire emerged: an office tower in Manhattan, a waterfront estate on Long Island, palatial properties in the Philippines.

In the court of public opinion, the First Lady was even more vilified than the President. An anecdote related how President Marcos and General Fabian Ver encountered each other in hell. The general inquired, "Boss, I've committed treacherous acts, but yours were far worse. So how come I'm covered in burning tar up to my neck, and you're only covered up to your knees?" Marcos replied, "I'm standing on Imelda's shoulders."

After Ferdinand died in exile, Imelda was devastated when the Philippine government refused to allow her to bury him in the sacred soil of their homeland. However, dictatorial Rodrigo Duterte, who became president of the Philippines in 2016, permitted Ferdinand's reburial in the Heroes' Cemetery in Manila.

The woman who had graced magazine covers found herself pictured in mugshots. In New York, Imelda stood trial on charges she had plundered the Philippines National Bank; Billionaire gal pal Doris Duke bailed her out to the tune of $5 million. The tobacco heiress also lent Imelda her Boeing 737 to fly her and her entourage from Hawaii to New York for her trial. Unsurprisingly, Imelda painted herself as a martyr: "There I was in a foreign country to face the sword of justice. I faced the trial of the century alone, widowed, and orphaned from my country." Perhaps her butterfly sleeves held Teflon since the court acquitted her of all charges. The yo-yo, a Philippine invention, provides an apt metaphor for Imelda, who continues to spin without stopping. The Marcos money allowed Imelda to return to the country that once elected her as a congresswoman for Leyte. Perhaps due to historic amnesia, in 2022, her son Bongbong became the seventeenth president and, as of this writing, still holds that office.

At the time of this writing, the now ninety-five-year-old Imelda can no longer comfortably fit into the shoes of yesteryear. She has lost Ferdinand, her partner in crime, and she is pursued by the shadow of having orchestrated one of the greatest thefts in history. Her name is a byword for greed on steroids, and she is known as a tyrant who hastened the end of millions of her opponents. In token of an added dollop of karma, her once-legendary beauty has deserted her. As a coping device, Imelda relies on her old crutch of reinvention, a landscape where reality and fantasy merge. While professing to be a penniless widow, she presses a button to summon servants. Her Manila penthouse is a treasure trove of masterpieces by Picasso, Michelangelo, and Gauguin; priceless antique statues abound, as does the glint of gold. There is an odd juxtaposition of buddhas and Catholic icons, as if their owner was trying to hedge her bets. Rather than focusing on her king's ransom of possessions, she rues the lost trappings of her previous wealth. Her coffee table art book showcases pieces she once owned, about which she has stated, "We had a Raphael and a Botticelli, [and] at least a thousand pieces of silver, including a piece given by the King of Morocco for our silver wedding anniversary." The government that ousted her from power auctioned them off to recoup the country's emptied coffers.

If an interviewer could ask questions of the nonagenarian, some might be: Did you arrange the assassination of political rival Benigno Aquino? What fueled your endless quest for wealth? Do you fear the biblical passage, "For what shall it profit a man, if [she] shall gain the whole world, and lose [her] own soul?" Whatever the answers, what is certain is that Imelda Marcos will forever mourn her shattered glass slipper.

CHAPTER 15

Basia Piasecka Johnson: The Polish Pharmaceutical Princess (1937)

"I come from a noble family."

—BASIA PIASECKA JOHNSON

Johnson & Johnson

The name of the behemoth corporation Johnson & Johnson carries connotations of comfort: bandages to heal cuts, talcum to soothe rashes, "No More Tears" shampoo to prevent burning eyes. The company was transformed into Johnson *versus* Johnson with the advent of Barbara "Basia" Piasecka Johnson. Her rags-to-mega-rich story provides hope to all middle-aged Polish maids.

The American dynasty originated in 1887 with band of brothers Robert, Edward, and James, three of the eleven children of Sylvester Johnson, a poor Pennsylvania farmer. Aware that the staggering majority of Civil War casualties had resulted from poor medical care, they concentrated on products that promoted healing. For inspiration, the siblings turned to British surgeon Dr. Joseph Lister, the pioneer of antiseptic surgery. James' cursive writing provided the red Johnson & Johnson calligraphy script found on their merchandise labels. The Red Cross logo had been the brainchild of Civil War nurse, Clara Barton, who lobbied Congress for a bill granting her organization the sole right to its symbol. In one corner were the powerful Johnsons; in the other was the Civil War heroine. Pro-business President Grover Cleveland sided against the nurse known as "The Angel of the Battlefield." Magnanimously, the Johnsons awarded Clara a dollar. Another example of Johnson & Johnson's unauthorized use of a name concerned "Lister's Antiseptic Gauze," so called after Dr. Lister. An illustration of the wealth of the Johnson clan was their descendant, Robert Wood Johnson IV, who purchased the New York Jets for $635 million. *Fortune 500* described the Johnsons as America's "most dysfunctional family."

The contemporary Cinderella who embodied the American dream on steroids was born in Staniewicze, a village in what was then eastern Poland, now Belarus. She recounted an episode from her childhood when Bolshevik soldiers armed with machine guns forced her family up against a wall. Another recollection occurred on Christmas Eve in Warsaw, where Barbara, who went by Basia, was in the hospital. A nurse offered her white chocolate if she would say, "Heil, Hitler;" Basia responded, "I don't like chocolate." World War II uprooted the family, and Basia mourned the loss of their home and possessions, lamenting, "Begin again. Begin again." When Basia was thirteen, the Piaseckas relocated to Wroclaw, where, along with her father and brothers, she ran their farm from 1958 to 1965. To better her station, Basia left home to study art history and philosophy at Boleslaw Bierut University of Wroclaw, followed by a doctoral program at Jagiellonian University in Kraków. After completing her courses, Basia received one of the first Vatican scholarships for art in Rome and Florence. Under her father's advice not to return to communist Poland, Basia landed in the United States on Labor Day, 1968, with $100 and a smattering of English. The Polish American Immigration and Relief Committee found her a room in a dingy hotel.

Friends in the Polish community of Perth Amboy, New Jersey, introduced Basia to Zofia Koverdan, a cook for the Johnson family, who worked at their farm in Oldwick, New Jersey. Zofia told Esther (Essie) Johnson that she needed another set of hands in the kitchen, and Basia ended up in the employment of J. Seward Johnson, Jr., the son of company founder Robert Wood Johnson.

Had Basia been more adept in the kitchen, she would have sidestepped a singular destiny. When Essie noticed her new assistant cook's culinary incompetence, she made her an upstairs maid. As Basia explained of her transfer of duties, "She wanted that I take care of the grandchildren when they come. She knew that I have a very good attitude toward children, as well as toward the animals." In her new position, she caught Seward's wandering eye. Basia first learned that Seward thought of her as more than just 'the help' when his daughter, Jennifer, told her that her father had nearly run his yacht aground when he saw her walking on the beach. Basia explained of her stroll in her new twenty-dollar bathing suit that she "relied on her ability to enchant and captivate."

In 1969, feeling she had not obtained an art degree and moved to America to work as a maid, Basia moved to Manhattan and enrolled in New York University. A week later, she returned home to three messages from Seward. On a fourth call, he told her he had "something very important to discuss." Seward sent his limousine to bring her to his office at Johnson & Johnson. He told her he was impressed she had been able to save money while in his employment and that she reminded him of American pioneers. Seward explained he intended to start collecting art and, as she had a degree in the field, he offered to pay her $12,000 a year for her expertise (over $100,000 annually in present-day currency). He added that he foresaw a future for her in his oceanographic institute, which was why she would need to take scuba diving lessons in preparation for a trip. At the time Basia was engaged to Peter Ejsmont, a world-class sailor; when her fiancée perished at sea, her relationship with Seward departed from the platonic plane.

The thirty-two-year-old Basia and seventy-four-year-old Seward left on the *Ocean Pearl* for the Bahamas. The trip segued into a life of luxury as Seward took his new mistress on vacations to Paris, London, Rome, and Ireland. They visited galleries where Seward purchased a $250,000 Mondrian, a $100,000 Picasso, and a $250,000 Cézanne. Of her avid collecting, Basia stated, "When I came here, I pick up tradition very quickly of American life to build a monument for the Johnson family, an art collection...like Mellon, Rockefeller, Frick." Basia often outbid the Getty Museum for acquisitions and bested French national museums when she bid $1.5 million on a cabinet that had once resided in the Palace of Versailles. The purchase set a record for the highest bid for a single item of furniture. The next highest price items were $935,000 for a desk and $23,284 for two petit point cushions. They paid $4.8 million for a black chalk sketch by Raphael, the highest ever paid for an artist's drawing. The Johnsons' art collection was estimated at $100 million.

The following year, Seward set up Basia in a Sutton Place apartment. When his daughter visited, Seward announced, "I found the ideal woman for me. She can't speak English, so I can't talk to her, and therefore I don't have to listen to her."

For Christmas, Seward gave Essie, his second wife of thirty years, a locket that she took as a sign his affair had run its course. She knew she was wrong when her husband moved into Sutton Place and instituted divorce proceedings. On Basia's birthday, spent in São Paulo, Brazil, Seward proposed with an oval amethyst and diamond ring. His six children did not receive invitations to the wedding. The bride's terms of endearment for her husband were "Romeo" and "Sewardo." Adorably, the newlyweds engaged in affectionate games and baby talk. Smitten, Seward purchased his wife a dark-gray Mercedes. When she mentioned she had wanted the light-gray color model, the following day he bought that one as well.

Seward felt the third time was the charm when he married Basia. He stated, "I can't believe my luck; someone like Basia, a beautiful young girl, and she's in love with me. She's sexually attracted to me!" The newly minted Mrs. Johnson proved that you could teach an old dog new tricks. Seward started wearing turtlenecks and a Bulgari medallion; he replaced his Dodge with Mercedes-Benzes and Bentleys. Real estate acquisitions included a private Bahamian island and two houses in Ansedonia, Italy; the second Italian home was scooped up because their dogs, a boxer named Prince and a mastiff named Clara, enjoyed walking in its olive grove. Seward bought a Gulf Stream jet so that his dogs could fly to their homes nonstop.

Mr. and Mrs. Johnson built their real estate crown jewel on a 140-acre lot in Princeton, an undertaking that took four years. Their residence, the country's most expensive, cost $30 million, or $174,162,825 in contemporary currency. Their architect, Wallace Harrison, had supplied the blueprints for the United Nations. The Johnsons christened their princely palace Jasna Polana, Polish for "Bright Meadow," a nod to the name of Leo Trotsky's Russian estate. Bronze busts of Seward and Basia had spots in the foyer near the front doors, along with a pair of sixteenth-century Italian door knockers shaped like lions. There was also a seventy-two-foot-long swimming pool surrounded by Greek and Roman antiquities, a $78,000 orchid greenhouse, heated marble floors, a twelve-foot-square marble bathtub, and his-and-hers Italianate gardens. The Johnsons' doghouse had seasonal air conditioning, heated bronze steps, a kitchenette, and a passageway led to the main house, giving a twist to the adage, "It's a dog's life." Jasna Polana held $50 million in art. One of Basia's witticisms was to inform guests, "You are standing on the king's carpet." The royal in question was King Louis XIV. As Basia supported Poland's Solidarity party, fearing Russian reprisals, the windows were bulletproof.

Just as the Fifth Mughal emperor, Shah Jahan, built the Taj Mahal for his adored wife, Mumtaz Mahal, Seward's version of that love legacy was a $5 million tomb for himself, Basia, Prince, and Clara. In pharaonic fashion, they planned a Raphael-style mural for the ceiling and adornments of paintings and antiques. Alas, to paraphrase poet Robert Burns, the best laid plans of mice and men and millions of others often go awry. Neither spent eternity in the mausoleum.

When Seward died in 1983, a public tug-of-war ensued. Seward Jr. described his stepmother as a combination of Marie Antoinette and Hetty Green; Basia viewed her late husband's children as King Lear did his eldest daughters. Seward had bequeathed his wife a fortune estimated at between $400 million to $1 billion. The only child earmarked for an inheritance was Seward Jr., who received $1 million and a boathouse in Chatham, Massachusetts. He called his share "a cold fish in the face." His bitterness was evident in a remark against the woman he felt had stolen his birthright, of whom he said, "When Basia was asked to come and clean house, she took it idiomatically instead of literally."

The children—all of whom were multimillionaires from trusts their father had set up years before—challenged the will. They claimed the chambermaid had exerted undue influence on her ill, elderly husband. Of the proceedings, which left the media collectively licking their lips, Seward Jr., stated, "It's going to blow high, wide, and handsome, and it's gonna be a lulu."

The lawsuit ushered in a three-year, $24 million legal battle that involved the country's leading law firms, ones that had represented Kennedys, Mellons, Rockefellers, and Carnegies. Witnesses for the disinherited heirs testified that Basia had emotionally and physically assaulted her diminished-capacity husband. She countered there had only been tiffs such as when she had admonished him over not taking his medicine and he'd criticized her for squeezing the toothpaste tube from the middle. A journalist covering the case described it as "the largest, costliest, ugliest, most spectacular, and most conspicuous probate battle in American history." Court transcripts held the statements of the seven main dramatis persona and those who had interacted with Seward during his last three years. The depositions included those of two former secretaries of state, a Chief Justice, several Rothschilds, a Rockefeller, a Roosevelt, Gregory Peck, and Barbara

Sinatra. The widow's contention, "I know my husband's dream. That is why he want to leave it all to me."

Of course, there was the mandatory mudslinging. Camp Johnson painted their stepmother as the younger woman/gold digger/chambermaid who had estranged their father from his wife of three decades. An enraged Basia directed her lawyers, "Slam the door in their face and give them not the dust from a penny." Camp Basia painted her husband's children as suffering from the harmful effects of wealth. Her attorney referenced newspaper clippings of their past exploits, which reportedly included suicide attempts, drug addiction, and divorce. The unfortunate spotlight was especially harsh on Mary Lea, Seward's oldest daughter—the original model for the infant who had first appeared in advertisements for Johnson & Johnson baby powder. A not-very-well-kept family secret was Mary Lea's claim her father had sexually molested her from ages nine to fifteen. Then there was the accusation her ex-husband had hired his homosexual lover to kill her due to a monetary motive. One grandson was a drug addict whose parents had kicked him out of the house after he had injected the family dog with heroin. His brother had planned to blow up the Far Hill, New Jersey, police station. Seward Jr.'s divorce settlement stated his ex had forced him to serve her lover breakfast in bed.

The outcome of the trial: Each of the six children received $6.2 million after taxes, with an additional $8 million to Seward, Jr. One positive consequence of the horror show was expressed by Elaine Johnson Wold, who observed it had united the estranged siblings. Basia's share exceeded $350 million, in addition to her extensive holdings. Having survived what she termed her "American Hell," before she drove off from the courthouse in her bulletproof Mercedes, Basia stated, "Most people can't have their dreams.

I have made my dreams come true." Then she thrust her hands above her head and made the Polish Solidarity sign: V for Victory.

Basia promised to invest $100 million to rescue the Lenin shipyard in Gdansk, home of the Solidarity Movement. Along with Polish president Lech Walesa, she appeared on the cover of The New York Times under the headline, "Lech's American Angel." But when she demanded too many concessions from the workers, the plan collapsed.

The widow moved to Monaco—the principality Somerset Maugham described as "a sunny place for shady people." In the glittering principality, she held exhibitions of her art collection of Monets, Picassos, and Rembrandts and organized a foundation supporting Polish students in America. Before she left the States, Basia had transformed Jasna Polana into a private golf club house; golf pro Gary Player designed the greens. Members enjoy antique French chairs, sixteenth-century Flemish tapestries, and European fireplaces. In 1996, with the aid of her friend Prince Albert of Monaco, Basia baptized the club with her first golf swing—the ball landed on the fence. She visited her former mansion once a year, at which time she would walk her dachshund amongst the rose and gardenia trees.

In 2013, a Polish daily newspaper named *Rzeczpospolita* announced Basia's passing after "a long and serious illness." The seventy-six-year-old, who had not remarried, died near Wroclaw; there was a funeral Mass for her in its cathedral. The woman who had started life with the mantra, "Begin again. Begin again," ended up the forty-second richest woman in the world, with a net worth of $3.6 billion.

The weaving sisters worked overtime when they wove the threads of Basia Piasecka Johnson's destiny: to transform herself from a victim of the communists and the Nazis into the Polish Pharmaceutical Princess.

CHAPTER 16

Lily Safra: A Gilded Lily (1934)

"When you support people who are making a real difference in the world, you end up receiving far more than you give"

—LILY SAFRA

In *Twelfth Night,* William Shakespeare wrote, "Some are born great, some achieve greatness, and some have greatness thrust upon them." While the first part of the quotation does not apply to

Lily Safra, she both achieved greatness and had greatness thrust upon her—in terms of wealth—through her judicious choice of husbands.

Born in Porto Alegre, Brazil, Lily Watkins led such a star-filled yet star-crossed life that she could have emerged from a Danielle Steel novel. She was born, allegedly, in 1934; she always took pains—and cosmetic surgery—to hide the date on her birth certificate. Her mother, Annita, had fled her native Ukraine to escape its virulent anti-Semitism. Her father, Wolf White Watkins, had left Britain to capitalize on Latin America's railroad boom. Wolf owned a factory in the town of Mesquita, outside Rio de Janeiro, where he manufactured railway carriages. His over-the-top spending left him in financial crunches that he evaded through deals that were well south of legitimate. A doting dad, Wolf lavished gifts on sons Rodolpho, Daniel, and Artigas, as well as his daughter, named after the French soprano Lily Pons. The Watkins enrolled Lily in the Colegio Anglo-Americano, a British-American private school located on the former property of a Portuguese duke. Because of her prominent nose, students called her "Lily *nariz*," which translates to "Lily the nose;" a plastic surgeon curtailed the cruel nickname.

What Lily lacked in wealth, she compensated for in beauty. Her I-never-ate-a carb frame, classical features, and green eyes ensured her position as a Brazilian queen bee. Suitors surrounded her at the Clube Israelita Brasileiro, a Jewish community center in Copacabana. Extremely accomplished, she was fluent in Portuguese, English, Spanish, and French. The family left for a vacation in Uruguay, ostensibly to visit Annita's family, but actually undertaken to distance their daughter from Izidor, a boy with whom she was smitten. The Watsons hoped Lily would find her match amongst scions of the monied Jewish community in Uruguay. In the country's capital, Montevideo, the seventeen-year-old Lily met Argentinian Mario Cohen, who had made a fortune in nylon stockings. After their wedding, due to the repressive measures against Jews under Argentinian president Juan Peron, the couple settled in Uruguay, where they had children Claudio, Eduardo, and Adriana. During a shopping spree, Lily spent thousands of dollars on lingerie; but rather than whetting Mario's passion, her purchases ignited his fury at her spendthrift ways, and he ripped up the little garments with the big price tags. When Mario bought Lily a Morris Minor, a middle-class British import, a disgusted Wolf bought her a Cadillac.

Bored and unhappy, Lily longed to return to Rio—without Mario. However, she did not want to do so as a single mother living in her parents' Copacabana apartment. Mario remained committed to the marriage but was not savvy enough to understand the price for plucking a lily.

The ticket out of the marriage was Alfredo João Monteverde, the millionaire owner of Ponto Frio, Brazil's most successful appliance store chain; born Alfred Iancu Grunberg in Romania, he was the son of a prominent Jewish banker to the Romanian royal court. After his father's suicide, and with war looming in Europe, the family fled to Brazil, where they exchanged the name Grunberg for Monteverde, Portuguese for "green mountain." After a ceremony in Manhattan's Office of the City Clerk, Alfredo took his bride to the French jeweler Boucheron, where he purchased a serious diamond ring for her.

Doña Lily possessed an enviable life: Alfredo was handsome, and he was a good father to both her children and Carlos, his son from a former marriage, as well as an indulgent husband. He was also one of Brazil's richest men; he whisked her away on vacations to Switzerland, Italy, and France, and wonder of wonders, he did not begrudge her shopping sprees. The walls of their luxurious home displayed a van Gogh. Four years later, while considering a divorce, Alfredo committed suicide. His will left his widow $230 million. Suspicions swirled regarding his death: He had shot himself twice in the chest when one bullet would have proved fatal, and no gunpowder residue was found on his hand. Alfredo's mother and his adored sister Rosy launched a lawsuit against Lily over his will. On her late husband's tombstone, Lily had these words engraved: "Merci d'être né, Puchi." ["Thanks for being born, Puchi."]

Anxious to distance herself from her husband's death, Lily decamped for London, leaving behind her designer dresses. To manage her assets, Lily turned to Edmond Safra, head of Banco Safra. While the Rothschilds were an enormously wealthy European Jewish banking family, the Safras were the descendants of Lebanese Jewish bankers. Their surname, Safra, means gold in Arabic, and the family's camel caravans bearing gold had flourished since the Ottoman Empire. Edmond was the go-to man when the wealthy wanted to hide their money from Brazil's military dictatorship.

Financial affairs turned to a physical one when the blonde bouffant beauty began a relationship with the short, stocky, shy bachelor. As Lily had her own fortune, Edmond felt she was not a gold digger. Although his family had wanted Edmond to marry, the religious Sephardic Safra family disliked his secular Ashkenazi girlfriend. His brothers were fierce in their condemnation of the divorced and widowed Lily. They railed she was too old to bear Edmond heirs, thereby ending his hope of a son who would carry on his dream of a thousand-year-old Safra dynasty. Bowing to their pressure, Edmond ended their relationship.

Brilliant at shopping, less so with rejection, Lily cast her eye about for a new romance and found it on a London visit to her dentist where she met a fellow patient, Moroccan-born businessman

Samuel Bendahan. Attracted, Lily raised her hand to her hair, making sure it was perfectly coiffed. (The gesture went on to become their go-to signal for a bedroom tryst.) Twenty minutes later, Lily asked Samuel out on a date. After a dizzying courtship, the couple wed at an Acapulco registry office. The common consensus held that Samuel was a toy-boy gigolo, which was not the case. He kept their finances separate and paid half of the expenses for their French home. As quickly as she had fallen for Samuel, Lily checked out with the same speed. Her relationship with the younger, better-looking Samuel had whetted Edmond's jealousy (which probably was part of her ploy), and he agreed to make her Mrs. Safra. Upon being served with divorce papers, Samuel asked for compensation for his investment in their home. After steadfastly refusing to see him, Lily agreed to a meeting in New York. As Samuel stepped off the plane at the John F. Kennedy Airport, plain-clothes policemen took him to Rikers Island jail as Lily had charged him with extortion. Safra attorneys threatened if he caused further trouble, he would be incarcerated for a lengthy period. One attorney warned, "Imagine how popular a good-looking boy like you would be with all those violent Negro criminals." Lily applied for a divorce in Reno, Nevada, where she asked the judge that she not be required to be present in court with Samuel. They did appear separately, although they crossed paths in the Second Judicial Court of the State of Nevada. At that time, Lily raised her hand, not as a signal for sex, but to cover her face. Despite any residue of guilt, that year Lily made the list of London's Best-Dressed Women.

Despite his family's argument that Lily had embarrassed herself yet again with her gigolo third husband, Edmond presented his lover with a rectangular-cut, 34.05-carat diamond ring, as well as a 600-page prenuptial agreement. They tied the knot in 1976; guests included Ronald and Nancy Reagan and the Aga Khan. The Safras lived in Manhattan, where she attended soirees in designer dressers and priceless jewels; her bouffant hair was always meticulous. Known for her over-the-top gifts, Lily instructed her secretary to find out her friends' shoe sizes: they all received $500 Manolo Blahnik pumps.

Lily threw fabulous parties for their circle, and guests included Wall Street financiers and designers Hubert de Givenchy, Valentino, and Karl Lagerfeld. She hobnobbed with Prince Charles and Jacob Rothschild. When not attending galas or brokering deals, the Safras luxuriated in their palatial residences in Brazil, London, New York, Geneva, and Monaco. The crown jewel of their real estate—the continent's most pricey property—was Villa Leopolda, which overlooked the Mediterranean. The villa had once been the domain of the genocidal King Leopold II of Belgium, who had financed his lifestyle through his chokehold on the Congo.

To celebrate Edmond's fifty-six birthday, Lily invited three hundred guests for a Leopolda soiree. She flew in flowers from Holland as well as musician Sergio Mendes and his orchestra from California. Designer Valentino arrived on his newly purchased 152-foot yacht, along with dancer Mikhail Baryshnikov. Prince Rainier and his daughter Princess Caroline of Monaco insisted they not make an entrance until everyone had been seated. Other royals were Princess Firyal of Jordan and the Amyn Aga Khan; a French SWAT team provided security. John Fairchild, the snobbish publisher of *W* Magazine and *Women's Wear Daily*, wrote, "They have taken the Riviera, Southampton, New York, the Metropolitan Opera, Geneva—all in a space of five years. What's next?"

What was to come next was tragic. The apple of Lily's eye was her son Claudio, who she referred to as "Jesus Christ, Esquire." In 1989, Lily became a member of the world's least enviable club—those who bury their child. After an argument between Claudio and his wife Evelyn, the couple had taken separate cars to their friends' summer home in Angra dos Reis. Claudio and his four-year-old son Raphael traveled in one vehicle; Evelyn and their son Gabriel in another. While speeding, thirty-five-year-old Claudio collided with a speeding police truck. Father and son perished in the crash. Lily was inconsolable at the sudden loss of both her son and grandson.

In the mid-1990s, doctors diagnosed Edmond Safra with Parkinson's. Terrified he was already a target for his enemies and now even more vulnerable due to his illness, Edmond hired Samuel Cohen, who had trained with the Israeli intelligence force Mossad, as his head of security. Cohen's staff consisted of twelve bodyguards, all former Israeli soldiers. The Safras' twenty-room, 10,000-square-foot oceanfront penthouse was an impregnable Monaco fortress with its bulletproof windows, fifteen security cameras, and alarms connected to Monaco Sécurité.

With mortality approaching, Edmond increased his charitable work. In 1996, the Safras hosted a magnificent gala to commemorate the gift the couple had made to the Israel Museum in Jerusalem. The donation consisted of a seventy-two-page manuscript authored by Albert Einstein in which he had laid out his theory of relativity, including his famous E=MC2 equation. The Safras had purchased the artifact at Sotheby's for an undisclosed price; its presale estimate was $4 million.

At age sixty-seven, Edmond had not long before completed negotiations to sell his 29 percent of the Republic National Bank of New York—a financial institution that he had founded—to the London-based banking form HSBC Holdings for $9.9 billion. In December of 1999, one of Edmond's nurses, Ted Maher, an American and a former Green Beret, sounded the alarm: bleeding from abdomen and thigh wounds, Maher alerted his employer that two masked intruders wielding knives had entered his home and that a fire was raging. A panic-stricken Edmond dragged Vivane

Torrent, a nurse from the Philippines, into a bathroom and locked her in with him. When the firefighters arrived, they could not locate the bathroom because, having been designed as a panic room, it seamlessly blended into a wall. Inside, Edmond refused to open either the window or the door. During the investigation that followed, marks on Vivane's neck showed that he had prevented her from escaping. After forty-five minutes, when the rescuers finally broke through, they found that Edmond and Vivane had died from smoke inhalation. Lily and a granddaughter, who were in a bedroom in another wing, were unharmed.

Questions swirled as how armed intruders could have entered an impregnable penthouse with no sign of a forced entry. The fact that the municipality of Monaco was known as one of the safest havens in the world—a place where crime was a rarity—fed the frenzy of the international press. Was the responsible party the Russian Mafia, Palestinian hitmen, Muslim terrorists, or even Lily Safra? Suspicion hovered over the widow when the news leaked that Edmond had changed his will two months before his passing, making his wife his chief beneficiary. The fact that she had lost an earlier husband under questionable circumstances further fueled suspicion regarding her statements of innocence. Another damning factor was that despite strong ties to his family, Edmond had left nothing to his siblings.

A few days later, another bombshell burst onto the international press. Ted Maher, the American nurse who had been a Green Beret, confessed that *he* had started the fire in a garbage can and that his wounds had been self-inflicted. His motive was to save his employer from "the intruders," thereby winning Edmond's gratitude, as well as a hefty reward. His plan had backfired when the flames raged out of control; a judge sentenced Ted to ten years. Although Edmond's relatives desired that he be buried at their family plot in Mount Herzl in Israel, Lily arranged a Geneva interment.

Despite a flurry of lawsuits, Lily lived an unimaginably rich life. What rattled her rarefied existence was when the royal biographer, Lady Colin Campbell, published *Empress Bianca,* a novel whose plot revolved around a social-climbing billionairess who killed her second and fourth husbands and got away with their murders. Lily's lawyers threatened publisher Arcadia Books, which pulled all copies from the shelves and ceased further publication. Lady Campbell sued Lily for loss of income and vehemently declared that Ted Maher had been set up, citing his confession in French, which was a language he did not speak.

Once again anxious to distance herself from her husband's death, Lily decamped to London, where she purchased a six-floor Belle Époque townhouse in exclusive Belgravia, where bodyguards trailed behind her armor-plated car. The courtyard fountain held fifty-five jets of water; this was because five had been Edmond's lucky number as he believed it warded off the evil eye. To woo the British upper crust, she organized a charity dinner for three hundred at Somerset House to raise money for its restoration. In 2001, *Vanity Fair* displayed a photograph of her sitting beside Prince Charles at a dinner at Buckingham Palace. The following year, she and Jacob Rothschild cohosted a 5,000-pound-a-plate charity event, "An Evening With Elton John." Age did not diminish Lily's thing for bling. In 2010, she bought the Giacometti sculpture *Walking Man* for $104.3 million at Sotheby's.

In *King John,* Shakespeare wrote of the foolishness of painting a lily, as it is futile to enhance something that requires no embellishment. In the same vein, the Brazilian billionairess did not need to be a gilded Lily.

CHAPTER 17

Barbara Black: Gain the Whole World (1940)

"A planet can take billions of years to form, but it can shatter in an instant when something veers off course and the collision destroys it."

—BARBARA AMIEL

The fictional seventeenth-century aristocrat Lady Macbeth employed emasculation on her husband in order to gain the throne. Similarly, in the twentieth-century, Barbara Joan Estelle Amiel, Lady Black of Crossharbour in Britain, employed her wiles to pressure her spouse into using his company as a personal piggybank. While Lady Macbeth and Lady Black both satiated their ambitions, they paid a steep price.

The world of conspicuous consumption was far removed from Lady Black's modest beginnings. Barbara was born in Watford, England, to Jewish parents: mother Vera Amiel and father Harold Amiel, an attorney. She spent the war years with her grandparents in Hertfordshire; in 1945, she and her younger sister returned to Watford to the scene of another battle—one waged over her father's affair. At age eight, the Amiels divorced, and Vera went on the prowl to find another man. Her daughter later recalled, "I'm a bit of a hard-headed b**** now, but as a child, I really wanted to please." Vera's second marriage, this time to a Canadian draftsman, resulted in relocating to Hamilton, Ontario. Relations with her unstable mother broke down; Vera informed her fourteen-year-old daughter she could not deal with her anymore and moved her to a boarding house that was populated by prostitutes. A year later, Vera phoned Barbara to inform her of her father's death, "He killed himself... He went mad... I expect you'll go mad too." His last desperate act was motivated by the consequences of his embezzlement of his clients' funds. The only photograph on Barbara's wall was of her father Harold.

Barbara attended the University of Toronto, where she majored in philosophy and English; one extra-curricular activity was shoplifting. Of her old habit, she philosophized, "Perhaps there is some truth in the idea if you shoplift when young, you become a shopaholic when old." She dropped acid with Leonard Cohen, who later gained fame as Canada's singer-poet icon; he penned a poem for Barbara. Barbara fell for Robert Hershorn, who even though he used and sold heroin, hailed from a wealthy Jewish family in Montreal. She also followed a sexy reporter to war-torn Mozambique where they ended up behind bars.

She wed law student Gary Smith, a union that lasted seven months, and later tied the knot with a former refugee from Hungary, CBC radio producer George Jonas. His violence left her with a dislocated jaw, motivating her to tell the "I bumped into a door" story to cover up the true cause of the injury. After divorcing the domestic abuser, in the hope the third time would prove the proverbial charm, Barbara married David Graham, describing him as "so physically perfect a specimen that you really wanted to put him nude on the mantlepiece." Perhaps he was *too* handsome; hubby's infidelity unraveled the marital bond.

Career satisfaction arrived with a job at the Canadian Broadcasting Company, coinciding with a pregnancy that ended in a backstreet abortion since the procedure was against the law. Unable to conceive due to complications of the unregulated operation, she regretted her decision. Although Barbara participated in same-sex relationships, she was unable to sustain an emotional attachment to women.

Serendipity stepped in when Barbara fell for Montreal-born Conrad Black, the CEO of publishing company Hollinger International, which owned the *Spectator*, London's *Daily Telegraph, the Chicago Sun-Times*, and the *Jerusalem Post.* He had relinquished his Canadian citizenship in 2001 to accept a peerage in the British House of Lords that made him Lord Black of Crossharbour. At the time, Barbara was a renowned columnist who had made a meteoric rise through the publishing ranks with both her provocative articles and provocative attire. Before a London dinner date with Algy Cluff, chairman of the *Spectator*, she informed him, "But there's one thing I have to tell you. I won't be wearing any knickers."

The power couple of Barbara Amiel and Conrad Black began at a 1991 party where Conrad informed the British beauty his marriage could be referred to in the past tense. After her coy response, "London's girls will be falling out of trees for you;" Conrad's comeback was, "Don't restrain yourself, Barbara." The smitten media baron described Barbara as "brilliant...both vertically and horizontally." With a twenty-six-carat, $2.6-million sparkler on her finger, Barbara's variation of Dorothy's chant was: "Jets! Mansions! Jewels! Oh, my!" Her final marriage brought wealth, a title, a column in *The Telegraph*, and a ticket to high society. The wedding reception was at Annabel's in Mayfair; glitterati wedding guests included Prime Minister Margaret Thatcher and the Duchess of York. For their Maine honeymoon, Brooke Astor hosted a dinner.

Their life included various star-studded occasions, such as when the newlyweds attended the US ambassador's annual summer lunch at Claridge's. Aristocrats abounded; the Queen Mother was the guest of honor, and Conrad sat next to her. Meanwhile, the girl who had come of age in a Hamilton boarding house felt lost in the blue-blood gene pool; she experienced a kind of stage fright when the Duke of Edinburgh visited, prompting her to hide upstairs. Due to anti-Semitism, Palm Beach proved a hostile environment. The fabulous upscale zip code also had its share of unsavory socialites. While walking on the beach with Ghislaine Maxwell, a fellow Brit—and Jeffrey Epstein's lover and sidekick in exploitive crime and abuse of minors—remarked, "I bet I'm in charge of more bathrooms and lavatories than you are." When Barbara said her homes had thirty-nine restrooms, Ghislaine gloated, "I win." Competition was a common denominator among much of the upper echelon, as evidenced by Barbara's comment, "I used to sit in our plane and I would see their planes on the runway, and everyone would be sizing up each other's planes."

Marriage made Barbara the Right Honorable Lady Black of Crossharbour and a member of the international jet set. Guests who received the Blacks' coveted wedding invitations included Joan Collins, Elle Macpherson, the Rothschilds, and royalty. Guest speakers at the couple's later black-tie and designer gown events included Richard M. Nixon, Henry Kissinger, Ronald Reagan, and Margaret Thatcher; the Black photo album has snapshots of Barbara with Princess Diana, President Nixon, and US Secretary of State Henry Kissinger.

The Lord and Lady maintained a jaw-dropping real estate portfolio. The couple's Toronto residence was Conrad's 23,000-square-foot childhood mansion in the Bridle Path zip code. A prolific biographer, Conrad's three-story library held 15,000 books, and its ceiling had a copper cupola patterned after the dome of St. Peter's Basilica in Rome. In Manhattan, the couple maintained a Park Avenue apartment; however, the American jewel in their real estate crown was their 17,000-square-foot, six-bedroom oceanfront spread in Palm Beach. An Andy Warhol silkscreen of Marilyn Monroe adorned its walls. In London, they owned a four-story, eleven-bedroom estate where a giant portrait of Napoleon hung in the stairwell. A consummate collector, Conrad owned a chair that had belonged to the French emperor. Staff included a chef, butler, chauffeur, and maids. For the Blacks, 'frugal' was an ugly word.

Other perks of being Mrs. Midas included the use of two corporate jets and a $53,000 holiday in Bora Bora with a stopover in Seattle to view a Wagner opera. And then there was Barbara's surprise sixtieth birthday bash at the New York restaurant La Grenouille. A-listers in attendance were a veritable who's who: Michael Bloomberg, Donald Trump, cosmetics tycoon Donald Lauder, Anna Wintour, Lynn Rothschild, Henry Kissinger, Peter Jennings, Oscar de la Renta, Ghislaine Maxwell, Barbara Walters, and Happy

Rockefeller. The tab: $62,869.57. For a soiree at Kensington Palace, Lord Black dressed as the power-crazed Cardinal Richelieu of France; Barbara came as Marie Antoinette. The uxorious Conrad was oft heard to repeat the remark, "I think I better ask the little woman."

Lady Black's "Let them eat cake" moment occurred in 2002 in a *Vogue* magazine interview, during which she gave a journalist a tour of her vast haute couture wardrobe housed in her Kensington mansion. The article disclosed she had "a fur closet, a sweater closet, a closet for shirts and T-shirts, and a closet so crammed with evening gowns that the overflow has to be kept in yet more closets downstairs." The reporter spied a dozen Hermès bags and more than a hundred pairs of Manolo Blahnik shoes. Barbara dropped the disclosure, "I have an extravagance that knows no bounds." The ensuing column made readers feel like retching into one of the Hermès bags and Manolo Blahnik shoes. Barbara's rebuttal was that designer dresses served as "sexual armor" as an explanation of why she'd forked over $75,000 on a gown. As for her show-stopping jewels, Barbara explained that bling was *de rigeur* in her social circle and that jewels were a "defining attitude, rather like your intelligence." While the public gave the boyishly handsome Conrad a pass, the press was not kind to his missus. The Canadian media referred to the couple as "Mr. Money and Attila the Honey."

Their mansions transformed into houses of cards after Hollinger shareholders questioned the lifestyle of Lord and Lady Black. Although Conrad had inherited wealth and a $6.5 million annual salary, skepticism ran rampant as to the source of the Blacks' over-the-top expenditures. Margaret Wente, a columnist at Toronto's *Globe and Mail,* summed up the swirling suspicions, "Only a few hundred women in the world can afford to dress like Mrs. Black, and Mrs. Black may not be among them."

The Palm Beach estate became a pre-Revolution Versailles when those who felt cheated of $84 million cried out for the Blacks' heads. After his ouster from his company, an incident that launched a thousand headlines, Conrad countered the criticism, "The attempt to portray her as a Marie Antoinette and me as a supine lovestruck spouse, like most comments on the subject, is a complete fiction." An internal investigation disagreed. An audit revealed that despite Barbara's annual company salary of $300,000, she did little more than read the newspaper, take lunch breaks, and chat/canoodle with her husband. Another smoking gun was the revelation that Hollinger had paid $8 million for a collection of letters from Franklin Delano Roosevelt—the president who had been the subject of Conrad's biography: *Franklin Delano Roosevelt: Champion of Freedom.* Christopher Browne, upon investigating the charge of corruption, concluded, "If this was a cow, there wouldn't be an udder that wasn't sore."

Lord Black faced seventeen charges of fraud, money laundering, tax evasion, racketeering, and obstruction of justice. During the trial, a study in *schadenfreude*, Barbara dressed in pant suits accessorized by a Hermès purse. On the second day, while sharing an elevator with deep pocketed mean women who had come to witness the bloodbath, the North London girl told the ladies they were vermin. Before reaching the ground floor, she had also called one of them a slut.

The couple's defense team read a letter from Sir Elton John that stated his AIDS foundation had received a sizable donation from Mr. Black. His words did not carry weight since the money came from the coffers of the *Daily Telegraph*. The court cleared Conrad of nine counts but found him guilty on three charges of mail fraud and one of obstruction of justice. Although prosecutors had been pressing for a sentence of twenty-four to thirty years, the judge decided on a term of six and a half years. The press skewered the media baron who had once been its lord. In Toronto, T-shirts showed Black behind bars with the label: "ExConrad." In the backlash, the headlines pilloried Barbara.

After fainting at Conrad's sentencing, the little lady—all five feet and eight inches of tooth and claw—proved a heavyweight grudge-holder in her 608-page memoir, *Friends and Enemies*. She wrote of the emotional ambush from her former society friends, "I must have been wearing the Tarnhelm, the magic helmet from Wagner that renders one invisible." Her hairdresser dropped her; and when she phoned her go-to shop assistant, the manager of the Manhattan Manolo Blahnik shop, to request a pair of "mood-lifting shoes," the woman sneered, "You've got quite enough," and hung up. Barbara said of the Frigidaire treatment, "I never realized how hated I was." Lady Black's poisoned pen lampooned her former friends as women who lunch but barely eat. She wished for a revenge that entailed her enemies either being guillotined or injected with Ebola. Bitter was the new Black. However, not everyone bailed from the sinking ship. One of the ever-faithful friends was fellow Brit Elton John, who gifted Barbara a Theo Fennell pavé diamond star pendant and chain to soften the shock; Anna Wintour, the editor of *Vogue*, flew to Chicago in a show of solidarity. Similarly, Melania Trump proved to be a friend in both fair and foul weather.

As the scandal unfolded, most people assumed that Barbara would be on the prowl for her next husband. Instead, she was waking up at three am to make the twice-weekly 440-mile round trip to visit Conrad in his Florida jail. Conrad's jailhouse calls pained her deeply as she heard shouts from inmates and cell doors clanging. Barbara stoically sold off assets to pay astronomical legal fees. She claimed she would never leave Conrad, though he told her that she should, that he would understand. She explained, "He's everything to me. If I knew everything that was going to happen,

I would marry him all over again." For her column in *Maclean's*, Barbara quoted Lena Horne's lyric: "Stormy weather, since my man and I ain't together." In addition to a marriage that brought her wealth, title, and prestige, Barbara had found love. In 2019, President Donald Trump granted a full pardon to the Canadian Icarus who had flown too near the sun. Trump's leniency could have stemmed from Conrad's flattering biography of him: *Donald J. Trump: A President Like No Other.*

After the horror, the couple began living under the public radar, assuming a far more austere lifestyle. She ruminated of her new reality, "I have a soft spot for Edith Wharton's novel *The House of Mirth*, and I identify like mad with Lily Bart, who ends up killing herself in dire poverty. It will only be my husband's genius that ensures I don't end up the same way, because I've never saved a penny in my life." However, one can imagine that their Louis Vuitton suitcases remain packed, the Cardinal Richelieu and Marie Antoinette outfits awaiting their resurrection. At age eighty-four, Barbara retains her fierce spirit if not her former wealth, asserting, "I am going to try to enjoy the remaining time left to me. And bugger off to the whole damn lot of you! We're still here."

The lyrics of Whitney Houston's song "Didn't We Almost Have It All?" applied to Barbara. Gone were the heady days when she purchased emeralds that matched her green eyes and left others green with envy; when she lay down her gold credit card for an Hermès bag and when the butler shook the martini. In addition, she also has a connection with the song's lyric, "The ride with you was worth the fall my friend/Loving you makes life worth living." Although far from the grandeur of their former glory days, together, in a nod to their landed title, they have found a safe "harbour." Barbara recalled, "I think the happiest moment of my life was when I was alone with Conrad on a small boat in Turkey. We were swimming, and I thought, I am married to this wonderful man and life can never hurt me again." But even massive wealth fails to fully insulate its possessors from the suffering and surprises the Fates may have in store.

CHAPTER 18

Soraya Khashoggi: The Sad Eyes (1941)

"I have danced with a king on a beach under the stars and once Frank Sinatra sang just for me."

—SORAYA KHASHOGGI

◇◇◇◇◇◇◇◇◇◇◇◇◇◇◇◇◇◇◇◇◇◇◇◇

Some philosophical questions for historians: Can a person love a monster and not *be* a monster? Are the wives of evil men mere velvet gloves for iron fists? To what extent are spouses complicit in their husbands' misdeeds? This field of inquiry applies to Soraya Khashoggi, the wife of the arms dealer who made billions through bloodshed.

When a British-born girl from Leicester, a city north of London in England's Midlands, met a Middle Eastern billionaire, she felt he was a genie who would grant her every wish. Sandra (later Soraya) Patricia Jarvis-Daly described her childhood home in council housing (a British public housing project) as a "tiny, two-up, two-down house." She never knew her father, Stephen; her mother and her grandmother brought her up the best they could under straitened circumstances. Soraya later recalled, "I didn't know I was poor, and I thought everyone had an outside loo." Her mother Celia worked long hours at an ambulance station and as a waitress at the Grand Hotel. By hoarding her paychecks, Celia was able to send her daughter to a Catholic convent boarding school near Chertsey, Surrey. The nuns surreptitiously slipped her thruppence to put into the collection jar, though the other girls had more to give. Unable to keep up with the tuition, Soraya's mother reluctantly withdrew her from the school.

Life took a turn for the worse with her grandmother's 1949 passing, which left Soraya's grandfather in the role of babysitter. An abusive bully, he had beaten his wife and drowned Soraya's kitten; also an alcoholic, he stole money from Celia to gamble. Instead of taking his granddaughter to the park, he took her with him to the races, where she had to wait on the steps. Soraya blamed her lifelong insomnia on her grandfather, who left her alone when her mother worked a night shift. An audacious streak manifested itself in high school; she peeled back her dress to sunbathe in the athletic field, an outrageous act in the 1950s.

With an absentee mother and an abusive grandfather, at age sixteen, Soraya ran away, supporting herself as a telephone operator. Since her mother had provided her with French and German lessons, her next job was as a translator in London. With her savings, she bought a ticket to Kenya. In Africa, after making the acquaintance of missionaries, Soraya converted to Hinduism. The continent delivered romance when she fell for a law student who was the son of a maharaja, with whom she had a baby. Disapproving of the match, his father offered Soraya money to end the relationship. After putting her daughter up for adoption, she returned to Leicester.

In a nod to how life hinges on happenstance, when Soraya was in her late teens, her mother won a contest whose prize was a holiday for two anywhere in the world. Celia cast the fateful die in her daughter's life when she chose Paris as their destination. While staying at the King George V Hotel, the British women met the Saudi Arabian Khashoggi family, who invited mother and daughter to a New Year's celebration. Dr. Mohammad Khashoggi was the physician to King Abdul Aziz of Saudi Arabia. Six months later, in 1960, a Khashoggi cousin introduced Soraya to Adnan, known as 'Cashoggi.' He also went by his initials A. K., which were stamped on his plane's white-and-gold China dishes and the gold cufflinks he bestowed upon his employees at Christmas. Adnan was an uncle to Dodi Al-Fayed, who died in the car crash alongside Princess Diana, and to Jamal Khashoggi, the murdered journalist.

The warmonger—or, depending on perspective, whoremonger—Adnan Khashoggi had a life comprised of equal parts opulence, decadence, and depravity. When Saudi Arabia and other Arab states plowed oil wealth into weaponry, Adnan, who was often referred to as "Mr. Fixit," was their arms dealer, a role he took to as a camel does to the desert. Regarding the victims who died due to his machinations, for Adnan, in the words of Don Corleone, it was "just business." In the process, he became a billionaire who employed the services of his South Korean bodyguard—"Mr.

Kill." When there was a high-priced monetary scandal, Adnan was there. He left his DNA on both the Iran-Contra affair and the (rather successful) efforts of the Marcos family to spirit their ill-gotten fortune out of the Philippines. His empire included resorts in Kenya, shipping lines in East Asia, and an office complex in Salt Lake City. In 1987, *Time* magazine stated Adnan operated in "a shadowy sphere of deals, arms brokering, and billion-dollar investments." As Prince Alfonso Hohenlohe-Langenburg of Spain phrased it, "For A. K., there were no laws, no skies, no limits."

At their first meeting, the youthful Sandra did not like Adnan as she felt he was arrogant. Nevertheless, explaining she was a sucker for big brown eyes and long dark lashes, she soon fell in love. She worked for Adnan as a French translator, and on trips she modeled dresses so he could decide if they would make good gifts for his sisters. Later, she discovered the garments were for her, as her Svengali was already planning her wardrobe. In Beirut, Adnan proposed. He had not hedged his bets as he had already had their names engraved on their rings. Sandra converted from Christianity to Islam; she also traded English for Arabic, and even exchanged her first name, Sandra, for 'Soraya,' Arabic for "the brightest star in the sky." In 1961, they had wedding ceremonies in Saudi Arabia and in Lebanon, followed by a six-month honeymoon in Europe and America.

As the son of the doctor to the Saudi royals, Adnan was rich; however, his wealth skyrocketed in the 1960s when he bought the Saudi Arabian dealership of Rolls-Royce and Chrysler. In addition, he became an agent for Lockheed, which paid him $106 million in commissions over five years. However, the lion's share of his billions came from arms dealing. When asked about his dealing in death, Soraya would retort, "In my eyes, an arms dealer is someone who sells guns and bombs and weapons, something Adnan never did."

With his burgeoning bank account, Adnan indulged his beautiful wife. For her birthday, he rented a casino in Cannes where the champagne flowed. Of the magical time, Soraya recalled, "That night, sitting out on the terrace and watching fireworks explode over the Mediterranean, I thought I was the luckiest woman in the world." For another birthday, Adnan took over the Parisian restaurant Le Pre Catelan, and the cast of the musical *Hair* performed a private show for the party. As Adnan was not only prolific in his accumulation of wealth, the couple had daughter Nabila and sons Mohamed, Khalid, Hussein, and Omar. Of her husband, Soraya stated, "To the world, Adnan is a billionaire who dabbles in weapons and high-priced call girls, but to his children, he is 'Baba.' "

If living well is the best revenge, Adnan was the kingpin of vengeance. He and Soraya, self-described nomads, were jet-setters, flitting from Paris, Switzerland, Rome, and Cannes to faraway destinations like Africa. Rather than troubling his wife with flying to the French fashion houses, Adnan brought designers Pierre Cardin, Yves St. Laurent, and Hubert Givenchy, along with their models, to the Khashoggi home; Cartier delivered baubles to their hotel rooms. Soraya stated that she had lost count of how many homes they owned, but thought it was around seventeen. Their twelve estates included a $7 million ranch in Kenya, a $30 million apartment on Fifth Avenue with views of St. Patrick's Cathedral, and a flat near Buckingham Palace. Their Cannes villa was a haven-for-rent for the ousted Haitian dictator Jean-Claude Duvalier. Other zip codes they inhabited included: Marbella, Paris, the Canary Islands, Madrid, Rome, Beirut, Riyadh, Jidda, and Monte Carlo. For the First Couple of Armaments, their mantra was 'more is more.' They entertained Elizabeth Taylor, George Hamilton, and Joan and Jackie Collins.

To fly to their far-flung real estate, there were their three commercial-sized jets. Not restricted to the skies, they owned the 282-foot yacht the *Nabila*, a watercraft that made Queen Elizabeth II's *Britannia* pale by comparison. The ship appeared in the James Bond film *Never Say Never Again.* The rock group Queen based their song "Khashoggi's Ship" on the *Nabila.* The pleasure dome came with a disco—one whose laser beams projected Adnan's face—as well as a movie theater, a helicopter pad, an operating room, and a morgue with coffins. The floating palace welcomed Cheryl Tiegs, Raquel Welch, Henry Kissinger, Lee Iacocca, Prince Juan Carlos of Spain, Prince Constantine of Greece, and various Saudi royals. Adnan eventually sold his yacht to Donald Trump; he dropped a million dollars from the sale price with the proviso that the ship no longer display his daughter's name. As the new owner had already planned to rechristen his acquisition the *Trump Princess*, he remarked, "Khashoggi was a great broker and a lousy businessman."

The idylls of the king and queen of consumerism came to a grinding halt. Soraya's story is that her private detective caught her husband having an affair with her friend, a South African model. As Soraya was pregnant, she felt the need to forgive her errant spouse; but the next time he strayed, she filed for divorce. Adnan's counterclaim is that they had an open marriage, but Soraya went too far when she carried on with his friend, President Gaafar Nimeri of the Sudan. At the time, Adnan was canoodling with the seventeen-year-old Italian Laura Biancolini, whose wardrobe was not a nod to subtlety.

In 1974, in Cannes, Adnan promised to support Soraya for the rest of her life if she refrained from hiring an attorney. His addendum was if she did not cooperate, he would "declare her blood to be legal." Under Islamic shariah law, with such a declaration, she could be put to death. Soraya was caught between a rock and a hard place: their residence was in Saudi Arabia, where men held the legal rights, and he had control of billions of dollars—to which she did not have access. Moreover, as the world's most prolific arms dealer, he had any number of lethal weapons. The woman formerly known as Sandra may have rued taking her husband on.

While living in luxurious London digs that were even equipped with a basement swimming pool, she hired high-profile American divorce attorney Marvin Mitchelson, whose roster of clients included Joan Collins, Sony Bono, and Bianca Jagger. They requested a $42.5 billion settlement. In one bitter episode that left Adnan enraged, when a number of their children were in their DC-9 plane waiting to fly to their Swiss private schools, a court order prevented them from leaving. Perhaps Soraya should have abided by her husband's proverbs, "Flowers and light attract nightingales and butterflies"—his variation of "One catches more flies with honey than vinegar." The woman scorned explained she would not have gone on the offensive had Adnan not kept her from her children. At this juncture, the couple had been divorced for five years. In the interim, Soraya had married twenty-five-year-old Richard J. Coombes, ten years her junior. Richard had previously been dating her daughter, Kim Patrick, whom pre-Adnan Sandra had given up for adoption in Johannesburg, South Africa. Years before, Adnan had hired investigators who helped Soraya to find her lost child. The marriage to Richard fizzled.

The fight of Khashoggi vs. Khashoggi was so bitter their firstborn, Nabila, took an overdose of pills. She recovered and is married to the Cox Communications heir, James Cox Chambers, who has a 5.6-billion-dollar fortune. Soraya claimed she withdrew her suit because the publicity was damaging to her family. Although the media reported she received a $900 million settlement, she vowed no money was forthcoming. Her postscript was that she and Adnan had buried the hatchet and were committed to their children and grandchildren. Adnan's version was he would never have left her destitute since she is the mother of his children, and he gave her $3 million. Their divorce was finalized in 1974; in 1978, Adnan married Laura Biancolini of Italy, who changed her name to Lamia and traded Catholicism for Islam. They went on to have son Ali. Regarding her forty-carat diamond wedding ring, in heavily accented English, she asserted size is irrelevant: "It's the sentiment that counts."

The fact their future relations were not acrimonious was apparent when Soraya attended her ex's Christmas Eve party in his 5,000-acre Spanish spread overlooking the Mediterranean. For the event, Adnan had transformed his estate into a Moorish palace. The following day, he called Lamia to his all-white bedroom, where he presented her with a $1.9 million diamond, emerald, and ruby necklace. When she saw her gift, Lamia cried out, "Oh, Baba!" It is not known what Soraya said when she saw the new Mrs. Khashoggi's present. However, he did buy his ex a ruby necklace, a far less expensive one. Adnan's third walk down the aisle was with the Iranian beauty Shahpari Azam Zanganeh, a union that ended in divorce. Soraya claims the three ex-wives all get along, and that Adnan refers to them as 'Charlie's Angels.'

Despite having birthed six children and pledged vows in two marriages, the irrepressible Soraya was not ready to say "Never Say Never Again." In London, Soraya, in her position as a photojournalist, visited Jonathan Aiken, a British parliamentarian. Although involved in a relationship with historical novelist Antonia Fraser, he embarked on an affair with his alluring photographer. Soon Soraya was perusing the pages of *Bride* Magazine. What made her put the magazine down was when she met another politician: Winston Churchill, the grandson of Prime Minister Winston Churchill. He apologized for showing up late for their first dinner date at The White Elephant On the River restaurant, explaining that his wife, Minnie, had just delivered their son, Jack. The utterly smitten Winston accepted Soraya was still seeing Jonathan and offered to leave his wife to marry her. When news broke of the involvement of the famed arms dealer's former wife and the parliamentarian with the legendary name, the paparazzi had a field day. One anecdote involved Winston driving at 100 mph on an American freeway—during which she teased, "The faster you go, the more I'll take off." Needing space, Soraya embarked for America, where she gave birth to Jonathan's daughter, Petrina. Soraya did not tell Petrina the name of her father, just as she did not disclose the paternity of her subsequent two children, Oktavia and Nikolai. However, Petrina discovered the truth of her paternity when she befriended Jonathan's twin daughters, Victoria and Ally, also eighteen at the time. Jonathan's political career ended when he served eighteen months in prison for allowing the Saudi royal family to pick up his £1,000 bill at the Ritz Hotel in Paris. Post incarceration, he and his wife Lolicia divorced, and he became an Anglican priest.

Other romances were with Sammy Davis Jr., whom she met on a blind date at the White Elephant. They traveled the world together despite his marriage to his third wife, Altovise, but his heavy drug use proved problematic. She moved on to producer Roman Polanski and actor Warren Beatty. Perhaps in the hope three times would prove the proverbial charm, Soraya wed fashion designer Robert Rupley after meeting him through actor Tony Curtis. On her wedding day in New York, a man told her that she should not marry Robert because he had been his lover for many years. She did not believe him; she should have. Rummaging through his photographs after his passing, she saw Robert posing with sun-tanned, good-looking men. There was also a note, "To Darling Soraya—I am sorry." If Soraya ever decided to pen her memoirs, many elderly gentlemen, ranging from statesmen to stars, would be very anxious.

The eighty-three-year-old Soraya—in a nod to how life often comes full circle—is living in straitened circumstances in Britain. As she waits for her bus, she appears to be a run-of-the-mill, down-on-her-luck pensioner, no longer the high priestess of excess. Another Soraya, the former wife of the Shah of Iran, who lost her throne because she could not bear an heir, was tagged with an epithet that also applies to the former Mrs. Khashoggi: "the Princess with the Sad Eyes."

CHAPTER 19

Honey Sherman: Man Plans (1947)

"Even a blind squirrel can find a nut."

—HONEY SHERMAN

Saint Teresa of Avila warned, "More tears are shed over answered prayers than unanswered ones," words that would have resonated with Canadian billionaire Honey Sherman. Her life was as sweet as her given name suggests, until an unexpected event sent tremors throughout the provinces of her adopted country.

Honey's parents, Naftuli and Helen Reich, were Jewish Holocaust survivors who, at the conclusion of World War II, languished in an Austrian displaced persons' camp. Anna Debra Reich (known as Honey) was born into this limbo land as her parents awaited visas to let them escape a continent they viewed as a charnel house. Through a Jewish relief organization, the Reichs immigrated to Toronto, where their second daughter, Mary, was born. They settled in Bathurst Manor, North York, a predominantly Jewish neighborhood, many of whose residents were Holocaust survivors. To make ends meet, the Reichs rented out rooms. Although they spoke limited English, Naftuli and Helen opened Reichs Shoes.

Since the couple worked long hours, they tasked Honey with looking after Mary. But when the sisters went skating, Mary suffered a leg injury. Scared her parents would blame her, Honey told Mary, "You're fine, skate," something Mary did even though she had sustained a multiple fracture. Throughout their lives, when trouble loomed, the sisters' habitual response was, "You're fine, skate." Effervescent and attractive, Honey, who graduated in 1966, was a popular student at William Lyon McKenzie Collegiate Institute.

At the University of Toronto, Honey majored in psychology, though her mother Helen wanted her to 'major in MRS'—preferably to a nice Jewish doctor. At college, Honey became fast friends with Bryna Fishman; they were a Canadian Lucy and Ethel. On a 1960s trip to New York City, the two attractive mini-skirted brunettes were in their hotel lobby when some men invited them to a party. Bryna's knee-jerk reaction was to refuse; Honey, however, was unwilling to forego an escapade. On a later Chicago vacation, they went out on a double blind date arranged by Bryna's American cousin. When one of the men asked if Canadians lived in igloos, geek Geiger counter in high alert, Honey began speaking French. Bryna followed along even though they knew only a few words of French—a language that had just become Canada's second official tongue.

On a summer break from teacher's college, Helen suggested that Honey volunteer as a candy-striper at Toronto's Mount Sinai Hospital, a fertile hunting ground to meet a doctor with an unadorned ring finger. Helen shared her marital aspiration with nurse Cindy Ulster, whose husband, Joel, had a single business partner. Although not a medical doctor, Barry Sherman had a PhD; Honey declared, "Close enough."

The first time Barry visited the Reich home, he read a newspaper, ignoring Mary, who was not impressed with his lack of social graces. Honey, however, was taken with Chuck—she derived this nickname for him from his middle name, Charles—and was convinced he would go far due to his brilliance and pit-bull tenacity. Barry and Honey married at the York County Courthouse in 1971, a year after they had met. The newly minted Mrs. Sherman referred to herself as a trophy wife who "came about a little early."

After enduring a miscarriage, the couple was overjoyed with the 1975 birth of their daughter, Lauren. She remained an only child until age eight, at which time Barry and Honey turned to surrogacy. With the assistance of three women from three different American states, the family grew to include Jonathan in 1983, Alexandra in 1986, and Kaelen in 1990.

Barry had studied at the Massachusetts Institute of Technology, where he received a doctorate in astronautics. He followed in the footsteps of his uncle, Lou Winter, owner of Empire Laboratories, the first Canadian company to manufacture generic drugs. Lou had passed away from an aneurism; his wife, Beverly, died seventeen days later from leukemia, leaving behind children Dana, Kerry, Paul, and Jeffery. Barry assumed control of Empire Laboratories, a company that he parlayed into Apotex, which became a major pharmaceutical concern. When his friend Fred Steiner asked Barry to describe his operation, the mogul replied, "It's very simple. I'm a counterfeiter; I take other people's pills and I make them cheaper." Apotex grew from two employees to 17,000 with branches in Mexico and India. The pharmaceutical empire became the country's largest and furnished Barry with a net worth of $4.77 billion, making him Canada's fifteenth richest person. According to a company insider, the Shermans' fortune was closer to 10 billion. Cindy's matchmaking had not only helped Honey obtain her 'MRS,' it had also made her Madame Midas.

In 1990, the Shermans moved into a custom-built home at 50 Old Colony Road in North York. The six-bedroom, 12,000-square-foot mansion had outdoor and indoor pools, a tennis court, and a six-car underground garage, a far cry from the Reichs' Bathurst Manor home. Feeling his contractors had done a shoddy job, Barry sued and recouped $2 million of his $2.3 million costs.

Apotex launched hundreds of lawsuits against competitors such as the behemoth Pfizer Inc. Barry claimed he was on a crusade against the Bayers and other 'Big Pharma' corporations so he could provide the public with cheaper generics. He declared, "If we're thieves, we're Robin Hoods." Barry told his employees they worked for a legal company that happened to sell prescription meds. One Barryism went: "They're full of s**t. Sue them."

A particularly acrimonious legal conflict occurred when the Winter brothers, spearheaded by Kerry, launched a $1 billion lawsuit against their cousin, who claimed Barry owed them a "fiduciary duty" after profiting from their deceased father's company. A judge dismissed the Winters' claim, calling it "wishful thinking and beyond fanciful." The loss was a bitter pill for the siblings to swallow; they said their father had taken Barry under his wing, and Barry had repaid the kindness by stabbing his uncle's orphaned children in the back. An even more bitter pill followed: Barry countersued them for more than $8 million to recoup loans he had made to Kerry. Barry Sherman always came out swinging, armed with his unswerving belief he was right about everything and smarter than anyone else.

At Honey's urging, Barry sometimes took time off, though he insisted he would rather keep working. Honey's BFF Bryna and her husband Fred Steiner were Barry and Honey's closest friends, and the couples vacationed in Florida during the winter. Honey arranged an outing to the Crazy Horse Saloon, a male strip club. Six men dressed like the Village People gyrated on stage; Barry kept marveling at their "equipment." As Bryna recalled, "Honey did not want to miss out on anything." Honey's parents Helen and Naftuli had a condominium in Florida, compliments of the Bank of Barry. He also helped Honey's sister and her husband, Allen Shechtman; he provided them $32 million to invest in a jewelry business that went bankrupt.

Honey and Barry were also close to Cindy and Joel Ulster, whose four children were fond of Uncle Barry. In 1973, although homosexual acts had been against the law just a few years earlier, Joel, possessing the courage of his sexual convictions, came out of the closet when he fell in love with Michael Hertzman, the owner of a clothing store. Canadian Prime Minister Pierre Trudeau, who had passed legislation decriminalizing gay sex, had remarked, "There's no place for the state in the bedrooms of the nation." Over the years, Barry and Honey provided financial assistance to the Ulster children.

What made Barry tick was not the trappings of money, but the quest to amass it. Second-in-command at Apotex Jack Kay drove a Mercedes-Benz that he parked beside his boss' rusty convertible. The world according to Barry was revealed when Jack asked him about his old jalopy, to which Barry responded, "Jack, you just need four tires and a carburetor to go from A to B." For his fiftieth birthday, Honey threw him a party. In front of their guests, she presented him with a red sports car bearing a bow. His response, "Take it back." Barry cared as much about clothes as he did about cars; the same applied to watches. Asked why he was not wearing a Rolex, Barry replied, "I buy my watches at a flea market, and for an extra few dollars, I get one with the date on it. Why spend money on something you don't need?" When flying to their Florida condominium, they saw their friend Ed Sonshine and his wife, Fran. When Ed expressed shock the Shermans were not flying first class, Barry responded, "It's only a two-and-a-half flight. Ed, if I could get a cheaper fare and fly standing up, I would take that one." When Jonathan and his husband, Fred Mercure, wanted children, he approached his father to pick up the tab for his future grandchildren. In an email, Barry wrote that the cost (for IVF, surrogacy, etc.) "seems very high," but he paid for the $330,000-dollar procedure.

Honey's spending habits were more complex than those of her husband. While golfing, she astounded her friends when the billionaire wandered off, plastic bag in hand, to collect stray golf balls. She drove a ten-year-old SUV, yet on shopping sprees, she would buy multiple items of anything that caught her fancy, including Louis Vuitton and Jimmy Choo designer purses. Most remained in her closet, unused.

For those gazing upon the Sherman mansion, they might have mouthed a variation of Eliza Doolittle's "Wouldn't it be loverly?" Even billions of dollars, however, could not keep trouble at bay—

thereby giving truth to the saying, "The bigger the house, the bigger the problems." Lauren had confided to a close friend that her mother's controlling behavior was tantamount to "psychological abuse." Kaelen was hurt that Honey often berated her for being fat and told her that she needed to go on a diet. Often caught in the middle between his children and his wife, Barry was "the good cop," though he was mostly devoted to business. An absentee parent, he worked six days a week at Apotex; the seventh, he worked at home. When fellow philanthropist Lou Bregman asked Barry what he did for fun, Barry replied, "I work." In compensation, Barry showered his children with millions of dollars to buy houses, cottages, and cars. His two oldest received $100 million each to invest in businesses and real estate. As an adult, Jonathan went into business with his father, and title records show at least $127 million in loans from father to son. Jonathan purchased a large, wooded property north of Toronto for $2 million in 2006 when he was twenty-three and developed it with the help of a $5 million mortgage. Jonathan shares the property with Fred and their two children.

The Shermans were respected and loved by the Jewish community, where they were prominent philanthropists. A United Jewish Appeal official revealed that the couple donated $150 million dollars over the years. In tribute, the UJA named a recreation center the Sherman Campus. The project was close to Barry's heart since he had grown up in an era when health clubs did not accept Jewish members. Giving to the less fortunate was a lesson not lost on their son. When he was in grade one at the United Synagogue Day School, Jonathan went to his parents' room because he needed money for its Jewish charity. Half asleep, Barry told his son that his wallet was on the bureau and to take what he needed. Several hours later, a teacher called Honey and informed her that Jonathan had put nine $100 bills into the jar.

In addition to writing checks, Honey donated her time. She served on many boards, including Baycrest Health Sciences Center in Toronto, a facility for the aged that has an Apotex wing, the York University Foundation, the Mount Sinai Women's Auxiliary. As the child of Holocaust survivors, Honey volunteered at the Friends of Simon Wiesenthal Center and participated in the March of the Living, a pilgrimage to Poland that traces the journey to Auschwitz-Birkenau, the site of gas chambers.

When Honey was seventy, wanting a grander home, the Shermans put their Old Colony home on the market for $6.9 million; *Toronto Life* magazine described it as a "poured-concrete colossus." Barry was not keen on the move but acquiesced, acknowledging, "You know, I wish I was staying here, but my wife wants to move, so we're moving." Honey decided to construct a sixteen-thousand-square-foot estate in the exclusive Forest Hill zip code that would cost $30 million. Plans for their new residence entailed an elevator and a massive forty-one-foot retractable glass roof over an indoor pool that would transform into an outdoor one with the flick of a switch.

While not excited about this move, Barry was pleased when he received recognition for public service, as evidenced in an email he sent to Fred Steiner and Joel Ulster: "I was advised today by the Governor General's office that I have been appointed to the Order of Canada." Other wonderful events on the Sherman horizon were Kaelen's forthcoming wedding and the arrival of a third grandchild. Planning a vacation to Florida, Honey emailed her friends about dinner and golf dates, "Looking forward to hearing back a.s.a.p. xoxo Honey."

On the morning of December 15, 2017, veteran real estate agent Elise Stern was showing the Old Colony house to prospective buyers from China. As she walked ahead of her clients on the basement level, she noticed a bizarre tableau—one that led her to think the Shermans must have been practicing yoga. Sensing something was amiss, and too nervous to approach, Elise told Claire Banks, who was in the house to water the Sherman's plants, to investigate while she waited behind. A few moments later, Elise called the police, "Someone killed my clients! They are dead!" The police found Barry, seated, legs outstretched, his back to the lap pool. Beside him, Honey was in a similar position. They had been dead for a day. The reason they had not fallen was because each of the Shermans had a man's leather belt around their necks, tethered to a three-foot-high railing. Honey's face showed evidence that she had suffered an injury. Yellow tape went up around the property, with some affixed to the For Sale sign. The news ignited international headlines: "Murder-Suicide Suspected in Deaths of Toronto Billionaire and Wife." Toronto homicide detectives concluded that Barry had murdered his wife before committing suicide, a finding furiously countered by the grieving Sherman children. They railed their father had adored their mother and at the time of their deaths had been upbeat about their future. The public consensus was the pharmaceutical czar would have used pills. The Sherman siblings hired Brian Greenspan to conduct a private investigation; Jonathan offered a $35 million reward for information that would lead to his parents' killers. The Sherman children arranged for the demolition of their childhood home. Approximately 6,500 people attended the double funeral; among the mourners was Prime Minister Justin Trudeau and Toronto's mayor at the time, John Tory. To date, the police have agreed it was a double homicide, and their murders remain an unsolved mystery.

After the funeral, the Sherman siblings turned on their aunt Mary after she insisted they should give her $300 million, claiming her sister had promised her that amount. An infuriated Kaelin struck her aunt's name from her wedding list. Mary's children sued the Sherman estate over several trusts.

St. Teresa's haunting words are echoed in a Yiddish saying that Honey's friend Dahlia Sherman shared after the murders, "*Mann tracht und Gott lacht*," which means, "Man plans and God laughs."

CHAPTER 20

Ivana Trump: The Ivana (1949)

"Looking good is the best revenge."

—IVANA TRUMP

The story of how Ivana Marie Zelníčková slipped through the Iron Curtain and ascended the pinnacle of the American social hierarchy is the stuff of which a Brothers Grimm fairy tale could have been made. The differences between Ivana and her storybook counterparts are that instead of a castle, she lived in a tower, and her prince had a wandering eye.

Cut from the mold of a heroine from the novels of Joan Collins, Ivana grew up as an only child in Gottwaldov (renamed Zlin), Czechoslovakia. Her father, Milos, was an electrical engineer at a power plant; her mother, Marie, worked as a telephone operator. At age four, Milos taught her to ski in the foothills of the Carpathian Mountains. At Prague's Charles University, Ivana received a master's degree in physical education. Entranced with actress Brigitte Bardot, Ivana dyed her hair light blonde.

At age fourteen, Ivana met George Syrovatka, a competitive Czech skier; together they ventured beyond the borders of their communist country. When attending one of her western world ski competitions, she could have defected, but that would have meant never seeing her parents again and possibly placing them in danger.

In a "Cold War marriage," she wed her friend Alfred Winklmayr, an Austrian ski instructor who gave her the prized possession of a passport to the Free World. She claimed they never consummated their union. Her heart lay with Czechoslovakian poet Jiří Štaidl, who died while driving under the influence. A newspaper reported his passenger—identified only as I. Z.—emerged unharmed. Deeply shaken, Ivana headed to Montreal, Canada with her black poodle Chappy. By day, she worked as a ski instructor for George, who had defected from Czechoslovakia, and she spent nights at McGill University improving her English. For a time, she stayed in Toronto with her aunt and uncle. They treated her to a Caribbean cruise where, for a costume party, Ivana dressed as a Playboy bunny. She later trilled, "I won first prize!"

As a Canadian model, she left for New York on a promotion campaign for the Montreal Olympics. Along with fellow models, she visited the restaurant/bar Maxwell's Plum. The bevy of beauties caught the eye of then-twenty-nine-year-old Donald Trump, who zeroed in on the blonde bombshell with the red minidress. When Donald placed his hand on her arm, she was about to give him "the commie death stare," but desisted as he picked up the models' $400 dinner tab.

Dating Donald opened a vista into a world of wonder. "I came here and I saw the houses, the cars, the bananas and the strawberries in winter," Ivana recalled, "and I knew what I wanted. With Donald, I found [those things]. I may be blonde, but I'm not stupid." On the *Oprah Winfrey Show*, she gushed, "I love a good-looking man, but you know it's really with the look and the brain and the energy and really the potentials, and, you know, Donald always had a great head on his shoulders, and I saw the potential there." The tycoon remarked, "She speaks a little lousy, but she's gorgeous, and I'm going to marry her."

In her memoir, *Raising Trump*, Ivana wrote that during their dating days, Donald rented a ski chalet in Aspen, Colorado. She recalled, "It was a very sexy chalet. I know Donald had picked it for my benefit. I'm a realist, but I have a strong romantic streak and can see the moon and the stars. Donald wouldn't see the moon if it were sitting on his chest." Regardless of whether Donald could see the firmament, he could foresee the financial repercussions of a divorce. He did present Ivana with a three-carat Tiffany diamond ring. Before their walk—Ivana no doubt floated—down the aisle, Donald's attorney, the notorious Roy Cohn, drew up four prenuptial contracts. They married in 1977 in the Marble Collegiate Church in a ceremony presided over by the Reverend Norman Vincent Peale, the famed author of *The Power of Positive Thinking*.

"The Donald" was a moniker Ivana gave her husband. With her flamboyance and his finances, the Trumps became media magnets. Although they had reached the pinnacle of Manhattan society via divergent roads, they shared common ground in their relentless pursuit of fame and fortune. Ivana boasted, "In fifty years, we will be the Rockefellers."

The mogul's model wife appeared in the leading publications in her signature style of lacquered, blonde bouffant hair; her conversations were peppered with her preferred term of endearment, "*Dahling.*" Ivana felt furs were fabulous, and her mammoth-sized closets held chinchilla coats, sable jackets, and *Dynasty*-worthy outfits with padded shoulders. During a Christmas vacation, she called designer Dennis Basso and told him she was in Aspen and wanted a red sheared mink suit. The designer warned her that if she fell, the mink would get wet and would not be a good look or scent. Ivana responded, "*Dahling*. I don't fall."

Although the Trumps owned many splendored properties, their main residence was their Manhattan skyscraper, Trump Towers, a three-story, fifty-three-room penthouse that included his-and-her bathrooms: Donald's décor was dark brown marble; Ivana's was translucent pink onyx. The toilet was furnished with gold-covered seats.

The Trumps' crown jewel was their 115-room Winter Palace in Palm Beach, Florida, Mar-a-Lago. The former owner, Marjorie Meriweather Post, heiress to the cereal fortune, had named it after the Spanish for 'Sea to Lake,' as the storied address stood between the Atlantic Ocean and a lake. Whenever the couple increased their real estate portfolio, Ivana oversaw its interior redecoration, her variation of Barbie's playhouse.

Not content to be a mere Housewife of Manhattan, Ivana kept her lacquered finger in her husband's pies. By 1988, she was the CEO of the Trump Plaza Casino in Atlantic City, where she held her own in the male-dominated financial world. She commuted to the casino in a black helicopter with the word "*Ivana*" printed in white across its door. She also was a one-of-a-kind executive, as illustrated when she summoned the head of the Trump administration, Richard Wilhelm, with the question: "Where's the Dick? I need the Dick now!" After the Donald bought New York City's Plaza Hotel for more than $400 million, he appointed his wife president. Her annual salary was one dollar—plus all the haute-couture clothing she desired, a wardrobe which reportedly cost $500,000 per year. Ivana was also raising their three children, Donald Jr., Ivanka, and Eric. She stated that parenthood fell squarely on her shoulders as Donald "was not the father which would take a stroller and go to Central Park." Maternity leave was of two days' duration. In a nod to his wife's work ethic, Donald observed Ivana was his "twin as a woman."

The Trumps reigned at Le Cirque, The Pierre, and Studio 54, where photographers captured Ivana with Estée Lauder, Luciano Pavarotti, and Michael Douglas. In one shot, model Fabio carried her in his arms—a scene that could have sprung from the cover of a Harlequin romance novel. The press captured the king and queen of corporate America on the deck of their 282-foot yacht, *The Trump Princess*.

Fearful of time's toll, Ivana underwent extensive cosmetic surgery. Gossip columnist Liz Smith wrote that Ivana had had so many operations that she was unrecognizable—until she spoke in her distinctive accent.

The 1972 song "The Night the Lights Went Out in Georgia"—if altered to "The Night the Lights Went Out in Colorado"—occurred during a Trump family Christmas ski vacation in Aspen. Ivana was in her hotel suite when she overheard her husband's phone call, which led her to inquire, "Who is Moolah?" The truth was outed when Ivana spied Donald eating lunch with Marla, a former beauty queen. Marla approached Ivana and stated, "I'm Marla Maples and I love your husband. Do you?" Ivana hurtled Donald's clothes out the window, into the snow, along with his Rolex watch. She also delivered the Donald an ultimatum—his wife or the showgirl. Donald married Marla, with whom he had daughter Tiffany—so named after the jewelry emporium.

Ivana's 1990 divorce proved blood to the paparazzi sharks of the media. The wife spurned became a heroine for discarded starter wives, a position that earned her a cameo in the 1996 film *The First Wives Club*. In the movie, Ivana told her fellow jilted women—actresses Diane Keaton, Goldie Hawn, and Bette Midler—"Don't get mad, get everything!"

The divorce trial played out in a public arena. Outside the Plaza Hotel, fans of Ivana held candlelight vigils and waited for hours to catch a glimpse of her as she left the courthouse. She recalled that as the lawyers lobbied verbal grenades at one another, she put on her headphones and listened to Gloria Gaynor's lyrics from "I Will Survive." The dissolution of their marriage provided funds to survive: Ivana received $14 million, their forty-five room Greenwich mansion, an apartment in Trump Tower, and one month's use per year of Mar-a-Lago. In addition, her ex had to pay $650,000 yearly in child support.

Not one to fade into the cast-aside spouse sunset, Ivana used her celebrity status to build her own business empire: the House of Ivana. Her venue was the Home Shopping Network, to which she brought her invariable enthusiasm for each item, whether it be earrings or a women's tuxedo-style garment. She appeared in a milk commercial in which she quoted from the Duchess of Windsor, "You know what I say, *dahling?* You can never be too rich or too thin." Three secretaries waded through her fan mail, and she was a regular on daytime talk shows.

In 1993, Ivana acquired her own residence, an 8,725-square-foot townhouse a block from Central Park. As it was not up to her 'more is more' style of décor, she hired George Gregorian, the designer who had worked with her on the rejuvenation of the Plaza. Some of its over-the-top features were a leopard-print sitting room, a pink marble bathroom, a bedroom with a gold-embossed fireplace, and Chinese murals. The top floor mainly consisted of a closet that Ivana dubbed "Indochine," because "by the time you get to the end of it, you might as well be in another continent." A treadmill faced onto the street, and she often waved to neighbor Donatella Versace. Fearful of getting stuck in her elevator, Ivana always used the five flights of stairs. Although her marriage had imploded, Ivana still carried the romantic torch. When her daughter became engaged to the Orthodox Jewish Jared Kushner, she wrote, "If Ivanka was willing to give up lobster and bacon, she must really love him."

Other plum properties were a 12,000-square-foor hacienda in Palm Beach, which was named Concha Marina (Spanish for 'seashell marina'), and a ninety-eight-foot yacht she christened the *M. Y. Ivana*. To distance herself from the pain of the divorce, she rented a house in London's Eaton Square. At this point, she had a craving for Italian—and not of the culinary variety. Ivana was true to her earlier declaration, in which she said she liked "Italian men, Italian food, Italian mountains, Italian sea, everything Italian." She met her *numero uno* Latin lover, businessman Riccardo Mazzucchelli, at the Ascot races. Prior to their wedding at Manhattan's La Cirque, when Ivana's attorney asked him to estimate his net wealth for the prenup, Riccardo said, "Five million, more or less;" her attorney guessed it was “less.” Donald rated him “a zero.” For their Mayfair Regent marriage in New York, the thrice-wed bride wore a blue satin dress with a rock-sized diamond nestled in her decolletage. As soon as the ink was dry on their wedding contract, problems reared their ugly heads. He complained people viewed him as ‘Mr. Riccardo Trump’ and that no one referred to his wife as Mrs. Mazzucchelli. The death knell of their relationship occurred at a Las Vegas concert where Wayne Newton announced, “Ladies and gentlemen, my dear friend Ivana Trump is here!” Riccardo left; divorce followed.

Numero due was her romance with Count Roffredo Gaetani dell’ Aquila d’ Aragona di Laurenzana Lovatelli. Dating a man with a title was titillating, especially as he hailed from one of the most eminent families in Italy. He had grown up in a palace, and his family tree held two popes. If his social credentials were not aristocratic enough, Ivana described how they would make love on her townhouse’s piano, stating it was the best sex she had ever had. Donald, who (intentionally?) mispronounced “Roffredo,” stated, “Wilfredo is a terrific guy. I hope they both have a good time spending the money that I gave Ivana.” While driving to visit his mother in her palace in Tuscany, Roffredo’s car rolled over several times when he fell asleep at the wheel, resulting in his death.

Ivana’s next relationship was with the thirty-year-old Italian Rossano Rubicondi, who revived the spirits of the fifty-seven-year-old Ivana, known to her grandchildren as ‘Glam-ma.’ When asked if their age disparity presented a problem, Ivana responded, “I’d rather be a babysitter than a nursemaid.” They planned a multimillion-dollar wedding at Mar-a-Lago that included four hundred guests, a twenty-four-piece orchestra, twenty-five bridesmaids, and a twelve-foot-tall, tiered cake imported from Germany, all paid for by the bride. But two weeks before their vows, police stormed Ivana’s Palm Beach house due to a domestic disturbance. As Ivana had earned $2.5 million from wedding-related sponsorships, Rossano was fighting over his share. His intended ponied up $75,000. The groom charged down the aisle fist pumping to the *Rocky* theme, and they appeared on the Italian version of *Dancing with the Stars*. The marriage was rocky from the beginning, and matters did not improve in St. Tropez when Ivana discovered her husband carrying condoms in his travel bag even though they were no longer intimate. Their marriage did not reach the one-year mark, though they remained in close contact; Ivana nursed him through the cancer that claimed his life.

When Donald became president, Ivana was furious when she received a poor seat at the inauguration. Ivana also rued she was not the mistress of the White House; mentioning in an interview that she still spoke with him every fortnight, she added, "I'm basically first Trump wife, OK? I'm First Lady, OK?" Although denied the perks of the First Lady, strangers accosted her with invective against her ex-husband. While Ivana probably rued losing out to Donald's third spouse, Melanija (a.k.a. Melania) Knaus, who was also from Eastern Europe, Ivana wrote, "I wouldn't want to be in Melania's Louboutins right now."

In July 2022, scheduled to fly to St. Tropez the following day, Ivana died of her injuries after she fell from the top of her townhouse's stairs. The only witness to the horror was her Yorkie, Tiger II. Mourners, along with her family and Secret Service agents, gathered at New York City's St. Vincent Ferrer Church. Her Catholic burial in a gold-hued coffin was at the Trump National Golf Course in Bedminster, New Jersey.

Of her past glory days, Ivana reminisced, "I used to be Eloise of the Plaza..." an allusion to the six-year-hellion heroine of Kay Thomson's childhood classic. The book made the Plaza a literary landmark, and the hotel displayed a portrait of Eloise with her trademark smirk. Every morning, Eloise picked up the telephone in her pink suite and ordered room service saying, “It’s me. Eloise. Charge it please.” No doubt, the other famous Plaza denizen’s trademark call would have been, “It’s me, *dahling*. The Ivana.”

CHAPTER 21

Princess Gloria von Thurn und Taxis: Forever Loyal (1960)

"What do you get with showing off? A lot of envy."

—PRINCESS GLORIA

The closing page of a fairy tale generally delivers the scene where the handsome prince carries the beautiful princess to the land of happily ever after. The books never describe the storybook castle, but had there been any depiction of such a royal residence, it would have fallen short of the nonfictional ancestral home presided over by Princess Gloria von Thurn und Taxis.

The blue blood whose glass slipper transformed her into a royal party animal, formally known as Countess Mariae Gloria Ferdinanda Joachima Josephine Wilhelmina Huberta von Schönburg-Glauchau, started out with this impressive name and title in Stuttgart, West Germany. Her mother, Beatrix, was a dispossessed Hungarian aristocrat; her father, Count Joachim von Schönburg-Glauchau, was a member of the nobility. Although the young countess was to the manor born, a manor was not to be her birthright, because in the aftermath of World War II, the communists had confiscated their family castle. The count, a foreign correspondent, relocated his family to Togo and Somalia—the latter nation was the family's residence for five years. Between the ages of six and ten, Gloria and her older sister, Maya, attended an Italian missionary school in Mogadishu, Somalia; classmates nicknamed Gloria "Pummel," which means "Pudgy." Their younger brothers Carl-Alban and Alexander were born in Africa. In 1970, the Schönburg-Glauchaus again pulled up roots since the Somalians were now aligning themselves with the communists. Count Joachim found a position in Munich as an editor of a small hunting magazine and held a seat in the German parliament. The couple eventually separated after the count left his wife for his secretary, with whom he fathered a child.

In 1979, the nineteen-year-old countess, along with two school friends, was at the Universitärs-reitschule, a trendy Munich college café, waiting for the start of a Supertramp concert when fifty-three-year-old Johannes Baptisa de Jesus Maria Louis Miguel Friedrich Bonifazius Lamoral, the eleventh prince of Thurn und Taxis, walked in. Recognizing Gloria as his distant cousin, he joined the friends. Money and power had long been associated with the Thurn und Taxis dynasty. In 1695, Emperor Leopold I bestowed upon Johannes's ancestor Eugène Alexander the title of Imperial Postmaster, followed by the even more impressive title of Prince of the Holy Roman Empire. After conversing for a while, Johannes suggested she ditch the concert so he could take her to dinner.

A few weeks later, Johannes took her to Regensburg, a Bavarian town located on the Danube River, whose architecture heralds its 2,000-year-old history. His *schloss* ("castle"), the 500-room St. Emmeram Palace, "turned out to be rather intimidating." (Gloria said it made Buckingham Palace look like a hut.) Part of the intimidation might have stemmed from the St. Emmeram's seventy-five employees, including a brigade of liveried footmen. The palace held three hundred clocks, necessitating a full-time winder. Wrapping Gloria in a whirlwind courtship, Johannes wanted to whisk her away to foreign lands. As the countess was not interested in finishing her education and was aware she might never have another such travel opportunity, she acquiesced. In St. Moritz, he popped the question that was to turn the countess into Her Serene Highness Princess Gloria.

The von Thurn und Taxis 1980 wedding in Regensburg was, in Gloria's words, "an incredibly grand party. Johannes's friends came from all over the world." The bride wore a couture gown by Valentino, topped by Marie Antoinette's diamond crown. A French friend remarked, "It was really something to see. Half the Rothschilds were there, and then all those Prussian counts and barons covered with medals and Iron Crosses." Johannes's circle was taken aback at their engagement. The playboy prince had long been known for his carefree jet-set lifestyle, enacted on three or four continents, often accompanied by male paramours. A fellow Bavarian described the blue-blooded billionaire as having "some highly unusual tastes." When a journalist for *The Telegraph* asked Gloria if Johannes' bisexuality had presented a problem, her response was she believed she had been the only woman her husband had ever loved.

Princess Gloria said palace life was not strange to her because as a child, she had spent a great deal of time with cousins who lived in castles. She stated, "Well, nobody in our family is as rich as Johannes. But *who* is as rich as Johannes in Germany? I mean, who?" Gloria nicknamed her hubby Goldie; she said the term of endearment was not a nod to his wealth, but because in German, it translates to "sweet." While some viewed the May-December relationship as a storybook romance, others felt it was a mercenary marriage. Gloria's family suffered from straitened circumstances, and Prince Johannes had to abide by a Thurn und Taxis tradition that limited inheritance to those who marry members of other Roman Catholic princely houses. The couple had one son, Prince Albert, heir to St. Emmeram Palace, and daughters Princess Maria Theresia and Princess Elizabeth.

Gloria arrived at events wearing a necklace comprised of marble-sized pearls, diamond and ruby earrings, and a matching brooch. In the world according to Gloria, "It's bad luck for a woman to buy jewelry. She should be given jewelry. It doesn't matter what it's worth if he spent a lot of time picking it out." However, she had no problem spending money on clothes. Along with hubby's real estate portfolio, which included ten castles in Bavaria and Wurttemberg and a chunk of Brazil, she owned a couture collection. Prince Michael of Greece observed that Johannes and Gloria lived on a scale rivaled only by the Queen of England and the Queen of Holland. The Thurn und Taxises spent half a year in Regensburg; in the winter, they vacationed in Brazil, or travel destinations such as St. Moritz, Manhattan, Kenya, Paris, and London. One New Year's Eve they stayed at Adnan Khashoggi's villa in Marbella; on another occasion, Gloria set off to Buckingham Palace to have a private dinner with Prince Charles and Princess Diana.

Marital life was an endless succession of parties, as well as pranks that led a *Vanity Fair* journalist to dub Gloria 'Princess TNT.' Along with her Bavarian bisexual billionaire hubby, the aristocrat became catnip to the paparazzi. At her twenty-fifth birthday party at a New York club, she danced on tables clad in a Paco Rabanne chainmail dress that had a reported cost of £18,000. At a Chanel fashion show, she whistled at Jerry Hall as the supermodel sashayed down the runway. Entering the American embassy for a reception, she told a marine guard, "The way you hold a gun turns me on." The press delighted in showcasing her riding her Harley motorcycles to discos, her hair a blue Mohawk crowned with heirloom jewels, wearing garish goth frocks that seemed as if they were borrowed from the Bride of Frankenstein. On one occasion, she wore a pointed witch's hat to High Mass at St. Emmeram's in Bavaria. In New York City, she socialized with pop star Prince and pop artist Andy Warhol; in Hamburg, she hung out with hookers. The press had a field day when the princess appeared in court after Munich airport officials discovered ten grams of hashish hidden in her hatbox. The Teutonic Terror barked, doggy style, on the *David Letterman Show*.

Johannes was also no slouch when it came to flouting decorum. At a black-tie dinner in Newport, hosted by the reigning *grand dame*, Mrs. John Slocum, after her comment that she only invited second-generation-or-longer Newporters to her home, he responded, "It is a pleasure to see that the traditional conservative values so revered by my grandfather are being maintained here in Newport by you, my dear Mrs. Scrotum." At a Parisian party, he asked his dinner partner, the wife of a South American metals mogul, "Who is that pre-Columbian troll?" When she replied that the troll was her husband, Johannes' rejoinder was, "Well, I can see you didn't marry him for his looks." At a ball where the dress code mandated white attire, while Princess Margaret was on the dance floor, he dribbled red wine on her seat.

Perhaps the pinnacle of their extreme spending sprees occurred when Gloria threw Goldie a three-day, million-dollar extravaganza for his sixtieth birthday known as "The Ball of the Century." Among the guests were Mick Jagger, Jerry Hall, Malcolm Forbes, Ann and Gordon Getty, Adnan Khashoggi, and the Maharaja of Baroda. Those who received the coveted invitations arrived in eighteenth-century attire complete with powdered wigs. The cake held sixty pink marzipan phalluses. The hostess, dressed as Marie Antoinette in a $10,000 pink gown, accessorized by a two-foot-high wig and—"oh, *mein Gott*!"—wearing the former queen's pearl tiara, descended into the ballroom on a gilded cloud attached to a wire to the accompaniment of the Munich Opera's performance of "Don Giovanni." Princess Gloria sang "Happy Birthday, Johnny" in the style of Marlene Dietrich.

Four years later, Johannes' death snuffed out the candles of his widow's former lifestyle. The prince had passed away following two unsuccessful heart transplants. Twenty thousand people filed past his open casket to the accompaniment of six servants in powdered wigs and eighteenth-century livery. The funeral, which cost $500,000, took place in the ninety-five-year-old basilica that adjoined the *schloss,* filled with mourners from the royal houses of Europe.

The widow was left in charge of three minor children, the maintenance of a 500-room castle, and her husband's debts of more than $500 million. Although still stratospherically rich, with assets of more than a billion, Gloria needed cash. The princess explained her plight to *Stern* magazine, "If you consider the truly rich people, not a poor devil like me but rather people who have billions, then you see that they don't have burdens around their necks like I do." With her castle echoing her loneliness and loss, the princes spent time at Schloss Garatshausen, the family's forty-room retreat on the border of Lake Starnberg in southern Bavaria. For a time, her sister Maya, her brother-in-law, and their three children were her guests. Maya had also won the marital lottery with her marriage to Friedrich Christian Flick (known as Mick Flick), a Daimler-Benz heir.

To regain her financial footing, Gloria trimmed off some of the von Thurn und Taxis fat: she sold off a bank, two breweries, and twenty-four of her twenty-seven cars, and reduced her staff from twenty-seven to ten. Sotheby's held an estate sale at the Hotel des Bergues in Geneva, describing the event as its most important one since the one held for the Duchess of Windsor. What fell under the hammer were works of art, eighteenth-century German and French silver, suits of armor, servants' livery, fifty snuff boxes, seventy-five bottles of wine, and thirty-six candle holders that the Thurn und Taxis family had used when the Holy Roman Emperors dined at St. Emmeram. Among the crown jewels of the sale was the pearl-and-diamond tiara that Napoleon III had made for Empress Eugenie for their 1853 nuptial, the twenty-seven-carat-each emerald drop earrings of Tsar Nicholas II's aunt, the Grand Duchess Vladimir, and Frederick the Great's jeweled snuffbox. The princess' gems were even more sensational than those of the duchess since Lady Simpson's jewels were mainly modern pieces from Van Cleef & Arpels, while Gloria's were three centuries old and came from a lineage that included pieces from the Austrian Hapsburgs, the Bavarian Wittelsbachs, and the Portuguese Braganzas. Throughout, Gloria proved stoic: "Let's face it, we don't wear tiaras so often, so why keep so many?" Relatives were infuriated that Gloria was selling off her husband's heirlooms. Johannes' uncle, Father Emmeram, a ninety-year-old Benedictine monk, publicly denounced the princess as "a ruthless minx" and led a protest march comprised of local parishioners. *The Daily Mail of London* quoted her as saying, “My fairy story is over. You can’t be a fairy and meet a payroll.” The sale reaped $19.3 million. The choicest treasures remain intact, and she also held onto her Bavarian castles, as well as residences in Manhattan, Rome, Paris, and Kenya.

Another way of generating income was to open St. Emmeram as a home museum. The castle, whose formal garden extends to the Danube River, is approximately the same size as the Palace of Versailles. Despite the preponderance of clocks, time seems to have stood still within the *schloss* as various wings recall yesteryear with their Gothic, Baroque, and Victorian designs. In the white-and-gold Hall of Mirrors, Johannes and Gloria threw dinner parties for eighty where a liveried footman waited on each guest. Those who received the coveted invitations were from the circles of the stratospherically rich and bore such names as the Aga Khan, Agnelli, Niarchos, Rothschild, and Flick. Pop star Michael Jackson once arrived with an entourage of ten. Quincy Jones stayed two times, and he and Gloria went together to the Wagner festival in Bayreuth. Other celebrities who made an appearance in the ancient castle included Steve Martin, Elton John, Liza Minnelli, and Plácido Domingo. The dining room resembles a salon in a world-famous hotel—except for the portraits of various Würstenbergs and Fürstenbergs. The Throne Room contains an actual throne, raised on a dais, in the contingency of a royal visit. The Baroque Room, a blend of crimson and gilt, holds portraits of the Wittelsbach family, the siblings of Empress Elisabeth of Austria. There is a solarium where Johannes tanned, an Olympic-size indoor pool, and a bowling alley. Its transformation into a home museum left the castle with its resident ghosts, such as Duchess Helene, the wife of Prince Maximilian von Thurn und Taxis, and her sister Elisabeth, Empress of Austria, known as Sisi.

One eclectic touch is a coffee table originating in Kenya whose base consists of a three-ton box of elephant bones under glass.

What truly changed the life of the former punk princess was when Gloria, in a move to reconnect with religion, swapped pop stars for cardinals. Her parents had raised her in the Catholic faith, and she had spent several summers in her youth visiting her grand aunt, a Benedictine nun, in the Black Forest. Johannes's death sent her on a spiritual sojourn, and she embarked on a pilgrimage to Lourdes, France. She appeared on the cover of *Point de Vue* clad in a nun-like habit, pushing the wheelchair of an elderly miracle seeker headed toward the Shrine of the Virgin. The goth girl who once danced on tables in Manhattan's trendiest spots is now most at home in her *schloss*' ornate chapel where von Thurn und Taxis ancestors lie, including her great-grandmother-in-law, Crown Princess Helene. As she kneels before the altar's Carrara marble Jesus, colored light beams pour through the six stained glass windows. Her ecclesiastic views hold that abortion equates to murder; on her countertop is a bowl of miniature plastic fetuses that pro-lifers handed out at a German Catholic conference. Another political stance is that the government should pay women to stay home and raise their children, and that the money should correspond to the number of dependents. St. Emmeram provides three hundred daily meals to the destitute.

Through the trials and tribulations of the Teutonic princess, Gloria maintained her sense of humor. Her favorite joke concerns a rich couple who had suffered a change of financial circumstances. The man said to his wife, "Listen, if you knew how to cook, we could get rid of the chef." His wife responded, "Yes, and if you knew how to make love, we could get rid of the chauffeur." In addition to her sense of humor, what helps Gloria navigate her unusual path is the message inscribed on her ring, one that is comprised of her and her late husband's wedding bands welded together with a silver strip inscribed with the Thurn und Taxis motto: "Forever Loyal."

CHAPTER 22

Wendi Murdoch: The Shackles of Shanghai (1968)

"As for what other people think of me, I could worry about that every day, but choose not to."

—WENDI DENG MURDOCH

In 1972, the group Hall and Oates released their hit song with the famed refrain, "You can rely on the rich man's money." The lyric could have applied to Wendi Deng, whose "old man" was billionaire media mogul Rupert Murdoch. Their relationship could have been fodder for the Austrian aristocrat's tabloid outlets.

Wendi Deng was a legend within a group known as 'the Shanghai Girls.' Their hope of fleeing their communist country was a wealthy western man who would whisk them away to the land of milk and honey—that is, money. Wendi surpassed even their wildest dreams.

The mistress of reinvention was born Deng Wen Ge: Wen'ge translated to "cultural revolution" during Mao Tse-Tung's dictatorship. As a teenager, she changed her name to Deng Wen Di (called Wendi), which translates to "cultural enlightenment." Wendi grew up in Xuzhou, a polluted factory town of three million where hot water, telephones, televisions, and refrigerators were mirages; she never owned a doll or a toy. Her father, Dehui Deng, and her mother, Xue Qinie, earned a combined monthly salary of $43. Their 500-square-foot apartment housed her parents, three siblings, and her aunt, whose feet had been bound. New shoes for Wendi arrived as a present for Chinese New Year. Her dream was to one day eat meat on a regular basis.

At five feet and ten inches tall (a height that was Amazonian among her peers), the athletic teen excelled on the local volleyball team; its coach, Wang Chongshen, remembered her competitive spirit. When her father transferred to the city of Guangzhou (formerly Canton), Wendi shared a bunk bed with her friend in her team's dormitory. At age sixteen, to please her parents, Wendi enrolled in medical school. An inspiration for Wendi to see the world was the movie *The Sound of Music*, in which the family escaped a brutal regime by trekking through the Alps.

The genie in the bottle appeared when Wendi met Jake and Joyce Cherry. One afternoon, the Cherrys' interpreter asked if they would be interested in meeting a teenager who wanted to improve her English by conversing with native speakers. Joyce ended up volunteering to tutor the young woman; the lessons ended when Joyce returned to California to enroll her children in school. An infatuated Jake continued to see Wendi—and not to improve her communication skills. When Wendi shared her dream of studying in America, the Cherrys served as her sponsors. She roomed with the family, sharing a bunk bed in their San Fernando Valley home with their five-year-old daughter. After school, Wendi worked at the Sichuan Garden, where she had as much soup as she wanted. She gained ten pounds.

The living arrangement imploded when Joyce discovered suggestive photos her husband had taken of Wendi in a Chinese hotel room. Joyce evicted Wendi but was heartbroken when her husband moved in with his teenaged lover. To make an honest woman of his mistress—and provide her with a green card—Jake wed Wendi. Four months later, the newly minted Mrs. Cherry was canoodling with David Wolf, who, like her, was in his mid-twenties. Two years and seven months later—her legal status secured—Wendi told fifty-year-old Jake that he was a father figure to her. The couple divorced, leaving Jake crushed.

Soon Wendi was passing herself off as Mrs. Wolf, although that was not reflective of her marital status. She earned a bachelor's degree in economics from California State University at Northridge; rumor had it that David and his mother paid Wendi's tuition when she enrolled in a Master of Business Administration at Yale. Whatever sounded the death knell of their affair, David said it had left him "deeply wounded."

To fulfill Yale's requirement that students complete an internship, Wendi landed a coveted summer slot at Star TV, the Hong Kong station owned by Rupert Murdoch's News Corp. The position not only fulfilled the Ivy League's academic requirement, it set the stage for the Shanghai Girl's permanent state of shock and awe.

Through her position, Wendi met media baron Rupert Murdoch, the possessor of a fortune estimated at between $11 and $20 billion. His vast holdings included the 21st Century Fox film studio, Fox News, the *Times of London*, *National Geographic*, the *New York Post*, Harper Collins, and so forth. At this juncture, Rupert's crusade was to institute free market television in China that would lure a billion new viewers. When questioned about the direction of his company, he responded, "China, China, China, and China."

During a meeting at Star TV's Hong Kong headquarters, as his employees posed safe questions to their boss, Wendi, in heavily accented English, asked one of the world's greatest businessmen, "Why is your China strategy so bad?" Her lack of sycophancy, along with her beauty, proved an aphrodisiac. What also made Rupert susceptible was that his marriage to his second wife, Anna, the mother of three of his four children, had reached an impasse. His mother, Dame Elisabeth Murdoch, age ninety, had told her son that if he left Anna, he would fall prey to the first designing woman who crossed his gold-strewn path.

Soon Rupert was hot to trot for his intern and was shocked when Wendi spurned his advances, explaining she had no interest in becoming the other woman. Rupert reassured her with the four most beautiful words a billionaire could utter: "I will marry you." A headline heralded, "Viagra-chomping Rupert Murdoch has been dating a Cantonese cutie." A Murdoch employee stated, 'The boss may be old enough to qualify for a bus pass, but they giggled like lovestruck teenagers.' "

Two weeks after his divorce, Rupert wed wife number III aboard the Murdoch yacht moored in New York Harbor. Gathered for the ceremony were eighty-two guests, such as Russian billionaire Boris Berezovsky. For entertainment, Rupert had flown in the Welsh singing sensation Charlotte Church. The groom toasted his barefoot bride and promised he "loved her and would take care of her, forever."

The press had a field day; an article in *The Washington Post* eviscerated Wendi, especially for the manner in which she had amputated the joy from the life of Joyce Cherry. Ex-wife Anna confided to an interviewer, "I began to think that the Rupert I loved died a long time ago. The Rupert I fell in love with could not have behaved this way." To lessen the sting of terminating his three-decade-long marriage, he provided Anna with $1.7 billion in assets and $110 million in cash. Murdoch's mother vowed she would never meet the scheming siren.

While the Austrian former nun Maria von Trapp once said that her favorite things were raindrops on roses, the Chinese former volleyball player's favorite things were far more exotic; Wendi favored couture, yachts, and jet-setting. Through IVF, the couple had daughters Grace and Chloe. The Murdochs christened their girls on the banks of the Jordan River in an approximation of the spot where Jesus had undergone the same ceremony. In attendance were godparents Queen Rania, Nicole Kidman, Hugh Jackman, and British Prime Minister Tony Blair. While the media head honcho has been called "the big, bad, bastard," Murdoch the Munificent gave his six children $100 million in shares of his News Corporation empire. The sale of his media empire to Disney provided each child with a further $2 billion.

Although Wendi's Everest-sized disposable income could buy almost anything that struck her fancy, she could not always find acceptance in the economic stratosphere. Several of the mothers whose children attended the same school as Chloe and Grace made fun of Wendi's heavily accented Chinese accent. They mocked her *nouveaux riche* pronouncements delivered in rapid-fire speech, "Rockefeller apartment, fifty-point-eight million. But we had to put twenty million into it. Gut renovation." Another of her oft-repeated comments was, "Look at my daughters! So beautiful and so rich!" During the occasions when the Murdoch sisters arrived in a chauffeur-driven car in the company of their nanny, the mean-lady moms turned the screw, "Those poor things. They never see their parents."

The Shanghai Girls must have shrieked, "Dang Deng!" as they mythologized the Chinese Cinderella who had undergone a metamorphosis from Wen Di Deng to Wendi Murdoch. The Murdochs' Manhattan base was a $44-million Fifth Avenue triplex, once the property of Laurance S. Rockefeller, which contained twenty rooms and 4,000 square feet of terraces overlooking Central Park. Other American beauties were located in the zip codes of Beverly Hills and Carmel. The Murdochs also owned properties in London and Melbourne. As a love token, the devoted husband purchased a mansion near the former imperial palace in China's Forbidden City. Described as "fit for an emperor," the estate consisted of 21,500 square feet, and featured an underground swimming pool, golf course, and billiard room.

The Murdochs socialized with the world's glitterati, evoking the Chinese concept of *guanxi* ("connections"). Place settings bore the names David Geffen, Larry Ellison, Bono, Diane von Fürstenberg, Barbara Walters, Vera Wang, and Arianna Huffington. When the Murdochs lived in a condo on Trump Park Avenue, they were friendly with neighbors Jared Kushner and Ivanka Trump. Jared and Ivanka's daughter, Arabella, practiced her Mandarin with Murdoch heiresses Grace and Chloe. Ivanka invited the Murdochs for Sabbath dinners where Wendi enjoyed "braided bread." On one occasion, the Murdochs met with Queen Elizabeth II. In St. Barts, where they sailed on their 180-foot sailboat, Wendi informed her husband she preferred cruising with Russian oligarch Roman Abramovich as he had a bigger boat. When Rupert balked at buying an upgraded model, Wendi sniped, "His whole family like this. They so cheap." For the couple to reach their innumerable homes and international playgrounds, the Murdochs' Boeing 737 remained on standby.

Marriage to Wendi resulted in a tycoon's metamorphosis: Rupert darkened his hair and traded his suit and ties for black slacks and turtlenecks. However, marriage did not change Rupert as greatly as it did Wendi, a fact she revealed when she and Arianna Huffington cohosted a book release party for Kathy Freston's weight-loss book *The Lean*, an event to which they invited Martha Stewart and Harvey Weinstein. In deference to Kathy's vegetarianism, the caterers served hors d'oeuvres of tofu, quinoa, and kale. Wendi toasted her guests by sharing, "I grew up so poor in China that one day I aspired to have meat regularly. Now that I can have meat three times a day, Kathy tells us we can't have any meat at all."

In 2011, Wendi was catapulted into the spotlight when Rupert testified before a British parliamentary subcommittee that was investigating the illegal phone hacking of his *The News of the World.* While Rupert's 20th Century Fox had produced *The Devil Wears Prada*, Wendi wore Chanel—a pink blazer along with a black pencil skirt. Seated behind her husband, Wendi noticed a man hurling a shaving-cream pie at her husband. Switching to tiger-wife mode, channeling her youthful volleyball skills, she sprang from her chair and delivered a right-handed hook at Jonathan May-Bowles, known by his stage name, Jonnie Marbles. The image of Wendi literally leaping to her tycoon's defense transformed her from harridan to heroine.

Whether due to their age difference or divergent childhoods—Rupert was brought up in wealth in Australia—the couple began to lead separate lives. While he often retired early to bed, Wendi was regularly seen at the Oscars, the Met Gala, or the White House at a dinner for Chinese president Hu Jintao. Wendi produced the movie *Snow Flower and the Secret Fan*, based on a Lisa See novel; the plot centered on two women, old friends who find in each other the connection lacking in their marriages. At Parisian fashion shows, sheathed in Chanel, Wendi sat beside Anna Wintour, the editor of *Vogue*, and dined with Karl Lagerfeld, Chanel's head honcho.

Cracks formed in the Murdoch marriage when rumors circulated that Wendi had embarked on affairs with Chris DeWolfe, the founder of Myspace, and Eric Schmidt, the former CEO of Google. What really set tongues wagging was when former British Prime Minister Tony Blair, who had business dealings with Rupert, dropped by when only the missus was at home. Because Tony always arrived accompanied by his security detail, he could not slip unobtrusively though the back door. Rupert's private humiliation became public when the police investigated his newspaper's phone hacking allegations. To counter the charges, Rupert's employees sifted through millions of emails, where they found one from Mrs. Murdoch: "Oh, s**t, oh, s**t. Whatever why I'm so so missing Tony. Because he is so so charming and his clothes are so good. He has such good body and he has really really good legs [and] Butt... And he is slim tall and [has] good skin. Pierce blue eyes which I love. Also I love his power on the stage...and what else and what else and what else..." The email also gave way to press scrutiny: Was the "Butt" a misspelt pronoun or an allusion to the politician's backside?"

In response to the smoking-gun email, then eighty-year-old Rupert Murdoch ended his association with Tony and filed for divorce from Wendi in 2013. He confided to his oldest son Lachlan that marrying her had been a mistake. Forever had, it turns out, come with an expiration date. The tycoon's attorney was Ira E. Garr, whose previous high-profile client had been Ivana Trump. From New York to Los Angeles to Washington to London, the tabloids indulged in a feeding frenzy. One could imagine the horrified whispers of the Shanghai Girls. In the divorce settlement, Wendi received the Manhattan triplex (worth $60–$70 million), the Beijing home (estimated at $10–$40 million), and a cash settlement of $14 million, i.e., one million for each year of the Murdoch marriage, along with jewelry, a yacht, and art.

Wendi has never remarried, though she has had relationships, such as with British violinist Charlie Siem, who accompanied her to a Parisian fashion show. When the press asked if he was her date, Wendi replied, "Why not? Am I supposed to be shy?" One of the most shocking controversies about Wendi Deng concerned accounts of a romance she had post-divorce with Russian head of state Vladimir Putin, although she denied the rumors. At age forty-eight, she had a two-year affair with a twenty-one-year-old hunky Hungarian model, with whom she cavorted on a St. Barts beach.

Wendi is a polarizing figure. Is she a Machiavellian Murdoch whose prey is men she uses as stepping stones? Her detractors have labeled her the contemporary Yellow Peril and an Olympian opportunist. But for the Shanghai Girls from whose sisterhood she came, having fulfilled hopes of marrying well enough to lift her out of an economic backwater, she is the golden girl who escaped from the straitjacket situations of communism to the shining citadel of capitalism. Can one sit in judgment on Wendi Deng, who used whatever means at her disposal to escape the shackles of Shanghai?

CHAPTER 23

Crown Princess Marie-Chantal of Greece: Rumpelstiltskin (1968)

"It's statistically proven that children who have beautiful manners do better in life."

—QUEEN MARIE-CHANTAL

In a Brothers Grimm fairy tale, a miller boasted his daughter could weave straw into gold. An avaricious king locked her in a room, tasking her with proving her father's claim. Failure would result in her execution. When the royal saw she had succeeded, he made her his queen. Marie-Chantal also possesses an alchemic ability because she can turn her any wish or whim into golden reality. She is Robert Miller's daughter, billionaire heiress to his Duty-Free Shopping Emporium. Like her fairy-tale namesake, Marie-Chantal married into royalty.

Travelers might drop into an airport's duty-free shops; because such shops are exempt from taxes, owners offer less expensive prices. The realization made Robert Miller an entrepreneurial tsar. Imelda Marcos, First Lady of the Philippines, once emptied the world's duty-free shops of her favorite perfume so no one else would wear her signature scent. In the *Seinfeld* episode, "The Airport," George Costanza was not a fan, declaring, "Duty-free is the biggest sucker in retail." Then the two Stooges chanted, "I want to stop at the duty-free shop!"

A modern-day "once upon a time" story began on the Hong Kong estate of the 'King of Duty-Free,' Robert Miller, and his Ecuadorian-born wife, Maria Clara (known as Chantal), rumored to be the last Inca princess. The couple's three daughters—all future "It Girls"—were the winners of a financial and genetic lottery. Not limited by one zip code, the Millers owned houses in Paris, London, New York, Switzerland, and England. The couple's three daughters were all born in different countries: their eldest, Pia, in New York; middle child Marie-Chantal in London; and the youngest, Alexandra, in Hong Kong. With the duty-free dollars raining down, the Millers had a rarefied life in what was, at the time, a British Crown Colony where servants attended to their every wish. A boating aficionado, Robert took his family on sunset excursions in Hong Kong's harbor in one of his four boats, all christened *Mari-Cha*. Vacations consisted of exotic locales such as the Philippines, Thailand, and Europe; the world was truly their oyster.

When it came to education, the Millers wanted top echelon educational experiences for their daughters. At age nine, Marie-Chantal attended a Swiss boarding school, Institut Le Rosey, in Gstaad. After five years, when her parents purchased property in Paris, they enrolled their girls in the Ecole Active Bilingue in Paris. For her senior year, Marie-Chantal attended the Masters School in Dobbs Ferry, New York. What was far more important than any academic curriculum was that the Millers' art dealer, Jeffrey Deitch, introduced then sixteen-year-old Marie-Chantal to pop artist Andy Warhol. As part of her independent study program, she worked as an intern for Warhol at his studio, the Factory. The time with Warhol was straight out of a teenager's fantasy. Far from typical student digs, Marie-Chantal lived alone in her parents' luxurious Upper East Side apartment; parents Robert and Maria Clara were residing in Hong Kong, and sisters Alexandra and Pia were away at boarding schools. The Manhattan home held a collection of Old Master paintings, as well as a Louis XIV desk whose twin is ensconced is ensconced in Versailles. Despite the grandeur, when in the city, the Millers mainly resided on the twenty-second floor of the nearby Hotel Carlyle as Maria Clara preferred its view.

As part of her apprenticeship, Marie-Chantal accompanied Warhol to dinners, art gallery openings, clubs, and parties. Since the press covered the pop icon's every move, its flashbulbs also included the Hong Kong heiress. One afternoon, Warhol made the request, "Scarlett, would you like to pose for me?" (Scarlett was the nickname Marie-Chantal used at that time, likely chosen as a reference to the spitfire heroine of *Gone with the Wind*.) The artist painted three portraits of her, one of which he gifted to her as a high school graduation present. Robert bought the other two, something Marie-Chantal referred to as a "good investment." Glamorous as life was in the eye of the Warhol storm, after a year, she decided to take off to "figure out what I wanted to do."

One of the things Marie-Chantal wanted to do was choose her religion. Her father was Protestant, her mother Catholic, and they had not imposed either faith on their daughters. At age eighteen, Marie-Chantal embraced Catholicism and underwent a baptism at Manhattan's St. Patrick's Cathedral. Cardinal John O'Connor presided over the ceremony; Donatella Flick, the Millers' neighbor in Gstaad, then the wife of Daimler-Benz heir Mick Flick, was her godmother. To celebrate, the Millers threw a dinner at Le Cirque; they invited society columnist Aileen Mehle, because, as Marie-Chantal put it, "We have so much money and no one knows us."

An heiress in search of her purpose, she attended Sarah Lawrence then transferred to New York University, where she left before graduating. Afterwards, she left for Paris to breed horses, before embarking for Italy for an art history course. Then, on a 1992 night, the weaving sisters spun Marie-Chantal's destiny via a blind date. The matchmaker was billionaire New York investment banker Alecko Papamarkou, who had introduced Pia to Christopher Getty, the grandson of oil tycoon John Paul Getty. Hoping to duplicate his success with another Miller daughter, for a year, Alecko attempted in vain to arrange a meeting between Prince Pavlos and Marie-Chantal.

Prince Pavlos' father was the once and future king of Greece; King Constantine II had fled his country following a 1967 coup that resulted in the abolishment of the 140-year-old monarchy. The government seized the royals' 10,000-acre estate, Tatoi, its forests in central Greece, and their villa on Corfu. A 2002 European Court decreed that the confiscation had been illegal and ruled that the new republic had the choice of either returning the properties or offering financial compensation. Constantine stated that private appraisers had valued his real estate holdings at between $400 million and $600 million; the ousted king received $12 million. Constantine bestowed the money as a gift back to his homeland.

Prince Pavlos, the Crown Prince, was born in Athens' Tatoi Palace. On the day of his baptism, his father declared a national holiday. When forced into exile, the family fled first to Rome, then Denmark, and finally settled in London. Constantine maintained ties with his sister, Queen Sofia of Spain, and developed a close relationship with his second cousin, the current King Charles III. The British monarch chose Constantine as one of the godfathers to Prince William, heir to the British throne. Upon Constantine's passing, Pavlos and Marie-Chantal became the king and queen of Greece, rulers without thrones.

Still desirous of introducing the Crown Prince to the billionaire blonde beauty, Alecko invited Marie-Chantal to the fortieth birthday party that Greek shipping tycoon Stavros Niarchos was throwing in New Orleans for his son, Philip. Although reluctant to be set up on a date, Marie-Chantal borrowed her mother's navy-blue Chanel suit and admitted she "looked like a million bucks." Prince Pavlos agreed. The heiress said, "We clicked. It was love at first sight. I knew that he was the person I would marry." Equally smitten, Pavlos recalled, "Well, this is what I've been looking for. Alecko was right." Within two months of their meeting, Marie-Chantal had moved from Paris to the States to be closer to her beau, who was a student at Georgetown University's School of Foreign Service. His roommate was Prince Felipe of Spain.

On a Christmas vacation, Pavlos proposed while on a ski lift in Gstaad with an engagement ring that featured a seriously large sapphire enclosed with two heart-shaped diamonds. As part of her conversion to the Greek Orthodox faith, the couple flew to Istanbul,

Turkey, for a blessing by Bartholomew I, the Ecumenical Patriarch of Constantinople.

European bluebloods descended on London for the wedding festivities. Queen Sofia of Spain came to celebrate with her nephew, as did Pavlos' aunt, Queen Margrethe II of Denmark, who arrived with the Danish royals on her yacht, *Dannebrog.* Queen Elizabeth II held a tea for the couple. Wanting to contribute more than merely the dazzling $200 million dowry, the Millers hosted one of the most over-the-top pre-wedding and wedding receptions Britain had held since the nuptials of Prince Philip and Queen Elizabeth II. The first celebration was a dinner dance for 1,300 guests at Wrotham Park in Kent; the second was a garden party in a tent shaped like a replica of the Acropolis, held at Hampton Court Palace. The gala featured blue and white decorations as well as tents that resembled the Parthenon. The hosts imported 100,000 flowers from Ecuador, Maria Clara's home country. The Greek-born Duke of Edinburgh, along with Prince Albert of Monaco, danced far past the witching hour.

On July 1, 1995, the couple took their vows at St. Sophia, London's Greek Orthodox Cathedral. Designer Valentino—who had fashioned the wedding gowns of Jackie Kennedy and Athina Onassis—created the bride's $225,000 pearl-encrusted gown, one that took twenty-five seamstresses four months to complete. Adorning the dress was a fifteen-foot train composed of Chantilly lace with a scalloped edge, held in place with a tiara borrowed from the bride's mother-in-law, Queen Anne-Marie.

In addition to the British bluebloods, other guests wore the crowns of Spain, Sweden, Belgium, Romania, Bulgaria, and Jordan. The great Greek shipping dynasties—the Livanoses and Niarchoses—were present, as were tycoons Rupert Murdoch, John Kluge, and all four Forbes brothers. After the cathedral services, a thousand guests headed to a reception at Hampton Court Palace where they dined on lobster and sipped champagne. The cost of the festivities was in the vicinity of ten million dollars.

In New York, Marie-Chantal gave birth to Princess Maria-Olympia, Prince Constantine Alexios, and Prince Achileas Andreas. Their fourth child was born in London, though his parents held his christening in Athens in a thirteenth-century Byzantine chapel. Queen Sophia of Spain snapped digital photos while Crown Prince Haakon of Norway videotaped. Princess Olga of Greece had the honor of dipping her godchild into the gold baptismal font.

As royals in a deposed line, the couple may not live in a castle, but they do own five fairy-tale homes. In London, they live in Chelsea's Cheyne Walk, where Roman Abramovich owns a $134 million mansion. When they want a break from the city, they have the 32,000-acre Yorkshire hunting lodge they inherited from King Constantine II. An alternate British retreat is their Cotswolds getaway, nestled in the country. Currently, their main bolt-hole is their New York home, a residence that once belonged to the Millers. When they need sun, there is the holiday home on exclusive Harbour Island in the Bahamas, where the lawn displays a giant shell sculpture.

Not ones to rest on their well-padded laurels, Pavlos started a hedge fund with his brother in-law, Prince Alexander. For her husband's birthday bash, Marie-Chantal threw a "Roaring '20s" party at Harlem's Cotton Club in New York, where friends boogied till four in the morning. Another grand fête Marie-Chantal threw was an "Angels and Demons" bash for hubby's fortieth birthday. The heavenly and hellish guests included two Infantas of Spain.

However, one extravagant birthday soiree garnered negative press in which headlines employed the adjectives "decadent" and "extravagant." The occasion was the lavish joint birthday party for Marie-Chantal's husband and twenty-one-year-old daughter. High-profile attendees included King Felipe of Spain, Prince Charles's goddaughter India Hicks, and Paris and Nicky Hilton. The less than flattering reportage mentioned Princess Olympia's $858 Gucci running shoes. Of the media fallout, Marie-Chantal stated, "It's sad that it had to be misrepresented that way because it's not who we are as a family. But you can't win everybody's hearts, right?" She affirmed she had put that 'unpleasant incident' behind her.

The love affair between the Greek royal couple seems to have only ramped up its luster over the years. On Pavlos' fifty-seventh birthday, Marie-Chantal posted a photograph on social media of the couple with three of their children. She captioned the picture, "A little birthday celebration with our London lot. Happiest birthday to my numéro uno!"

While most people would feel they had enough on their plates managing five children and several households in various locales, Marie-Chantal wanted "to do something on my own merit." As she had always had a passion for fashion—having regularly appeared on magazine's best-dressed lists—she established a high-end children's clothing line in 2000. She christened her company Marie-Chantal; its signature logo sported a heart over the letter "I" in Marie. The brand's logo was a little prince with a crooked crown. Adding to the store's ambience was its location off King's Road, originally the studio of the Pre-Raphaelite painter Dante Gabriel Rossetti. The business expanded to several shops in several countries; when a Marie-Chantal shop opened in Athens, thousands turned out. The entrepreneur stated, "The business is what makes me *me*. That's why I called it Marie-Chantal—with no 'princess' or anything. It gives me my independence. It gives me incredible pleasure and focus. And it belongs to me 100 percent."

The shop's royal patrons included the Princess of Wales: Prince George wore a navy blazer for a Christmas outing and Princess Charlotte donned the brand's scarf for a first day at school. Other angel wing patrons were Princess Caroline of Monaco's grandchildren and the children of Crown Princess Victoria of Sweden. Celebrity customers included Victoria Beckham, Reese Witherspoon, Kim Kardashian, and Nicky Hilton.

Marie-Chantal's family takes meals at a table set as if it were a five-star restaurant—even when the meal consists of take-out. Her favorite China pattern is Royal Copenhagen. After-meal activities might include walking their dogs, Storm and Akila, or playing backgammon. In an article in The New York Times, "How Crown Princess Marie-Chantal Spends Her Time," she revealed another one of the myriad talents she has up her designer sleeve. In the newspaper she shared that as a child, in her home in Paris, her family played foosball. A competitive player, she can beat two of her children. The profile ended with Marie-Chantal reading to her youngest, Aristides, from C. S. Lewis's *The Chronicles of Narnia: The Lion, the Witch and the Wardrobe.*

CHAPTER 24

Clare Bronfman: Unhappy Chance (1979)

"I am truly remorseful. I wanted to do good in the world."

—CLAIRE BRONFMAN

As the French novelist Honoré de Balzac observed, "Behind every great fortune there is a crime." His words proved prescient for the Bronfman liquor dynasty behind the Seagram brand, a family that profited from Prohibition. A modern validation of his statement occurred with heiress Clare Bronfman, who proved that great fortunes can also carry in their wake transgressions stranger than fiction.

Canada's famous financial family began in 1899 in Saskatchewan, where Yechiel and Mindel Bronfman settled after emigrating from Bessarabia, in the Russian Empire. As Jewish surnames often derived from their occupations, the family likely honed their distillery skills in the Old Country: In Yiddish, "Bronfman" translates to "a maker of gin or brandy." Their son, Samuel, founded the distillery company and became a booze baron when his illegal liquor slaked the thirst of America via bootleggers such as Al Capone. One consequence of the rumrunners' operation was the shotgun death of Paul Matoff, Sam's brother-in-law. For the Bronfman godfather, the murder was the cost of doing business.

With an empire that encompassed ownership of the Montreal Expos and vast international oil holdings, the family dwelled in baronial splendor—in sharp contrast to a country mired in the Great Depression. Sam's four children, one of whom was Edgar, Claire's father, grew up in a Montreal mansion with staff that included a butler, cook, nannies, maids, chauffeurs, and gardeners. When Edgar was a boy, Sam built a bicycle path behind the wall that enclosed the Bronfman estate to safeguard his son from kidnappers.

With the passing of his father Sam, Edgar lost his emotional compass. He separated from his investment-banking heiress wife, Ann Loeb, with whom he had five children. His second spouse was Lady Carolyn Townshend, the daughter of the seventh Marquess Townshend. The relationship was on the rocks before their first anniversary; Edgar annulled the marriage on the grounds she refused to sleep with him. In 1975, on one of his mansion's lawns, Edgar married Rita Webb, whose father owned a pub, Ye Old

Nosebag, in Essex, England. She was a nightclub receptionist—who moonlighted as a social climber—twenty-three years his junior. The couple had met in Marbella, Spain, where he had fallen for the British beauty. Before her wedding, the bride converted to Judaism. She also changed her name to Georgiana after Edgar nicknamed her 'George.' The attention normally reserved for the newlyweds extended to Edgar's son, Samuel, as wedding guests kept telling him, "Thank God, you're safe." They were alluding to his recent kidnapping, when his father had paid a ransom of $2.3 million to regain him. After his safe return, Samuel said, "Thanks for everything, Dad." During a subsequent trial, the defense accused Samuel of staging his own abduction to shake down his father in retaliation for having chosen his younger son, Edgar Jr., as heir to the Seagram's throne.

The Edgar-Georgiana union ended when their daughter Sara was seven and Clare was four. In a decision he would later refer to as "really naïve," he remarried Georgiana "to keep my young girls with me." Despite his wanting to keep the family together, the marriage collapsed. Edgar moved on to his fourth wife, Jan Aronson.

As children, the sisters lived at a boarding school in England. During vacations, they stayed in Kenya, where their mother was reportedly in a romantic relationship with the famous paleontologist, Richard Leakey, or, alternatively, just in love with Africa. Another love affair was with Lorenzo Ricciardi, an Italian filmmaker in his sixties. The police arrested Lorenzo for trying to arrange Georgiana's murder. Georgiana went on to marry British television actor Nigel Havers, who appeared in the film *Chariots of Fire*.

The girls also visited their father at his estates outside Charlottesville, Virginia, as well as in Westchester County, Sun Valley, and on Fifth Avenue. They were the youngest of his seven children—their half siblings were in their late teens and early twenties—and Edgar may not have been in peak parenting prime. His distance from his daughters is reflected in the fact that they were barely mentioned in Edgar's 1996 memoir. One of his few references to Clare is how she had been subject to anti-Semitic bullying in her British school, and how he had the offender expelled. Edgar wrote that Sara had "gone through the normal phrase of rebellion especially from her mother." The Bronfman family dynamics echoed Leo Tolstoy's pronouncement in *Anna Karenina*, "All happy families are alike; each unhappy family is unhappy in its own way."

Clare did not graduate high school as her passion lay elsewhere. There seems to be a strong bond between heiresses and horses—one that goes beyond the Black Beauty/My Little Pony phase. Athina Onassis, heir to her grandfather Aristotle's shipping empire, became an Olympian equestrian and married fellow riding enthusiast Álvaro Afonso de Miranda Neto (known as Doda). Microsoft billionaire Bill Gates ponied up $15.82 million for a 124-acre horse farm for his daughter Jennifer. Laurene Jobs, widow of the founder of Apple, purchased a horse ranch in Wellington, Florida, for her daughter Eve at a cost of $15.3 million. Clare owned a horse farm, Slate River Farm, and was a show jumper in Europe who harbored Olympic aspirations. Riding a twelve-year-old gelding called Charlton, she won the Rome Grand Prix equestrian tournament and placed second in a show in Bremen. What derailed her dreams was an episode so bizarre it seemed to belong more in the realm of a bad batch of moonshine.

While the male branch of the Bronfman clan raised eyebrows, the female branch was more circumspect. The only exception was Clare's aunt, Holly Bronfman, who moved to India, converted to Hinduism, and changed her name to Bhavani Lev. But in terms of scandal, her niece went on to make her aunt look like a rank amateur.

In the early 2000s, Clare's older sister Sara became involved with Nxivm, an organization based in Albany, New York. She was twenty-five years old, self-described as a socially anxious multimillionaire with "patterns of self-loathing, insecurity, shame, and fear." The party girl drifted amongst various European capitals. Her four-month marriage to Irish jockey Ronan Clarke was heading to its finish line. Nxivm offered workshops designed to help its members obtain self-fulfillment by removing emotional and psychological roadblocks. Thrilled she had finally found her purpose, Sara introduced Clare to the organization to help her find her own. Another lure that might have drawn in the sisters is they felt feelings of inferiority compared to other members of the Bronfman family: Several of them held high-profile careers, such as their half-brother, Edgar Bronfman, Jr., who had served as a chief executive of Warner Music Group. Some of the female members had made brilliant marital matches, like their Aunt Aileen, a graduate of Smith College and Columbia University and the wife of Alain de Gunzburg, a Harvard University graduate and heir to a French barony.

An archetypal angry young woman, at her first Nxivm meeting in Mexico, Clare stated that she was going to spend the rest of her life with horses since she didn't like people. Several meetings convinced Clare that the group provided the road to enlightenment. What might have helped convince her is she likely had fallen for its Svengali-style leader, Keith Raniere, whose followers addressed him as 'Vanguard.' To bond with his two youngest daughters, Edgar also participated in Nxivm. However, when he discovered Clare had given Keith $2 million, feeling highly suspicious, he stated in an interview with *Forbes* Magazine, "I think it's a cult." To spy on her father, Clare installed malware on his computer that gave Nxivm access to Edgar's email.

Forbes featured Keith on its cover, and its article portrayed him as a dangerous demagogue and a spiritual heir of Charles Manson, the Reverend Jim Jones, and David Koresh. In contrast, his adherents likened him to Nelson Mandela and Archbishop Desmond Tutu. Some of the revelations were Keith had no bank accounts in his name even though his organization was raking in millions. There were accounts of former members who had experienced psychotic breakdowns and who claimed they had been victims of brainwashing and coerced alienation from their families. The article satirized Sara, who caressed her yellow Nxivm sash while gushing it was "the first thing that I had earned on just my merits."

More bombshells followed after publication of the piece in *Forbes*. Like the moon, Nxivm had a dark side, invisible to the naked eye. A women's only group within Nxivm, "DOS," stood for "Dominus Obsequious Sororium," which is Latin for "master over slave," meaning designated sex slaves. In secret ceremonies, the women submitted to branding with a symbol that consisted of Keith's initials on the area above their pelvises. During the initiation, they repeated, "Master, please brand me, it would be an honor." A celebrity who endorsed the ritual was Allison Mack, who played Chloe Sullivan, Clark Kent's friend on the decade-long Superman series *Smallville*. Using her celebrity status, Allison lured women with the promise they would be part of a female mentorship program. She admitted that she had come up with the idea of branding, "I was like: 'Y'all, a tattoo? People get drunk and tattooed on their ankle 'BFF,' or a tramp stamp.' "

Another high-profile member, India Oxenberg, who was the granddaughter of Princess Elizabeth of Yugoslavia and the daughter of *Dallas* actress Catherine Oxenberg, was a member for seven years. Due to her restricted diet, she was emaciated, her hair was falling out, and she had stopped menstruating. With a herculean effort, Catherine was successful in freeing her brainwashed daughter. In contrast, Georgiana was unable to extricate Clare. A former Nxivm member remarked of cult leader Keith Raniere, "He is what you would get if David Koresh and Bernie Madoff had a child."

Because Keith liked his women ultra-thin, he limited their food intake so that they took on an emaciated heroin-chic appearance. He also liked ladies with deep pockets, which was the reason he paid special attention to Sara and Clare Bronfman, whose trust funds endowed each of them with $200 million. The siblings bankrolled expenditures that included $30 million for properties in Los Angeles and New York, $11 million for a twenty-two-seat Canadair CL-600 jet, and $66 million to cover Keith's losses on failed investments. Millions more went to fight lawsuits against Nxivm's enemies. Sara and Clare took great pains to hide the fact that they were the organization's cash cows from their eighty-one-year-old father and the Bronfman family trustees. Trying to mend bridges with his daughters, Edgar emailed Sara and Clare, "Whether or not you want to believe me, I do not lie, and I love you two very much. Someone is not telling you the truth. Why don't you try and figure out who that might be? Who has something to gain? Certainly not me. What would be my motive? Tons of love, even if not requited, Pops."

Having taken heat from Nxivm for Edgar branding it a cult, before his passing, Clare visited her estranged father, accompanied by a camera crew. She wanted her father to go on record that he had been mistaken in his condemnation. An organization official, Mark Vincente, recalled Edgar was very sick and "appeared to be very saddened by her questioning." Edgar refused to renounce his statement; in this instance, father knew best. Unlike his father

Sam, Edgar was unable to build a "bicycle path" sheltered from the world to safeguard his daughter.

A 2009 event Nxivm hailed as a "victory" occurred when Sara arranged for the Dalai Lama to speak at an Albany, New York, gathering to an audience of three thousand. She had orchestrated the coup through Lama Tenzin Dhonden, head of the spiritual leader's US trust. The Bronfman sisters shared the stage with the Dalai Lama and watched in awe as the spiritual leader placed a *khata*—a Tibetan scarf—around Keith's neck. While the event proved a watershed moment, detritus followed in its wake: Clare was Lama Tenzin's lover, although the monk had taken a vow of chastity. Moreover, Clare had paid $1 million for her guest speaker's appearance. Amidst charges of corruption, the Dalai Lama Trust removed Lama Tenzin Dhonden as its executive secretary; the holy man also cut ties with Sara. Shortly afterwards, Sara began a relationship with Basit Igtet, a Libyan exile who had been born in Benghazi. When his father ended up in jail for embezzling millions of dollars from the Qaddafi government, Basit fled to Switzerland. As Sara was pregnant with Basit's baby, the couple married. At Keith's urging, although Basit had a Jewish wife and had not lived in Libya for years, he ran for the position of the country's prime minister, but lost by a landslide. Putting Nxivm aside to care for her daughter, Safia, Sara severed ties with the organization.

Clare remained and rose ever higher in Nxivm's hierarchy. In 2010, in her role as ATM., she organized a week-long celebration in upstate New York for Keith's fiftieth birthday called 'Vanguard Week.' The organization touted itself as "the prototype and blueprint for a new era of civilized humanity." The heiress purchased an island in Fiji for $47 million for Nxivm members to use as a retreat. That year, *Vanity Fair* reported that the Bronfman trust had contributed $150 million to bankroll Nxivm.

In 2018, Keith's house of cards began to collapse. A federal court charged him with coercing women into sex by threatening to reveal damaging secrets to which he was privy, information he had received as part of their initiations when they entered Nxivm. Prosecutors also indicted Clare with conspiracy and criminal racketeering and argued she had financed and pursued lawsuits against Nxivm's opponents and had also brought in an undocumented immigrant. Victims claimed she had filed spurious criminal complaints for the purpose of intimidation. A judge set bail at $100 million and ordered that she wear an ankle monitor while under house arrest.

During sentencing, Clare held hands with her mother and her sister's husband while several women begged her to denounce Keith. One victim, Susan Dones, said through her tears, "I pray that you will take the claws of Keith Raniere out of you and you will learn who Clare Bronfman really is." Another former Nxivm member, Kristin Keeffe, told the court that after she gave birth to Keith's son, Clare had pressured her into saying the baby had been adopted so he would not be saddled with child support. Judge Garaufis stated, "I don't know how many other multimillionaires are out there, ready to devote the limitless resources at their disposal to supporting pyramid schemes run by dangerous criminals." Clare refused to testify against Keith, saying she still believed in him, still believed in Nxivm. She addressed the court in a barely audible voice, "Your honor, I was afforded a great gift by my grandfather and father. With the gift comes immense privilege, and more importantly, tremendous responsibility. It does not come with an ability to break the law; it comes with a greater responsibility to uphold the law. I failed to uphold the following laws set forth by this country, and for that I am truly remorseful." The federal judge sentenced Clare to six years and nine months in prison. Upon hearing the verdict, Clare touched her throat, as if she were having trouble swallowing.

Samuel Bronfman had often quoted a line from Alfred, Lord Tennyson's poem "In Memoriam" that involved grasping "the skirts of happy chance." The $200 million question remains: how did Clare so misread her own "happy chance"?

CHAPTER 25

Athina Onassis: The Greek Chorus (1985)

"If I burn the money, there will be no problem. No money, no problem."

—ATHINA ONASSIS

No one ever mastered tragedy quite like the ancient Greeks—especially when they mined the arena of dysfunctional families. The legacy of billionaire heiress Athina Onassis could well have sprung from the Aegean world of the ancient Greeks.

This twentieth-century saga began with Aristotle Socrates Onassis. He had arrived on the docks of Buenos Aires, Argentina, with sixty dollars that he parlayed into a multibillion-dollar shipping empire. His Midas Touch earned him the epithet "the Golden Greek." Schadenfreude—inherent to human nature as it has existed since at least the days of the gladiators—went into overdrive with the Onassis dynasty.

Aristotle bequeathed his heirs his larger-than-life legacy: a fabulous fortune—and a family curse. His daughter, Christina, the essence of the poor little rich girl, was an expert at looking for love in all the wrong places. She was for a time smitten with the French-born Thierry Roussel—who was smitten with her bank account. Writer Taki Theodoracopulos described Thierry as "the most successful gigolo in the world" for his conquest of Miss Midas. While pregnant with daughter Athina, Christina held on to her husband—even after he had also impregnated his long-time mistress, Swedish model Marianne "Gaby" Landhage, with whom he had son Erik. The heiress' breaking point arrived when Gaby delivered her second child, Sandrine. Tired of serving as a cash cow for her husband and his lover, Christina filed for divorce. With the loss of her parents, brother, and lover, Christina doted on her little daughter, Athina Hélène. The indulgent mother decorated her daughter's three-room nursery with walls adorned with $600,000 in gold leaf. Athina's dolls dressed in Dior, and the child played with a diamond-studded rocking-horse and a $12,500 toy Rolls-Royce. As the toddler's favorite nursery rhyme was "Baa, Baa, Black Sheep," she had a zoo with a flock of real sheep watched over by a shepherd.

In the hope Buenos Aires would live up to its translated meaning of "Fair Winds," Christina planned to buy a ranch where she and Athina could live for several months of the year. Before tying the knot for the fifth time, Christina's life ended in a bathtub where she succumbed to years of dieting, depression, and pills. Christina's will had bequeathed her three-year-old child $300 million in cash, two apartments in Paris, a vacation home in Spain, a house in Geneva, a compound in Ibiza that contained eight swimming pools and a discothèque, and seaside homes in Athens. The crown jewel in the real estate empire was the Greek island of Skorpios, her grandfather's former fiefdom. The private island was in proximity to Lefkada, where the mythic hero Odysseus once roamed. *People Magazine* featured Athina on its cover with the caption: "The Richest Little Girl in the World."

Thierry raised Athina with a complicated family dynamic. His children with Gaby had her Swedish light hair and eyes, while the coloration of his daughter with Christina reflected her Greek heritage. Another difference was although his son and two daughters with Gaby were hugely affluent—mostly due to the millions Christina had lavished on him—the heiress herself had been a denizen of the one percent. Because of her exalted finances, whether attending her Swiss school or riding her beloved horse, Arco de Valmont, bodyguards trailed her every move and rode in formation behind her armor-plated limousine. Another unique aspect of Athina's upbringing was her estate was in the hands of the Alexander S. Onassis Public Benefit Foundation. On one occasion, Thierry accused the foundation, whom he referred to as "greybeards," of sending former Israeli commandos to abduct his daughter. They countered they had merely hired the Israelis to check if her British bodyguards were providing sufficient protection. Living under the constant threat of kidnapping, the heiress had remarked, "If I burn the money, there will be no problem. No money, no problem." The family moved amongst their two houses in Switzerland, three apartments in Paris, a château in the French countryside, and their estate in Marbella.

Another dynamic Athina faced was her exalted status in Greece; when her father agreed to take her to visit the family homeland on the tenth anniversary of her mother's death, although she had been raised far from its shores and was unaware of its culture and history, Greece afforded her the status of an absentee royal. Fluent in French and English, she did not understand the shouts of *"Koukla!"* ("doll!") and *"Chryso mou!"* ("My gold!")—the latter phrase a term of endearment Aristotle had used when speaking to Christina.

Four years later, at the urging of her father, Athina repudiated her Greek roots. Thierry's motivation was his antipathy for the foundation with whom he continued to battle for control of the Onassis gold. By encouraging his child to distance herself from her ancestral homeland, Thierry was in defiance of the stipulation he had signed when he assumed custody: to raise her in the Greek Orthodox Church and ensure she would learn to speak Greek.

At age seventeen, in a surprising move for the unassuming Athina, the teen who preferred horses to the high life dropped out of her Swiss high school near Lake Geneva and enrolled in a Brussels equestrian school. In her adopted city, she met Álvaro de Miranda Neto, a young man of her age with whom she bonded over their shared passion for riding. His friends called him 'Doda;' Thierry called him "my worst nightmare." Doda was a Brazilian two-time Olympic bronze medal winner who had garnered trophies in the Atlanta and Sydney Olympics. The cat was out of the bag when Athina and Doda vacationed in Thailand, where a Greek tourist took their photograph and leaked it to the press. The couple maintained their relationship had only begun after Doda had separated from his wife, Cibele—a Brazilian *Playboy* cover girl with whom he shared one daughter, Viviane. From her São Paulo home, his scorned wife raged that her estranged husband was hypnotized by the Pied Piper of the Onassis billions and that Athina had destroyed her marriage. To publicize her pain, she sent a "*J'accuse*!" letter to the Brazilian magazine *Caras* (meaning '*Faces*'), in which she ranted, "She can buy him horses and I can't. We were happy together until he met her. Our only problem was money, and Doda is useless with money. What he earns, he spends. She will hang on his every word, but she will learn, as I have." Cibele also gave a telephone interview to a journalist at the Greek television station STAR, where she poured out her heartache that she had to relinquish daughter Viviane to Doda and Athina.

Thierry was highly suspicious of this Brazilian man, who was twelve years older than his daughter. To exert his control, Thierry cut back on Athina's $9,000-a-month allowance. Probably encouraged by Doda, Athina decided to duke it out with her dad using legal tactics. On her eighteenth birthday, followed by an entourage of ten former SAS bodyguards, Athina drove in a bulletproof black limousine to a home she had lived in for her first three years: La Villa Crystal Boislande, an eighteen-room mansion, where she signed documents that changed her surname from Roussel to Onassis. She also severed the restrictions on her more-than-billion-dollar inheritance, a move that made her the world's richest teenager. In addition to cash and contemporary castles, Athina received a million ounces of gold and several Rodin sculptures, 217 bank accounts, companies in Argentina, Uruguay, Brazil, Japan and Iran, a Latin American airline, a tower on Fifth Avenue, a hotel in Monte Carlo. With the stroke of a pen, Athina's wealth surpassed the fortune of Queen Elizabeth II. To prevent protracted litigation, Thierry received an $85 million settlement.

Athina joined an Athenian equestrian club, Avlona, with the aspiration of competing in international competitions, including the 2008 Beijing Olympics, where she displayed the blue and white of the Greek flag. Her ever-present shadow was the six-foot-two-inch Doda, whom she followed to São Paulo, Brazil. Their residence was the $5.8 million Château Margaux, overlooking Parque de Ibirapuera, the city's version of Central Park. To visit their horses, they rented $1,300-an-hour helicopters that whisked them to their country farm. The doting Athina treated Doda to a $320,000 cow, Esperança (Portuguese for 'Hope'), for his cattle farm. The couple were joint owners of AD Sport Horses in Fleurus, Belgium. Also included in their real estate portfolio was their $12-million, 5.6-acre horse estate in Florida. She forked over an additional $12 million for a nearby twenty-stall barn, paddock, and all-weather ring, complete with grooms' accommodations and situated on more than five acres of land. Athina celebrated her twenty-eighth birthday at the nearby International Polo Club in Palm Beach.

Shortly after arriving in Brazil, Athina underwent a physical metamorphosis that included bleaching her hair blonde and losing weight. She underwent abdominal and derrière liposuction, a procedure performed by Dr. Ricardo Lemos, known for making Brazilian women thong-ready. Although she exited through the clinic's garage, journalists snapped a photograph of the heiress, her boyfriend, and her bodyguard.

The couple initially considered marrying on the isle of Skorpios, where a staff of ten maintained facilities on the island. However, in 2005, Athina and Doda exchanged vows in a big fat Brazilian wedding. The Roman Catholic ceremony took place at São Paulo's Maria Luiza and Oscar Americano Foundation, a garden and museum situated a few miles from the city's notorious slum. The cost of the venue was equivalent to 415 times the Brazilian minimum monthly wage. The garden décor depicted a pastoral scene; the air reverberated with the strains of a forty-piece orchestra. The bride wore a pearl-colored, bare-shouldered

Valentino gown, embroidered with flowers and adorned with Chantilly lace and a fifteen-foot train. To complement the dress, the bride chose a Spanish-style mantilla headdress and low Chanel shoes. Valentino stated, "I've known Athina since she was a child. Her greatest wish is to create a happy family with Álvaro, away from intrusive eyes." The groom was resplendent in gold and white. Six-year-old Viviane was the maid of honor while stepsister Sandrine carried the rings.

The security operation was worthy of a pope or a president: four hundred guards patrolled the grounds. For the lavish event, 1,300 guests from around the world attended; staff ferried them to the gala in fleets of limousines that had to pass through two security checkpoints. Cell phones and cameras were *verboten*. For those allowed entry, they indulged in a thousand bottles of Veuve Clicquot champagne, 2002 Bordeaux, and Brazilian Caipirinha cocktails. The cuisine offered included a chilled soup, salmon, shrimp in artichokes, and veal on risotto. As Thierry had not been invited, the groom's father gave the bride away. The vows took place at ten p.m., at which time the groom whispered to his bride, "You are everything to me." The party continued until four a.m. In Greece, however, the marriage was not viewed as a source of celebration. As the daughter of the dynasty took her vows far from her ancestral shores, the prospect of Athina bestowing her money on her new husband and his six-year-old daughter fueled fears that her union would enable a gigolo's quest to gorge on the Grecian's golden goose. To add insult to injury, most of Athenian society, including church leader Archbishop Chrysostomos, had been left off the guest list.

Post nuptials, the newlyweds stayed in a São Paulo hotel and honeymooned in Uruguay's Punta d'Este resort. The reclusive heiress, now known as Athina Onassis de Miranda, settled in her adopted city, where she was safer from the cult of celebrity than in Europe. She immersed herself in learning Portuguese, watching Brazilian soap operas, and frequenting health spas.

The fairy-tale wedding did not, however, segue into a happily ever after. Her marriage to Doda had made Athina the stepmother of Viviane and Fernando, Cibele's son from a previous relationship: suffering from the traumas of her broken marriage, loss of custody, drug addiction, injury from a car accident, and the suicide of her boyfriend, Cibele jumped from the window of her São Paulo apartment in 2011. She left behind a suicide note of apology to her two children and a damning letter against Doda.

Perhaps in a bid to divest herself from the tragic fates of those in the Onassis line, in 2008, Athina arranged for the sale of forty-four items of jewelry that had belonged to Christina. Under the hammer of Christie's auction house was a thirty-eight-carat D color flawless diamond that had originally been part of a necklace, a 4.15-carat diamond ring with a vivid yellow pear-shaped diamond, and a rare Buddha made by Carl Fabergé, once prominently displayed on the family yacht. The auction netted $13.3 million. In 2006, she bid adieu to her fifteen-room Paris residence whose penthouse had sweeping views of the Arc de Triomphe and the Eiffel Tower, a romantic ambience that had helped seduce Maria Callas and Jacqueline Kennedy. The Monet masterpiece that had once hung on the estate's walls also sold, as well as Christina's villa in St. Moritz. Athina's Brazilian marital home sold for $20 million. Another tie she severed from the House of Onassis occurred when Athina parted with Skorpios. Unsuccessful bidders were Giorgio Armani, Bill Gates, and Madonna. The new owner was equestrian Ekaterina Rybolovleva, the twenty-four-year-old daughter of Russian oligarch Dmitry Rybolovleva, who forked over $125 million.

Although Athina had freed herself from her family's ill-starred fate, not all was well in horse heaven. Despite the optimistic-sounding name of the prize cow, Esperança, marital trouble loomed. Rumor among the horse set held that Doda was seeing the sister of a fellow equestrian. When the Onassis security detail caught Doda at their Florida home in bed with a blonde, he explained it had been a meaningless one-night stand and that it should not be the death knell for their marriage. Her lawyers begged to differ and revealed proof that Doda had been straying within months of his wedding. The Onassis legal eagles prepared one hundred pages of evidence delineating a nine-year affair that Doda had carried on with "Nicky," a Belgian call girl who was the daughter of a French military official. The affair came to light after Doda dumped the young lady; however, what made Nicky more than the mistress scorned was that she never asked for money for her bombshell revelation. She said she only spilled the adultery beans because she wanted Athina to know the truth. Nicky provided smoking guns: airline tickets bearing their names on shared flights, VIP passes to horse shows, and text messages exchanged via their Instagram accounts, code-named Romeo and Princess Charlotte.

Athina departed their Florida horse farm and hired Manhattan celebrity attorney Robert Cohen, who had previously been retained by Ivana Trump, to represent her in her divorce. Cohen boarded a plane for Belgium, his heiress client's main residence. Initially, Doda declared he would "fight until the end" to win back his lost love. He told the Brazilian magazine *Epoca*, "I am really in the midst of a storm. But I will not give up on my love." The piles of adulterous proof against Doda negated his claim that as an abandoned husband, he merited $10,000 a day alimony. When he realized Athina would not take him back, Doda demanded $300,000 a month in alimony and $11 million in cash, as outlined in their prenuptial agreement. The couple settled in a confidential divorce agreement. Four months later, Doda stopped licking his wounds when he fell for a blonde Brazilian TV star; they soon married in a lavish ceremony in Portugal.

What final words the Greek chorus will chant as the last descendant of the Onassis dynasty lives out her life is a question whose answer remains in the murky world of tomorrow.

EPILOGUE

Getting Bored

After finishing *The World's Wealthiest Women*, the overriding question is this: Are the recipients of fabulous fortunes more or less fortunate than the 99 percent, many of whom indeed must borrow from Peter to pay Paul? Are their lives more blessed than those of more modest means? Does being the possessor of "eff-you" money make life a magical mystery tour?

While researching the profiled women, I discovered a variation of Dorothy's words as she journeyed along the yellow brick road superimposed on my keyboard: "Yachts, mansions, jewels...oh my..." How wondrous to have a many-splendored bank account that serves as a personal genie, allowing the rich to walk on golden-bricked roads. Evalyn Walsh McLean owned the world's most magnificent blue diamond; Marjorie Merriweather Post built and dwelled in Mar-a-Lago; Imelda Marcos' feet never had to wear the same designer footwear twice.

While Virginia Woolf wrote of the importance of a woman having a room of her own, these ladies had any number of magnificent mansions. The refrain "so not fair" marched in my mind as sugar plums do on Christmas Eve. When I was a teacher at a school on the San Diego/Tijuana border, my students regaled me with stories that showcased lives analogous to holding onto a cliff. Some of the more tragic included a family who lived in their van at the local Walmart, and the boy whose father, the sole means of support for his family, ended up deported. The kids said that a good meal was one where their moms could afford meat. Driving home, I witnessed those with their possessions loaded onto shopping carts. Homeless people held up signs: Help—Hungry; Will Work For Weed, Too Ugly to Prostitute.

Given the economic dire straits of the neighborhood, I was not surprised when a student showed me photographs on her phone filled with endless images of Kim Kardashian, where the "reality" star sat in front of her in-your-wildest-dreams mansion. Another was of Paris Hilton, who posed from her Barbie-hued Bentley, one that sported a pink exterior, pink interior, and pink wheels. I did not share with the student that Paris had custom ordered an additional touch: a $285,000 diamond-encrusted dashboard. Through the lottery of birth, Paris' grandfather was the founder of the Hilton Hotels. One descriptive phrase for such inherited paternal wealth could be 'the Lucky Sperm Club.' Fighting against empty bank accounts, the students were fortunate to have fierce family ties. As a teacher once mentioned, "Our school is not state-of-the-art—but it is state of the *heart*." She did not exaggerate when she said the facility was not state-of-the-art. For the first half of my career, although classes began in July during sweltering weather, there was no air conditioning. The classroom, rather than a venue for learning, was a study in surviving the unbearable heat.

In retrospect, great wealth is not a bulwark against pain and even the mighty are subjects to the Shakespearean "slings and arrows of outrageous fortune." Although Betsy Bloomingdale was the billionaire owner of the high-end department store that bore her name, all hell broke loose when the press played up the fact her hubby was into sadomasochism with a teenager who ended up murdered. The dual homicide of Canadian billionaires Honey and Barry Sherman sent shock waves throughout all ten provinces. Seagram heiress Clare Bronfman's billions ensnared her in a maniacal cult. Yes, a plentiful amount of green buys wondrous things, but the collateral cost is Damocles' Sword.

Children remain fans of Kay Thompson's 1955 book that centered on Eloise, the six-year-old poor little rich girl who lived at the Plaza, the august hotel that was once the domain of Ivana Trump. Eloise shared her suite with her pug, Weenie, her turtle, Skipperdee, and her British nanny. Every morning, Eloise phoned for room service and ended the call with, "Charge it please." The rest of the day, she wandered the halls of the hotel, finding ways to get into mischief.

Piggybacking on their famous fictional resident, the Plaza hung a full-length portrait of Eloise near its Palm Court. While staring at the portrait, a guest overheard a little girl asking, "Mommy, do we like Eloise?" The same question can be asked of the world's wealthiest women. Although they trod divergent paths, one commonality was they abided by Eloise's trademark pronouncement, "Getting bored is not allowed."

"Vases"
by Nan Terrell Reed

Two vases stood on the Shelf of Life
As Love came by to look,
One was of priceless cloisonné,
The other of solid common clay.
Which do you think Love took?

He took them both from the Shelf of Life,
He took them both with a smile;
He clasped them both with his finger tips,
And touched them both with caressing lips,
And held them both for awhile.

From tired hands Love let them fall,
And never a word was spoken.
One was of priceless cloisonné,
The other of solid common clay.
Which do you think was broken?

Acknowledgments

In my first book, *Once Again to Zelda: The Stories Behind Literature's Most Intriguing Dedications*, I explored the dedication pages of fifty classic novels. The concept was intriguing: when writing their magnum opuses, why did the authors choose to honor these individuals? The acknowledgments page also provides a venue for writers to pay tribute to those who inspired, those who provided guidance. Writing a book takes a village; the following are those who comprise mine.

The most revised section in a book is the acknowledgment page, as it depends on the ebb and flow of my interpersonal relationships. However, there are some individuals on whom I will never press the delete key. Brenda Knight's surname is serendipitous, for she has championed me on six prior books: an eighth waits in the wings. I am indebted to my literary agent, Roger Williams. Endless thanks for leading me to Brenda's door.

I never had a sister—not until I met Jamie Lovett, who I was introduced to through *Once Again to Zelda*. She has been the wind beneath my wings as she has seen me through the many threads that comprise the writing of a book. Irish poet William Butler Yeats must have had a friend such as Jamie when he wrote these words on which the dust will never settle: "Think where man's glory most begins and ends, and say my glory was I had such friends."

Lastly, let's end with a nod to the world's wealthiest women, whose stories seem drawn from the pages of fiction. Despite the commonality of fabulous fortune, they trod different paths. Several took to heart the ancient principle of *noblesse oblige*, the idea that there is a natural obligation on those more privileged to look after those less fortunate. Others, however, were reminiscent of F. Scott Fitzgerald's memorable characters in *The Great Gatsby*: "They were careless people, Tom and Daisy—they smashed up things and creatures and then retreated back into their money or their vast carelessness or whatever it was that kept them together, and let other people clean up the mess they had made." In either contingency, their stories part the curtain on their rarefied worlds.

Marlene Wagman-Geller
San Diego, California 2025

Photography Credit

1. Hetty Green: Hollinger & Rockey
2. Hetty Green, circa 1905: National Magazine
3. Madame C. J. Walker: Scurlock Studio
4. Sarah in her seven-passenger limited edition Cole touring car: photographer unknown
5. Helena Rubenstein: George Grantham Bain Collection (Library of Congress)
6. Rubenstein family childhood home, Kraków, Poland: Zygmunt Put
7. Diane von **Fürstenberg**, New York Fashion Week, 2008: Ed Kavishe
8. Diane von **Fürstenberg**'s 1970s wrap dress: Rhododendrites
9. Dolly Parton, Grand Ole Opry, 2005: Sgt. Cherie A. Thurlby
10. Porter Wagoner and protégée Dolly Parton, 1969: Moelle Talent
11. Donatella Versace, Los Angeles, 2003: Stephano Corti (Wikimedia Commons)
12. The Versace Boutique, Milan, Italy: Bahar
13. Portrait of Evalyn Walsh McLean wearing the Hope Diamond, 1914: Harris & Ewing
14. *Washington Post* heir Edward McLean, Evalyn, and their dog: Harris & Ewing
15. Marjorie Meriweather Post: C. M. Stieglitz
16. Mar-a-Lago, Palm Beach, Florida, 1967: Jack Boucher
17. The White House Rose Garden, landscaper Bunny Mellon: Jack Boucher

18. *Life* Magazine 1925 Listerine Advertisement: Britta Gustafson
19. Zsa Zsa Gabor Publicity Photo, 1954: Rogers & Cowen
20. Zsa Zsa Gabor Film Premiere, 1962: Wire Press
21. Bloomingdale's New York City: Ajay Suresh
22. Marella Agnelli, 1950s: Unknown
23. Italy's First Couple, Marella and Gianni Agnelli: Unknown
24. Four painted portraits of São Schlumberger by Andy Warhol: Bernard Gotfryd
25. A painted portrait of São Schlumberger by Salvador Dali: Carl Van Vechten
26. Official Portrait of First Lady Imelda Marcos: Philippine House of Representatives
27. First Lady Imelda Marcos' Signed Red Shoes Size 8 ½: David Stanley
28. Basia Johnson's mansion, Jasna Polana ("Bright Meadow"): Ekem
29. Johnson & Johnson original logo: Johnson & Johnson
30. Villa Leopolda, the Safra French Riviera Mansion: Miniwark
31. Banco Safra, São Paulo, Brazil: Mike Peel
32. Barbara Amiel, Canadian Film Center Annual Gala & Auction, 2013: Canadian Film Center
33. Lord Black of Crossharbour, Canadian Film Center Annual Gala & Auction: Canadian Film Center
34. The Nabila, the Khashoggi Yacht: Roger McNamara
35. The Custom-Made Monopoly Game of Khashoggi Properties: Roger McNamara
36. Apotex Pharmaceutical Headquarters: Raysonho
37. Ivana Trump Life Ball, Vienna, 2009: Manfred Werner

38. Ivana Trump, Estée Lauder, Red Cross Ball, Palm Beach, Florida, 1986: Bert Morgan
39. Princess Gloria und Prince Johannes of Thurn und Taxis: 8 mobil
40. Schloss Thurn und Taxis, Regensburg, Germany: PeterBraun74
41. Wendi Deng Murdoch (on right): UKinUSA
42. Wendi and Rupert Murdoch, *Vanity Fair* Party: Davis Shankbone
43. Queen Marie-Chantal, London, England: Frankie Fouganthin
44. Queen Marie-Chantal, King Pavlos, King Charles III: Ian Jones
45. Clare Bronfman: Government Exhibit in US v. Raniere trial
46. Seagram Skyscraper, New York City: epicgenius
47. Athina Onassis, Equestrian Competition: Michael Kramer
48. Skorpios, Greece, Island Fiefdom of the Onassis Dynasty: Shadster
49. The Plaza Hotel, New York, Eloise's Playground: Zinetv1
50. French Vase with Cover, 1788, www.metmuseum.org/art/collection/search/186835

A Note to the Readers

Dear reader,

Thank you so much for accompanying me on my writer's journey—my once and future dream. One of the most wonderful aspects of publishing a book is interacting with readers. I have received emails from wonderful people whom I would never have otherwise met, some of whom have become friends. In 2008, after I wrote my first book, *Once Again to Zelda: The Stories Behind Literature's Most Intriguing Dedications*, I received an email from Avis Weeks. She regretted that, instead of anyone dedicating a book to her, she only received shopping lists of groceries to pick up. When I spoke at Yale University Library, Avis let me stay at her lovely home, one where she had written literary quotations on her kitchen wall. Fellow English teacher Jamie Lovett contacted me about the same book; ever since, she has been the sister I never had.

If you would like to share an anecdote concerning a profiled "wealthiest woman," please do so. In addition, please let me know of any other women who could have been included in this volume. If you send me a photo of you and the book, I would love to share it on Facebook. (Please include your city and country with your photo.)

I would also be interested in readers' reaction to having extreme wealth. Do you feel it would be a blessing or a curse?

From the bottom of my heart, I want to thank you for your encouragement: it continues to provide the wind beneath my writer's wings. An author's world is chiefly one of solitude; you make it less so.

Please contact me through:

marlenewagmangeller.com
wagmangeller@hotmail.com
www.facebook.com/marlene.wagman.5/

Happy reading trails,
Marlene Wagman-Geller
San Diego, California (2025)

About the Author

Marlene Wagman-Geller received her Bachelor of Arts from York University and her teaching credentials from the University of Toronto and San Diego State University. She recently retired after teaching high school English and history. Reviews from her books have appeared in *The New York Times* and dozens of other newspapers such as *The Washington Post, The Chicago Tribune*, and *The Huffington Post.* When not researching or writing, she devotes her time to her guilty pleasures—a Starbuck's run (venti latte nonfat milk extra hot extra foam), reading, and volunteering at a cat shelter where she has to restrain herself from taking them all home.

About the Publisher

Books That Save Lives came into being in 2024 when the editor and publisher, Brenda Knight, heard directly from readers and authors that certain self-help, grief, psychology books, and journals were providing a lifeline for folks. We live in a stressful world where it is increasingly difficult not to feel overwhelmed, worried, depressed, and downright scared. We intend to offer support for the vulnerable, including people struggling with mental wellness and physical illness as well as people of color, queer and trans adults and teens, immigrants and anyone who needs encouragement and inspiration.

From first responders, military veterans, and retirees to LGBTQ+ teens and to those experiencing the shock of bereavement and loss, our books have saved lives. To us, there is no higher calling.

We would love to hear from you! Our readers are our most important resource; we value your input, suggestions, and ideas.

Please stay in touch with us and follow us at:

www.booksthatsavelives.net

https://www.instagram.com/booksthatsavelives/

www.ingramcontent.com/pod-product-compliance
Lightning Source LLC
Chambersburg PA
CBHW021137090426
42740CB00008B/824

* 9 7 8 1 6 8 4 8 1 8 2 1 1 *